HANDBOOK of the
TREATMENT of the
ANXIETY DISORDERS

HANDBOOK of the TREATMENT of the ANXIETY DISORDERS

Edited by
Carol Lindemann, Ph.D.

JASON ARONSON INC.
Northvale, New Jersey
London

This book was set in 12 pt. Centaur by Alpha Graphics of Pittsfield, New Hampshire, and printed and bound by Book-mart Press of North Bergen, New Jersey.

Library of Congress Cataloging-in-Publication Data
Handbook of the treatment of the anxiety disorders / edited by Carol
   Lindemann. —2nd ed., new and expanded.
      p.   cm.
   Rev. ed. of: Handbook of phobia therapy. c1989.
   Includes bibliographical references and index.
   ISBN 1-56821-805-2 (alk. paper).
      1. Anxiety—Treatment.   I. Lindemann, Carol G.   II. Handbook of
   phobia therapy.
      [DNLM: 1. Anxiety Disorders—therapy.   WM 172 H2374 1996]
   RC531.H285   1996
   616.85'22306—dc20
   DNLM/DLC
   for Library of Congress   95-51105

Manufactured in the United States of America. Jason Aronson Inc. offers books and cassettes. For information and catalog write to Jason Aronson Inc., 230 Livingston Street, Northvale, New Jersey 07647.

CONTENTS

PART I
TREATMENT OF THE ANXIETY DISORDERS

CONTRIBUTORS

Sander M. Abend, M.D.
Training and Supervising Analyst, New York Psychoanalytic Institute, New York, NY

Bonnie R. Aronowitz, Ph.D.
Assistant Professor of Psychology in Psychiatry, the Mount Sinai Medical Center, New York, NY

James C. Ballenger, M.D.
Chairman and Professor, Department of Psychiatry/Behavioral Science and Director, Institute of Psychiatry, Medical University of South Carolina, Charleston, SC

David H. Barlow, Ph.D.
Director of Clinical Programs and Director of the Center for Anxiety and Related Disorders, Department of Psychology, Boston University, Boston, MA

Aaron T. Beck, M.D.
University Professor Emeritus at the University of Pennsylvania School of Medicine and President of the Beck Institute for Cognitive Therapy and Research, Philadelphia, PA

T. D. Borkovec, Ph.D.
Distinguished Professor of Psychology at the Pennsylvania State University

Karen S. Calhoun, Ph.D.
Professor and Director of Clinical Training in the Department of Psychology at the University of Georgia

Cheryl N. Carmin, Ph.D.
Director, Cognitive-Behavior Therapy Program and Visiting Associate Professor, Department of Psychiatry, University of Illinois at Chicago

Michelle Craske, Ph.D.
Assistant Professor of Psychology, UCLA

Gary Emery, Ph.D.
Director of the Los Angeles Center for Cognitive Therapy

Edna B. Foa, Ph.D.
Professor and Director, Center for the Treatment and Study of Anxiety, Medical Center of Pennsylvania and Hahnemann University, Philadelphia, PA

Ruth L. Greenberg, Ph.D.
Private practice, Philadelphia, PA

Eric Hollander, M.D.
Professor of Psychiatry, Director of Clinical Psychopharmacology, Director of Compulsive, Impulsive and Anxiety Disorders Program, and Clinical Director Seaver Autism Research Center at Mount Sinai School of Medicine, New York, NY

Donald F. Klein, M.D.
Director of Research and Director of Therapeutics, Department of Psychiatry, College of Physicians and Surgeons of Columbia University and the New York State Psychiatric Institute, New York, NY

Janet S. Klosko, Ph.D.
Senior Therapist at the Cognitive Therapy Center of New York, New York City; Co-Director of the Cognitive Therapy Center of Long Island, Great Neck, New York, and private practice Kingston, NY

Harold S. Koplewicz, M.D.
Professor of Psychiatry, Vice Chairman for Child and Adolescent Psychiatry, New York University Medical Center, New York, NY

Michael J. Kozak, Ph.D.
Professor and Director, Center for the Treatment and Study of Anxiety, Medical Center of Pennsylvania and Hahnemann University, Philadelphia, PA

Ira Lesser, M.D.
Professor of Psychiatry, UCLA School of Medicine, and Director of the Residency Training Program, Harbor-UCLA Medical Center

Carol Lindemann, Ph.D.
Private practice, New York, NY

John Marshall, M.D.
Professor of Psychiatry at the University of Wisconsin Medical School and Director of the Anxiety Disorders Center

John Pecknold, M.D.
Director of General Psychiatry and Director of the Anxiety Clinic at the Douglas Hospital, and Associate Professor of Psychiatry at McGill University, Montreal, Canada

C. Alec Pollard, Ph.D.
Director of the Anxiety Disorders Center of the St. Louis Behavioral Institute and Associate Professor of Community and Family Medicine at St. Louis School of Medicine, MO

Ronald M. Rapee, Ph.D.
School of Behavioral Science, Macquarie University, Sydney, Australia

Patricia A. Resick, Ph.D.
Professor of Psychology and Director of the Center for Trauma Recovery at the University of Missouri, St. Louis, MO

Karl Rickels, M.D.
Stuart and Emily Mudd Professor of Human Behavior and Psychiatry at the University of Pennsylvania, Philadelphia, PA

Lizabeth Roemer, Ph.D.
Assistant Professor of Psychology at the University of Massachusetts.

Jerilyn Ross, MA, LICSW
President, Anxiety Disorders of America and Director; President, the Ross Center for Anxiety and Related Disorders, Washington, DC

Edward M. Sellers, M.D., Ph.D.
Professor of Pharmacology, Medicine and Psychiatry; Senior Scientist, Addiction Research Foundation, University of Toronto, Canada

Claire Weekes
Deceased

R. Reid Wilson, Ph.D.
Associate Clinical Professor, Department of Psychiatry, University of North Carolina School of Medicine, Chapel Hill, NC

Sally Winston, Ph.D.
The Anxiety and Stress Disorder Institute of Maryland, Towson, MD

Manuel D. Zane, M.D.
Director Emeritus, Phobia Clinic, White Plains Hospital Medical Center, NY

PREFACE TO THE
SECOND EDITION

This book is written for the psychotherapist who is not trained in behavioral techniques. There have been substantial gains in the treatment of the anxiety disorders in the past twenty years. Lifelong debilitating disorders that were rarely treated successfully are now much more amenable to treatment. In this volume, I have collected from the leaders in their respective fields a series of brief-treatment-oriented papers that will orient the reader to the components of the treatment techniques.

It seems remarkable that a new edition of this book is needed in only six years, since in the field of mental health change is so often slow and painstaking. But there has been a revolution in treatment of the anxiety disorders over the past twenty-five years and it continues unabated. The number of research articles, for example, on the anxiety disorders has rapidly expanded, estimated at a tenfold increase, with a logarithmic increase each decade (Norton et al. 1995).

Two main threads have dictated the changes in this new edition. The first, as mentioned above, is the voluminous amount of new research which has given us new, effective, and well-accepted medication and treatment protocols. The second impetus is the new *Diagnostic and Statistical Manual, DSM-IV* (1994), which reorganizes and redefines the diagnosis of anxiety disorder.

Part I of this volume is concerned primarily with description of the various disorders, while Part II is concerned primarily with treatment techniques. Chapter 1, giving a brief history of the treatment of anxiety disorders, has been updated to reflect the new trends in the field. Dr. Lesser's chapter on diagnostics has been extensively revised, reflecting greater emphasis on the developing new subfields within anxiety disorders, particularly panic disorders. The chapters on agoraphobia and on generalized anxiety disorder are new to this volume and present two excellent illustrations of the trend through-out the field for carefully researched and designed programmatic approaches to brief treatment. A second chapter on social phobia by Dr. Marshall has been added to Dr. Beck's original chapter to reflect the increased knowledge we now have about treating this phobia, which was first delineated in the *DSM-III* in 1980. Dr. Foa's chapter on obsessive-compulsive disorder has been extensively revised to include new material that reflects advances in theory and treatment of this complex disorder. Drs. Calhoun and Resick continue with a thorough discussion of issues of post-traumatic stress disorder, a section which was not included in the first edition.

Part II again includes two chapters from Dr. Barlow's work, one on cognitive-behavioral therapy for panic attacks (CBT) and one on psychoeducation. While the preface to the first edition called the advances in CBT "currently the state of the art," by this writing, CBT has become the standard of empirically validated treatment of the anxiety disorders. To amplify on the elements of CBT, the next few chapters detail the treatment components: Aaron Beck applies cognitive therapy to social phobia, making a cogent argument for seeing this disorder as primarily cognitive, Reid Wilson describes imaginal desensitization techniques of relaxation and visualization, and Jerilyn Ross describes in vivo desensitization techniques used in the field with the phobic person. Manual Zane's "Six Points of Contextual Therapy" and Claire Weekes's self-help contribution complete this section.

Medication is a most effective treatment option for the anxiety disorders, and Drs. Hollander, Aronowitz, and Klein's paper has been revised to expand upon the new medications available and the current research status of those in prevalent use. To amplify issues of medication in this edition, Dr. Ballenger's chapter discusses the difficult issue of medication discontinuation. The other excellent technique chapters in this section remain unchanged from the original edition.

Post-traumatic stress disorder was not included in the first edition of the book, which was more focused on phobias, and, to compensate, a second chapter on the disorder is included. The volume ends with Dr. Abend's thoughtful chapter on the psychoanalytic treatment of a simple phobia, reminding us that there are many treatments that, although they have not yet been validated by research, may be effective in the hands of an expert in that particular technique.

To make room for all this new material, several chapters have been eliminated. While these chapters may not add to the current configuration of the book, some of the concepts are timeless, and the reader is referred to the first edition to amplify the chapters in this current book. Also, by kind permission of the publisher, Jason Aronson, selected chapters from the first edition will be posted on the Internet. The Internet is in constant flux, but as of this writing this material can be found on the CyberPsych web page at http://www.cyberpsych.org.

REFERENCE

Norton, G. R., Cox, B. J., Asmundson, J. G., and Maser, J. D. (1995). The growth of research on anxiety disorders during the 1980s. *Journal of the Anxiety Disorders* 9:75–85.

PREFACE TO THE
FIRST EDITION

This book is written for the practitioner—psychologists, psychiatrists, social workers, and other mental health workers who wish to learn how to treat anxiety disorders. The collection of chapters will provide the therapist who is new to the field with an orientation to the major theoretical and technical issues, and a concrete, working understanding of how a number of specific techniques are applied.

For the psychotherapist, perhaps the most compelling aspect of these phobia treatments is their ability to rapidly bring significant improvement. The availability of (1) a set of specific interventions that can effect change in most people suffering from a specific complaint, together with (2) relatively precise knowledge of when and why to use these interventions, permanently changes one's perspective on therapy. Although many people seeking psychotherapy have general complaints, some seek therapy for specific, clearly delineated problems. For this latter group, exploratory psychotherapy often proves inefficient, and it can be argued that the patient is best served by therapy that provides rapid symptom relief.

For example, a person threatened with job loss because of phobic avoidance of a crucial segment of his job, or a person who has panic attacks and is too afraid to leave home alone, may be eager for symptom relief rather than a prolonged treatment involving exploration of underlying factors. In the latter case, particularly, it is most beneficial to treat the panic disorder directly, before a consolidation of phobic avoidance and agoraphobia occurs. Psychodynamic factors can, if indicated, be explored after the crisis has abated. It is gratifying to both the therapist and patient when the therapist can say that he has treatment methods that have helped over 80% of people with similar problems.

Chapter 1 is a brief history of treatment of anxiety disorders in the context of the evolutionary trends in general psychotherapy during the past fifteen years. Part I then begins with Dr. Lesser's chapter on changes in the diagnostic understanding of anxiety disorders.

Part I then addresses the specific subtypes of anxiety disorder for which special techniques have been developed. Agoraphobia, certainly the most dramatic subtype, is seen most frequently. Generalized anxiety disorder, or what has been called free-floating anxiety, is another common syndrome for which techniques are now available. Obsessive-compulsive disorder (to be distinguished from the obsessive-compulsive personality disorder) remains a difficult syndrome to treat. The simple phobias (those in which there is situation specific panic) are exemplified by fear of flying, and the social phobias are illustrated in the chapter on evaluation anxiety. The authors of these chapters advocate techniques that range from behavioral to psychoeducational, to an integration between dynamic and symptom-focused approaches.

Part II concentrates on technique, describing in detail components of the treatment program outlined in the first section, such as cognitive-behavioral therapy, desensitization, family therapy, hypnotherapy, psychoanalysis, and medication. The array of techniques described in this volume have certain similarities to bear in mind. The most consistent finding is that in any effective treatment program, the phobic person must reenter the phobic situation. The respective authors may vary in their strategies and procedures at three specific stages: how they prepare the patient to enter the phobic situation, what takes place in the situation itself, and how the experience is subsequently worked through.

Dr. Barlow and his colleagues present what is currently regarded as the most effective nonpsychopharmacological treatment. Their cognitive-behavioral therapy updates and further refines behavioral techniques and, as of this writing, is considered state of the art. The components of the behavioral package are then explored in a series of chapters including psychoeducation, imaginal and in vivo desensitization, the control of hyperventilation, and anxiety coping techniques.

All of the technique chapters address, to some degree, all three phases of treatment. Some of the early programmatic approaches, such as those originated by Drs. Zane and Hardy, integrate all three aspects. Both use groups in their time-limited programs, often employing aides who are themselves former phobics. The groups first learn a body of structured information, then enter the phobic situations together with the support of others who understand their struggle. When the patient is in the phobic situation, a number of techniques help reduce the levels of anxiety. These are generally called *anxiety coping techniques.* Examples of these techniques are presented in the training manual excerpt by Jerilyn Ross. Some are developed to help the patient feel more in control when in the phobic situation. Some work by suggestion, others through changing the focus of attention. Paraprofessionals often specialize in the in vivo work. Imaginal desensitization is usually conducted in a traditional office setting, as described by Reid Wilson.

The remaining chapters in Part II demonstrate broader-based techniques, often combining some behaviorism with other forms of therapy. As clinical practice has developed beyond the limits of the stricter behavioral orientation, phobia therapy has moved closer to general supportive psychotherapy, including employing some dynamic interventions. Phobia therapy is by no means synonymous with behavior therapy. Although it emerged primarily from behavior therapy, most therapists were skilled in using other therapeutic modalities before beginning to specialize in phobia therapy. They brought to the new task their experience with strategic, family, group, or psychodynamic therapy, modifying these approaches appropriately to suit the needs of the phobic patient.

With many patients, while the core of the treatment remains symptom-focused, it proves impossible to ignore certain intrapsychic issues, of which resistance is a prime example, since to do so might otherwise impede progress. Furthermore, as certain patients begin to recover, they seem to want to discuss dynamic material: dreams, insight into the meaning of the symptoms, interpersonal dynamics maintaining the symptoms, and aggressive and libidinal conflicts. Many patients express a desire to know why they have experienced these problems.

Whether the future holds an increasing synthesis of techniques and levels of integration not yet imagined, is beyond our power to see at this juncture. The dramatic developments of the past two decades show no signs of leveling off. New research, broader clinical experience, and the work of innovative therapists promise many more advances. At this time, these pages represent the breadth of current methodologies available to treat this challenging group of patients.

ACKNOWLEDGMENTS

This volume would not have been possible without the knowledge that has been gained from countless individuals with anxiety disorders with whom I have worked over the years. I have learned from each of those whom I have tried to help, and it is this wealth of clinical experience that is the basis for this volume. Every contributing author joins me in the hope that this book leads the reader to improved skills in the relief of still other patients' suffering.

I would like to acknowledge the role of my colleagues and of the Anxiety Disorder Association of America for providing a constant forum for new ideas over the past twenty-five years. Sometimes contentious and sometimes cooperative, the interaction of intensely committed colleagues, many of whom are represented in this edition, has provided a fascinating journey into the development of the field of anxiety disorders. Foremost among those whose help should be explicitly recognized are the authors of the chapters included in this book, all of whom are renowned experts in the field. Their invaluable time and efforts in preparing these excellent contributions cannot be overpraised.

I would especially like to recognize my publisher, Jason Aronson, whose continued confidence in the value of this edition was a constant spur to my efforts. I am grateful to the Aronson staff, especially to Judith Cohen for her invaluable assistance in all aspects of this project.

Finally, a special expression of gratitude goes to my husband, Sander Abend, who has been as generous with his time and expertise as with his encouragement and support.

Carol Lindemann
New York City
June 1996

Treatment of
the Anxiety Disorders

CHAPTER ONE

The Development of Treatment: From Phobias to Anxiety Disorders

CAROL LINDEMANN

Effective treatment of the anxiety disorders is relatively new to the therapeutic field. It differs from previous therapies in several ways: (1) it focuses on a diagnostic category rather than on a theory or method, (2) it uses specific techniques that have been developed empirically, and (3) it makes symptom relief a primary goal rather than subordinating it to broader treatment goals.

Treatment of a specific diagnostic category is not new; therapeutic approaches to drug addiction and alcoholism are of that nature. Other examples are Masters and Johnson's work, from which emerged specific therapies for sexual disorders, and the treatment of eating disorders. The development of highly effective treatments for specific disorders is the primary cause of this new special syndrome orientation. Earlier, all these disorders were approached with the same general psychotherapy techniques.

This chapter traces the developments in research and theory that made possible the new approach to treating anxiety disorders.

NEW DIAGNOSTIC CLASSIFICATION
OF ANXIETY DISORDERS

Freud, together with the variety of psychoanalytic schools to which his work gave rise, remains the chief source of a comprehensive general theory of psychology. Treatment of anxiety disorders represents a departure from a Freudian theoretical orientation, being based primarily on pragmatic considerations of "what works." Contributors from disparate orientations—behavioral, psychopharmacological, and psychodynamic—converged in their interest in treating anxiety. This diverse group, despite considerable jostling for dominance of one contributor over another, has developed an eclectic treatment orientation employing a blend of techniques. The initial lack of a theory that might give cohesion to this body of therapy techniques is rapidly being remedied as new information emerges.

The idea of symptom relief without attention to underlying dynamics initially evoked strong doubts among the psychodynamically oriented community. Pessimistic predictions of symptom substitution and of psychological decompensation after symptom removal, however, turned out to be groundless. On the contrary, successful symptom removal has been found in general to lead to increased self-esteem, assertiveness, feelings of well-being, and improved levels of functioning in patients who experience it. This finding has stimulated the promotion of symptom-focused psychotherapy, as well as encouraging a shift of emphasis toward discernible change through psychotherapeutic treatment.

In a very brief period the new work in phobias and related anxiety disorders gained such importance that it spurred a complete revision of the diagnostic classification of anxiety in the *Diagnostic and Statistical Manual* (*DSM-III* and *DSM-IV*). Because panic disorder is now seen as a physiological as well as a psychological phenomenon, the research accompanying the development of this new field has been on the cutting edge of psychobiology. Anxiety, as a major component of psychological life, has always been of primary importance, but the new ability to treat the symptoms quickly and successfully has made this a hot new topic.

FREUDIAN APPROACH

Freudian theory, which provides the historical foundation for our understanding of psychopathology, must be the point of departure for a review of the new understanding of anxiety disorders. In *Studies in Hysteria* (Freud and Breuer 1895) Freud described the role of repressed traumatic memories in the development of such symptoms as hysterical paralysis and phobias. In later revisions of his theory of anxiety and symptom formation he determined that unconscious fantasies as well as actual trauma were pathogenic. His technique was to understand with the patient the unconscious conflicts connected with those experiences and fantasies, relieving the symptoms through conscious recognition and resolution of unconscious irrational elements.

Freud's goal, however, soon shifted from symptom removal to the development of an understanding of how symptoms were formed and the elaboration of a general theory of psychopathology. His study of Little Hans (Freud 1909) still serves as a model for the psychoanalytic understanding and treatment of phobias. Little Hans had a fear of horses, and he resisted going out on the street where horses and carriages were numerous. Freud understood Hans's phobia in terms of an oedipal conflict that activated the defenses of denial, displacement, and projection. In this case, an understanding of unconscious conflicts and their resolution led to the disappearance of the symptom.

Although much of the early psychoanalytic literature emphasized oedipal conflicts in the development of phobias, more recently an equal emphasis has been placed on separation anxiety as pathogenic. For example, Frances and Dunn (1975) speak of agoraphobia as an attachment–autonomy conflict and understand the disorder in terms of object theory while minimizing the significance of infantile sexuality.

Freud discouraged symptom removal without an understanding of the intrapsychic conflicts involved because of the danger of symptom substitution. Theoretically, the symptom serves a purpose as an expression of psychic conflicts, and, as such, it plays a part in maintaining the psychic balance. If abruptly removed, it might be replaced with a less adaptive symptom. Further, as psychoanalytic theory has developed, symptoms and anxiety are seen as motivating the patient toward treatment and as indicating the areas where unconscious problems that require further exploration are to be found. Freud was fond of saying that "the better is always the enemy of the good" (Freud 1937, p. 231), meaning that too early a relief of distressing symptoms might lead patients to drop treatment before more extensive solutions were achieved. The analytic posture recommends that understanding the workings of the patient's mind be the goal, and that beneficial change be a secondary consequence of that process, albeit a desirable one.

It is not possible to take an analytic stance of trying to achieve understanding with symptom change as a byproduct and at the same time have as a goal the rapid modification of symptoms. Further, the analytic viewpoint that phobias are based on underlying conflicts, and that avoidance of the phobic situation is a symbolic avoidance and fulfillment of the conflicted impulse, directs the therapist to look away from the patient's concrete conscious experience of distress. On the experiential level, phobics understand their avoidance to be of the terrifying feelings that are experienced in the phobic situation. The phobic claims he is reluctant to walk the street, fly on a plane, or speak in public because he fears those situations will cause panic. Only rarely does he have, or is he interested in gaining, insight: he wants simply to be rid of the debilitating anxiety.

BEHAVIORAL APPROACH

From an entirely different perspective, the behaviorists' explanation of phobic symptom formation is based on the theory of conditioned learning. The learning theorists have attacked the disease model of mental illness. Psychic pain, or symptom formation, need not be thought of as indicating an underlying dynamic cause in the psychic structure parallel to the relationship between physical pain and the underlying cause of infection, inflammation, or injury. The behaviorists have been especially interested in phobias because a phobia can be induced experimentally and then successfully treated (Jones 1924, Watson and Rayner 1920), thus serving as a perfect model of experimental psychopathology. Wolpe's *desensitization* was the first treatment based on learning theory to gain wide acceptance in the psychotherapy of phobias. The crux of the theory is *reciprocal inhibition:* "If a response antagonistic to anxiety can be made to occur in the presence of anxiety-evoking stimuli . . . the bond between these stimuli and the anxiety responses will be weakened" (Wolpe 1958, p. 71).

Desensitization, also called counterconditioning or deconditioning, is derived from classical conditioning. Pavlov's (1927) classical conditioning model, it will be remembered, is as follows: the dog is given food and salivates, the sound of the bell is presented a few seconds before the food, and the dog becomes conditioned to salivate at the sound of the bell. The application of the classical conditioning model to phobias runs as follows: a panic attack occurs, for reasons unspecified, in the elevator. The person, on the basis of a "one trial learning," becomes conditioned to have a fear response when in the elevator. Reciprocal inhibition of this response means pairing a competing response, such as relaxation, with the elevator repeatedly until the fear response is "deconditioned." In practice, this was originally accomplished by relaxing the patient through the

Jacobson technique (Jacobson 1938) of progressively tensing and relaxing muscle groups. When the patient is fully relaxed, a hierarchy of images of feared situations is presented verbally. For example, an elevator phobic might be told to imagine, first, stepping off an elevator after a successful short ride; next, standing in an elevator with the door open. The top of the hierarchy might be imagining being stuck in a small, crowded elevator. When the patient can remain fully relaxed while contemplating each feared event, the next step of the hierarchy is presented. For maximum effectiveness, where feasible, this hierarchy is then repeated in the situation itself (in vivo).

MODERN PSYCHOBIOLOGICAL APPROACH

Panic attacks are a measurable psychophysiological event. The modern history of the treatment of anxiety disorders is firmly grounded in psychobiological research and the use of psychotropic medication. Klein presented the first major breakthrough in the psychopharmacological treatment of anxiety disorders in his paper on the effective use of the tricyclic antidepressant, imipramine (Tofranil) (Klein and Fink 1962). At first this discovery raised more questions than it answered. Why did antidepressants help anxiety? Anxiety and depression theoretically were distinctly different emotions; were they functionally the same? What was the common basis? What were the site of action and the mode of action? Some of these questions are now answered.

Separation Anxiety

In early speculations (Klein and Fink 1962) the panic reaction was explained in terms of the separation anxiety model as elaborated by Bowlby (1960). The initial reaction of infants separated from their mother is marked by crying and the increased motoric activity of anxiety, followed later on by the reduced activity and vocalization associated with states of anaclitic depression. The initial phase is thought to be genetically programmed in mammals as a search for the mother who has lost or abandoned the infant. This theory provided a teleological reason for the existence of panic in all mammals. The second phase is parallel to depression, indicating a substantial link between these two experientially different emotions. Separation anxiety as a core issue in agoraphobia has been emphasized in psychoanalytic studies. The idea also spurred considerable research in separation anxiety as a component of panic disorders, but studies have not confirmed that a higher-than-expected number of agoraphobics have early separation experiences, and other groups, such as obsessive-compulsives, may be as likely to experience early separation anxiety. The association of depression and anxiety disorders is now well documented (Lesser, this volume).

Blocking Panic Attacks

To return to the biochemical understanding pioneered by Klein, imipramine was thought to block panic attacks. Phobic patients on an adequate dosage reported that they felt a rising panic, just as before, but that the subsequent full-blown panic they were accustomed to experiencing no longer appeared. The hypothesized explanation derived from learning theory is that the person avoids the emotional experience of anxiety associated with being in the phobic situation, rather than the situation itself. The medication permits the phobic to enter the phobic situation without fear of panics, once he learns they are effectively blocked.

Anticipatory Anxiety

For several years hope was high that medication alone would be an effective treatment for phobias. Many medicated patients did overcome their former phobic avoidance, but a number did not. Despite assurance that they would not panic, they stubbornly refused to enter the phobic situation. A new concept to explain such cases developed: that of *anticipatory anxiety* (Klein 1964)—the anxiety experienced at the thought or other symbolic representation of the phobic situation. In the elevator phobia, for example, the thought of entering an elevator is believed to cause the person to anticipate that a panic will again occur there and consequently anxiety begins merely by thinking of approaching an elevator. Further, the patient fears that panic might occur under circumstances in which help is not available, such as when alone and far from home, and this anticipation leads to phobic restrictions.

New Distinctions within Anxieties

The finding that medication may block the panic attack, but not affect the anticipatory anxiety, led to the speculation that panic and anxiety are different. While they may be experienced as if they were on a continuum, the two affects are thought to differ physiologically (Klein 1962). The medications frequently found to be useful for reducing anticipatory anxiety are those in the benzodiazepine group (such as Valium). The treatment protocol that was initially developed treated the panic attacks with antidepressant medication, conjointly treating any residual avoidance attributed to anticipatory anxiety with minor tranquilizers and desensitization. Treatment for anticipatory anxiety currently relies less on tranquilizers because therapy techniques are more sophisticated. New developments in medications have also changed the options for treating the anxiety disorders considerably (see Chapter 15).

This distinction between panic attacks and other anxiety experiences was crucial to the new understanding of the etiology, the diagnostics, and the treatment of phobias and anxiety disorders. Panic attacks are separated from the *DSM-II* diagnostic category of "anxiety neurosis" in contrast to "generalized anxiety disorder." The understanding of the anxiety is no longer as a "neurosis," that is, based upon unconscious conflict, but rather becomes descriptive and empirical. The ramifications of this change supported the development of symptom relief treatment, since long-term exploration of underlying conflicts causing the anxiety was no longer crucial.

Uncued Panic Attacks

In a further refinement, it was found that imipramine is far more effective with agoraphobia than with certain specific phobias, such as animal phobia. The panic of agoraphobics often occurs spontaneously, for no apparent reason (Zitrin et al. 1975), rather than exclusively and inevitably when patients are in the phobic situation. Imipramine may be specifically effective in blocking these unexpected attacks.

The concept of a spontaneous panic attack was slow to gain acceptance, especially by clinicians who retain a preference for purely psychological rather than biochemical explanations for psychological events. The observation of what appeared to be uncued attacks, however, led to the idea that some forms of panic have no external antecedent and may be purely physiological events. Klein's idea that these can be differentiated by the response to medication supports the view that they constitute specific syndromes. The terms *panic disorder* and *anxiety disorder* have now emerged in common parlance. What is treated is no longer merely a symptom, but one or another syndrome.

Locating the Brain's Panic Center

The concept of the panic as a physiological discharge soon led to two new ideas: (1) there is a specific panic center in the brain; and (2) despite the subjective emotional experience of panic, the event is physiological or biochemical in origin.

The "panic center" was hypothesized to have a physical location in the brain, and, most important, the panic response involves deep brain structures rather than being an event of the cerebral cortex. This means that although conscious or preconscious thought may mediate panic, the panic attack itself occurs at deep primitive levels of the brain that can fire autonomously. The panic response is also thought to be an innate, genetically determined discharge phenomenon that follows a pattern relatively consistent for each person, although differing slightly from one individual to the next.

In panic disorder, panic occurs "untriggered" by an external situation, such as being far from home. The trigger mechanism appears to be altered to fire more frequently or more readily. Klein (1993) has advanced a theory of "suffocation alarm," proposing that untriggered panic attacks are a response to a false experience of impending suffocation caused by a hypersensitivity to elevated CO_2 levels. Indeed, a connection between breathing irregularities, such as hyperventilation and deep sighing, and anxiety is frequently noted. Although hyperventilation causes symptoms also present in panic attacks, and frequently accompanies panic attacks, the evidence is not convincing that hyperventilation is the single or primary cause of panic. Yet this intriguing link remains a possibility in the pursuit of a complete understanding of panic attacks.

Recent advances in brain imaging have allowed us to see which brain structures are active during a panic attack or during the symptoms of anxiety disorders. These include the limbic system, as suspected, as well as a complex network of systems and structures connected to the limbic system, the paralimbic belt (including the insular cortex, the posterior orbitofrontal cortex, and the anterior cingulate cortex). There may also be increased activity in the language, visual, sensory, and memory areas of the cortex, as might be expected, depending on the particular anxiety disorder provoked during the brain imaging.

One hope is that as the technology becomes even more sophisticated and the research can tease out some of the complexities of the brain systems responding to anxiety disorder stimulation, there will be more precise diagnosis of the disorder and a consequent better treatment decision for each individual.

CURRENT INTEGRATIVE APPROACH

Inherent in the assumption of the primacy of emotional-physiological discharge in the etiology of the panic attack is the idea that the phobia is not necessarily mediated by conscious or unconscious thought, nor must it necessarily have symbolic meaning or affective displacement. The panic attack *precedes* the thought. In 1890 William James had expressed a similar hypothesis. James's theory of emotionality reversed the notion that you run from a bear because you feel afraid: actually, you see the bear, you run, then you feel afraid. If the emotional experience of fear really follows, rather than precedes, the physical expression of the emotion, then if you change the expression, you may change the subjective feeling of the emotional state. On a very simple observational level this theory appears to hold true. For example, the act of running out of a phobic situation makes many phobics feel more panicky. If one is able to induce the patient to remain in the phobic situation, the anxiety will often gradually diminish.

Dr. Aaron Beck's very popular new theory and therapeutic intervention, cognitive restructuring, is compatible with these ideas, although he begins from a different theoretical basis. He advocates inducing the patient to change the thought in order to change the experience. For the elevator phobic, for example, the thought "I will surely panic if I am stuck in an elevator" is more likely to produce anxiety than is the thought "I can cope with whatever emerges." Beck's elaborations on this theme, together with the subtleties of technique, have rapidly penetrated the field of phobia therapy.

Skinner has asserted that the mind is a black box that can be known only indirectly through behavior. Cognitive theory has given the behaviorists a vehicle in which to emerge from the black box and investigate mental events as trial behaviors. The psychodynamic community has similarly become more accepting of behaviorism in recognition of the effectiveness of the treatment. The psychopharmacologist has become integrated into the treatment team, and conversely, begun to accept the effectiveness of certain well-documented therapies.

In summary, the treatment of anxiety disorders embodies a highly effective group of symptom focused techniques applied to specific diagnostic categories. It blends innovations in psychotropic medication, behavioral pragmatism, and the eclecticism of recent years. Exploration of the variety of therapeutic approaches has led to promising new ideas about the nature of anxiety and panic. Cross-fertilization is increasingly in evidence as data gathered from one approach informs and stimulates research and therapy from other vantage points.

REFERENCES

Beck, A. T., and Emery, G. (1985). *Anxiety Disorders and Phobias: A Cognitive Perspective.* New York: Basic Books.

Bowlby, J. (1960). Separation anxiety. *International Journal of Psycho-Analysis* 41:89–113.

——— (1973). *Separation.* New York: Basic Books.

Diagnostic and Statistical Manual of Mental Disorders. (1980). 3rd ed. Washington, DC: American Psychiatric Association.

——— (1987). 3rd ed., rev. Washington, DC: American Psychiatric Association.

——— (1994). 4th ed., rev. Washington, DC; American Psychiatric Association.

Freud, S. (1909). Analysis of a phobia in a five-year-old boy. *Standard Edition* 10:5–149.

———— (1937). Analysis terminable and interminable. *Standard Edition* 23:209–254.

Freud, S., and Breuer, J. (1895). *Studies on Hysteria.* New York: Avon Books, 1966.

Jacobson, E. (1938). *Progressive Relaxation.* Chicago: University of Chicago Press.

James, W. (1890). *The Principles of Psychology.* New York: Henry Holt.

Jones, M. C. (1924). Elimination of children's fears. *Journal of Experimental Psychology* 7:382.

Klein. D. F. (1964). Delineation of two drug-responsive anxiety syndromes. *Psychopharmacologia* 53:397–408.

———— (1993). False suffocation alarms, spontaneous panics, and related conditions: an integrative hypothesis. *Archives of General Psychiatry* 50:306–317.

Klein, D. F., and Fink, M. (1962). Psychiatric reaction patterns to imipramine. *American Journal of Psychiatry* 119:432–438.

Pavlov, I. P. (1927). *Conditioned Reflexes.* London: Oxford University Press.

Watson, J. B., and Rayner, P. (1920). Conditioned emotional reactions. *Journal of Experimental Psychology* 3:1.

Wolpe, J. (1958). *Psychotherapy by Reciprocal Inhibition.* Stanford, CA: Stanford University Press.

Zitrin, C. M., Klein, D. F., Lindemann, C., et al. (1975). Comparison of short-term treatment regimens in phobic patients: A preliminary report. In *Evaluation of Psychological Therapies,* ed. R. L. Spitzer and D. F. Klein, pp. 233–250. Baltimore: Johns Hopkins Press.

CHAPTER TWO

Diagnostic Considerations in Anxiety Disorders

Dr. Lesser's introduction to diagnosis is essential to orient the investigator new to this field as there has been considerable recent modification in the classification of anxiety disorders. The first major change took place between the *DSM-II* and the *DSM-III*, at which time the diagnostic category of anxiety disorders became a separate entity. Previously, various aspects of anxiety and phobias were grouped mainly under the "psychoneuroses." In addition to naming anxiety disorders as a diagnostic entity, the *DSM-III* also eliminated the dynamic implication of "neurosis" from the diagnostic category. Instead, the main defining characteristics are the presence of panic symptoms and of overt behaviors, such as phobic avoidance. In the further revisions of the *DSM-III-R* and the *DSM-IV*, the emphasis in this diagnostic category was shifted from phobic avoidance with panic attacks, then to panic as a separate category, and finally to a central position of panic attacks in the understanding of anxiety disorders.

This chapter has been revised considerably for this edition, presenting a lucid discussion of the place of panic disorder in the continuing rapid changes in diagnostic understanding.

Diagnostic Considerations in Anxiety Disorders

IRA M. LESSER

In the past two decades, the field of anxiety disorders has received increasing attention from clinicians, researchers from a variety of theoretical backgrounds, and the lay public. As a group, anxiety disorders constitute perhaps the most common psychiatric disorders in the population (Robins and Regier 1991), causing considerable morbidity and a staggering economic burden. However, the recognition of anxiety disorders, particularly in primary care settings where patients with anxiety disorders are likely to present, remains unsatisfactory (Eisenberg 1992).

Are we, as has been suggested, living in an "age of anxiety" such that more people suffer from anxiety disorders? Are these illnesses, now christened with new names, really different from those described a century ago? Has an increase in diagnostic acumen coupled with a new nomenclature and an effective armamentarium of treatments all converged to bring more people into treatment? Did the *DSM-III-R* (1987) and now the *DSM-IV* (1994), our most current diagnostic system, adequately separate out the variety of anxiety disorders? How directly does our diagnostic classification lead to effective treatment planning? These are questions that need to be examined in any attempt to evaluate diagnostic considerations in anxiety disorders.

This chapter will provide an overview of diagnostic issues in anxiety disorders, with an emphasis on the panic disorders. In so doing, clinical material relevant to differentiating anxiety disorders from other psychiatric disorders and from medical disorders will be presented, bolstered by research findings from clinical investigations. Treatment considerations, although beyond the scope of this chapter and covered in depth elsewhere, will be addressed as they are pertinent to the issues of diagnosis and sub-classification.

HISTORICAL PERSPECTIVE

Clinical descriptions of anxiety attacks and phobias have been noted for centuries and display a startling similarity to each other and to our current clinical reports. Robert Burton, in *The Anatomy of Melancholy*, wrote in the 17th century:

> this fear causeth in man, as to be red, pale tremble, sweat; it makes sudden cold and heat to come over all the body, palpitation of the heart, syncope, etc . . . it confounds voice and memory . . . Many men are so amazed and astonished with fear, they know not where they are, what they say, what they do . . . and makes their hearts ache, sad and heavy. They that live in fear, are never free, resolute, secure, never merry, but in continual pain. . . . Fear makes our imagination conceive what it list, invites the devil to come to us . . . and tyranizeth over our phantasy more than all other afflictions, especially in the dark. [1621, pp. 261–262]

This literary and eloquent description includes most of the salient features of panic disorder replete with symptoms of the attacks themselves, the anticipatory anxiety, and the depression that so commonly accompanies panic attacks.

Almost surely the equivalent of panic disorder, seen during the Civil War and described in cardiac terms, was Da Costa's syndrome. Patients with this syndrome were described as having precordial pains, palpitations, and giddiness, occurring during rest or during slight exertion. Da Costa, a military physician, concluded, "It seems to me most likely that the heart has become irritable, from its overaction and frequent excitement, and that disordered innervation keeps it so" (Uhde and Nemiah 1989, p. 453). A focus on the physical, primarily cardiac symptoms of this disorder was maintained over the next half-century, and it was variously called irritable heart, soldier's heart, effort syndrome, disordered action of the heart, and neurocirculatory asthenia.

Descriptions of panic attacks were not confined to the medical or cardiac literature. Pierre Janet (cited in Nemiah 1974) described the case of a woman who

> experiences phenomena that are always identical: she senses a tightness in her throat along with a desire to cry, and feels suffocated and labored breathing as in an attack of asthma. Her stomach and lower abdomen become distended, she trembles, has palpitations, and breaks into a cold sweat, etc. Simultaneously, her thoughts become vague and seem to escape her. She is afraid of something without knowing what it is. The attack generally lasts for a short time, a half hour or so. [p. 92]

Freud (1962), too, gave classic descriptions of anxiety attacks, which he described as often being superimposed upon the more chronic manifestations of anxiety. He said, "I call this syndrome *anxiety neurosis* because all its components can be grouped around the chief symptom of anxiety" (p. 91). Freud distinguished anxiety neurosis, which he termed an "actual neurosis," from psychoneuroses by asserting that the former was more biologically and not psychologically initiated, a view shared by many current-day leaders in anxiety research.

Thus, there is little doubt that for centuries clinicians from both medicine and psychiatry have recognized the existence of dramatic episodes of anxiety that have both cognitive and physiological components. The nomenclature chosen to label these episodes has reflected the point of view of the observer, thereby confusing classification but not calling their existence into question.

THE PLACE OF THE PANIC ATTACK IN DIAGNOSTIC PRACTICE

A major shift in classification of the anxiety disorders occurred with the publication of *DSM-III* (1980). Previously, the *DSM-II* category of "anxiety neurosis" was quite heterogeneous, without any distinctions made between acute attacks of anxiety and its more chronic manifestations. The newer classification system was greatly influenced by the work of researchers in the field of anxiety, notably Donald Klein and colleagues (Klein 1964, 1980, 1987). In the course of his studies, Klein noted that when extremely anxious and phobic patients were given the antidepressant imipramine, their acute episodes of anxiety dramatically lessened, although their chronic behavior pattern was barely altered. From these findings, he developed the concept that these patients suffered from two phenomenologically distinct types of anxiety: acute panic attacks, and chronic anxiety that developed in anticipation of having another panic attack. Their phobic behavior and avoidance was seen as an attempt to avoid further attacks by not entering situations where an attack was thought likely to occur or where, if one did occur, it would be difficult to receive help.

In *DSM-III*, the more acute, episodic type of anxiety was recognized as panic disorder (PD) and classified separately from generalized anxiety disorder (GAD), although patients with PD would usually meet criteria also for GAD. In addition, for those patients who had considerable phobic avoidance, the category agoraphobia with panic attacks was created and listed as part of the phobic disorders. Agoraphobia without panic attacks was also a separate category, although there is considerable debate regarding the frequency with which agoraphobia presents in the absence of a history of panic attacks. Completing the anxiety disorder section in *DSM-III* were the diagnoses of simple phobia, social phobia, obsessive-compulsive disorder, post-traumatic stress disorder, and atypical anxiety disorder.

DSM-III-R (1987) again modified the classification of anxiety disorders, though the changes were not as marked as they were in the transition from *DSM-II* to *DSM-III*. Because the utility was questioned of classifying agoraphobia as part of the phobias while panic disorder was a separate category, in *DSM-III-R* panic disorder assumed primacy, with agoraphobic symptoms listed as consequences of the PD. Once again, there remained a category for agoraphobia without panic attacks. The remaining categories stayed the same as in *DSM-III*. The time criterion for GAD was increased from one month to six months of continuous symptoms, making it more likely that it would be used to denote a chronic rather than a reactive condition.

DSM-IV (1994) once again refined the classification of anxiety disorders. The most salient changes are: subtyping the kind of panic attacks which may occur, creating a new diagnostic category (acute stress disorder), moving organic anxiety disorder from the organic mental disorders section to the anxiety disorders section and renaming it anxiety disorder due to a general medical condition or substance-induced anxiety disorder, and making slight changes in either the name (specific phobia replaces simple phobia) or the criteria for several of the individual diagnoses. In addition, *DSM-IV* includes specific cultural and gender features for each diagnostic category.

Stressing the importance of the panic attack as intrinsic to some diagnoses (e.g., panic disorder) and as often occurring in a variety of other disorders (e.g., social phobia), *DSM-IV* provides extensive information regarding the criteria for a panic attack. The essential feature of a panic attack is a discrete period of intense fear or discomfort, accompanied by a variety of physical and cognitive symptoms (see Table 2–1) at least four of which must have been present during at least some of the attacks. As can be seen, the majority of these symptoms are physical: cardiac, respiratory, neurological, or related to discharge of the sympathetic nervous system. Only two have a cognitive component: fear of dying or fear of going crazy and losing control. Attacks which meet criteria but have fewer than four symptoms are referred to as limited symptom attacks.

A further classification of panic attacks has been made depending upon the context in which the attack has occurred. Attacks can be unexpected or uncued (the attack occurs without a clear external trigger); situationally bound or cued (the attack invariably occurs upon exposure to a particular stimulus); and situationally predisposed (the attack is likely to occur upon exposure to the situation, but does not always occur in the situation). Different diagnoses are associated with these types of panic attacks. For example, PD requires the presence of unexpected panic attacks sometime during the course of the disorder, but patients with PD often have both other types of panic attacks as well. On the other hand, situationally bound attacks predominate in patients with social and specific phobias. The degree to which this distinction will be helpful in diagnosis remains to be seen, but it encourages clinicians to probe the specific situations that bring on the attacks. In clinical practice, it may make conceptual sense to target treatment strategies to the type of panic attack (e.g., medications could be utilized to treat unexpected attacks, cognitive therapy to treat situationally bound attacks, etc.).

A panic attack, especially the first one, is a dramatic event, which patients recount in exquisite detail. They often will recall the exact date, time, place, and circumstance of their initial attack. For

Table 2–1. Criteria for a Panic Attack

Palpitations, pounding heart, or accelerated heart rate

Sweating

Trembling or shaking

Sensations of shortness of breath or smothering

Feeling of choking

Chest pain or discomfort

Nausea or abdominal distress

Feeling dizzy, unsteady, lightheaded, or faint

Derealization (feelings of unreality) or depersonalization (being detached from oneself)

Fear of losing control or going crazy

Fear of dying

Paresthesias (numbness or tingling sensations)

Chills or hot flushes

---

most patients, especially those who had been previously healthy, this event "comes out of the blue" and "hits them like a ton of bricks," leaving them perplexed and worried about their health and safety. It is not clear why some patients can have recurrent panic attacks without developing overwhelming anticipatory anxiety and phobic avoidance, while others are almost immediately disabled. Certainly, one would suspect that pre-morbid personality factors would influence the course, but in some patients the illness seems to have a particular virulence that is difficult to explain.

To meet criteria for PD, the patient must have recurrent unexpected panic attacks, at least one of which has been followed by persistent concern about having additional attacks, worry about the implications of the attacks, or a significant change in behavior as a result of having had an attack. PD can present with or without some degree of phobic avoidance. Panic disorder with agoraphobia is diagnosed when the patient also meets the criteria for agoraphobia. The agoraphobic symptoms may range from enduring a situation with dread and anxiety to avoiding the situation entirely. Severe degrees of phobic avoidance may result in patients who are housebound, but this is not a necessary condition for diagnosing agoraphobia. Indeed, less severe though still limiting and disabling degrees of phobic avoidance are more common than total inability to leave home.

DIFFERENTIAL DIAGNOSIS
AMONG THE ANXIETY DISORDERS

Current diagnostic practices reflect our best approximation of discrete categories. However, both the boundaries between a disorder and no disorder and among the anxiety disorders themselves are not clear or rigid. As a result, there are significant numbers of patients having components of several of these illnesses or meeting criteria for multiple anxiety disorders simultaneously. Considerable work has been conducted in attempts to differentiate among these disorders from genetic, family history, biologic, and treatment response perspectives. This section will discuss differential diagnosis based upon symptom picture and the psychological factors that lead to the overt symptoms. Table 2–2 lists the anxiety disorders as enumerated in *DSM-IV*.

Although it is a truism that a diagnostic evaluation must have historical, intrapsychic, and symptom-oriented components, oftentimes the first two receive less attention in favor of the phenomenological approach. Anxiety disorders, by their very nature, may have an intrapsychic component deriving from what fuels the fear

Table 2–2. DSM-IV Classification of Anxiety Disorders

Panic disorder with agoraphobia

Panic disorder without agoraphobia

Agoraphobia without history of panic disorder

Social phobia

Specific phobia

Obsessive-compulsive disorder

Post-traumatic stress disorder

Acute stress disorder

Generalized anxiety disorder

Anxiety disorder due to . . . (specify the medical disorder)

Substance-induced anxiety disorder (specify substance)

Anxiety disorder, not otherwise specified

Reprinted with permission from the *Diagnostic and Statistical Manual of Mental Disorders, Fourth Edition.* Copyright © 1994 American Psychiatric Association.

or what fuels the avoidance behavior, and eliciting this information is crucial to making the correct diagnosis. The body has a relatively limited repertoire of responses to frightening situations. Therefore, many differing situations, some external, some intrapsychic, can lead to the physiological responses that we label as anxiety or as a panic attack. It is imperative to talk with patients not only about the symptoms that are most obvious (e.g., palpitations, shortness of breath, etc.), but about their inner world—their cognitions and the meaning of their cognitions—in order to make an appropriate diagnosis (and of course in order to design a treatment plan).

The attempt to subtype the nature of the panic attack is a move in this direction; a similar approach could be applied to non-panic anxiety as well. If the panic attack is unexpected or uncued, the most likely diagnosis is panic disorder (if all the other criteria are met).

If the panic attack or anxiety is cued, one must explore what situations bring this on; specific phobia (if the feared stimulus is a specific object or situation) and social phobia (if the feared situation is being the object of others' scrutiny) would be likely diagnoses. If the panic attack or severe anxiety is brought on by disturbing, intrusive thoughts, one could consider obsessive-compulsive disorder or post-traumatic stress disorder (if the intrusive thoughts relate to past trauma).

For the purposes of making a diagnosis, eliciting the patient's explanation for his or her behavior is akin to understanding the circumstances which bring about a panic attack. The behavior of the patient with OCD can seem incomprehensible and even psychotic unless the cognitions associated with the behavior are known. The avoidance of situations by a patient with PTSD so as not to re-experience the trauma is different from the avoidance of the patient with social phobia who fears humiliation. The issue of trauma and the need for exploration of proximal and more distant traumatic experiences is crucial for the diagnosis of PTSD and of the newly created category of acute stress disorder. The anxiety and avoidance behavior of these patients could be seen as meeting criteria for PD, agoraphobia, specific or social phobias if the experience of the trauma is not taken into account.

Generalized anxiety disorder (GAD) presents in a less dramatic form than most of the other anxiety disorders. Panic attacks are typically not present, the anxiety is relatively constant (as opposed to episodic or situational), and the patient may not be able to describe the circumstances which precipitate the anxiety. The six-month time frame for GAD is the longest for the anxiety disorders, making it more likely to be applied in chronic conditions. Also, there must be an effort to determine that the focus of the worry would not make the diagnosis of another disorder more likely (e.g., worry about social performance, worry about body image, etc.).

Finally, and similar to diagnostic practices with other disorders, one must explore whether the symptoms are secondary to a medical disorder and/or substance abuse. This is crucial for anxiety disorders (panic disorder in particular) because the majority of symptoms are physical ones and could mimic other medical illnesses (see below). The new category of anxiety disorder due to a general medical condition would be used when there is evidence that the symptoms of prominent anxiety, panic attacks, or obsessions and/or compulsions are the direct physiological consequence of an identifiable medical disorder (with the exception of delirium). Similarly, if the symptoms developed during or within one month of substance intoxication or withdrawal or medication use is thought to be related to the disorder, a diagnosis of substance-induced anxiety disorder can be made.

DSM-IV has added a section for each group of disorders relating to cultural variants of specific disorders. For the diagnosis of anxiety disorders in people from different cultures, the clinician must be aware of the patient's belief in spirits, witchcraft, and/or magic. Cultural beliefs may lead to avoidance of certain situations, which may appear to be a phobic disorder if not understood in the context of the culture. In addition to being sensitive to these expressions of culture, there are culture-bound syndromes, which *DSM-IV* defines as "locality-specific patterns of aberrant behavior and troubling experience that may or may not be linked to a particular *DSM-IV* diagnostic category" (p. 844). Examples of these syndromes that have the most similarity to the anxiety disorders are: ataque de nervios (Latin America and Puerto Rico); bilis and colera (Latino countries); shen-k'uei (Taiwan) and shenkui (China), resembling panic attacks; hwa-byung and shin-byung (Korea); nervios (Latino countries); rootwork (African-American [south US], Caribbean countries); and shenjing shuairuo or neurasthenia (China), resembling more chronic anxiety with a somatic focus; susto (Latino countries), having elements of PTSD; and taijin kyofusho (Japan), resembling social phobia.

In sum, there is reasonable agreement that grouping the anxiety disorders together has merit, but within this group several disorders share considerable symptom overlap. Given that the modern classification of anxiety disorders is only about 15 years old, it seems reasonable and healthy that acceptance of it is far from universal. As with classification in general, the system must be put to the test as more clinical material is gathered and data are collected regarding course, family incidence, co-morbidity, stability over time, response to treatment, and biological and genetic factors.

DIFFERENTIATION FROM OTHER PSYCHIATRIC DISORDERS

Despite its myriad symptoms, in its pure form there should be little problem distinguishing PD from other psychiatric illnesses. Certainly patients with PD, though extremely anxious, do not display psychotic symptoms or have a formal thought disorder. However, as Klein (1980) pointed out, it was only twenty-five years ago that "in the feckless habit of the time, they were then labeled schizophrenic because they had marked social impairment and severe symptoms" (p. 411). If there is a marked degree of phobic avoidance, the patient's overt behavior may appear similar to that of the patient with paranoid delusions. This distinction can be made by ascertaining the reasons for their not leaving home. Patients with PD fear a panic attack outside of their home or their "safety zone" rather than having a delusional belief about external forces causing them harm. The patient with PD often fears losing control or doing something "crazy," but there is not the actual fragmentation of the self as seen in schizophrenic disorders. The psychosocial function of severely agoraphobic individuals may be similar to a schizophrenic patient, but the symptoms and the explanation of their behavior should allow for distinguishing between these disorders. The boundary between OCD and psychotic states can, at times, be fuzzy. The degree to which patients feel their thoughts are ego-dystonic or that their behavior really makes no sense but they do it to relieve their anxiety are the distinguishing characteristics.

As noted above, there are a number of non-psychotic diagnoses, especially those in the somatoform group, which share symptoms with PD and GAD. Patients with recurrent panic attacks and high levels of intercurrent anxiety may experience multiple physical symptoms in a variety of body systems, making the diagnosis of somatization disorder a possibility. Alternatively, they may focus upon one symptom (e.g., palpitations or dizziness) with a tenacious conviction that there is something terribly wrong. In this case, confusion with hypochondriasis may occur. The important element to focus upon is not the presence of physical symptoms, but the crescendo-like, dramatic anxiety or panic attack, which typically is not present in either of these somatoform disorders. The worry in GAD is typically more broad than a focus upon health concerns.

Depersonalization experiences are noted by some patients during a panic attack, although this is not one of the more common symptoms. If present, it occurs only during an attack, and it is accompanied by a host of other more typical symptoms as detailed above. If the depersonalization is the sole symptom, or the most prominent symptom, then one could consider depersonalization disorder in the differential diagnosis.

The relationship of panic disorder with depression is more perplexing than it is for panic disorder with other psychiatric disorders. Here, the views range from their being variants of the same illness to being separate illnesses altogether (Lesser 1988, Stavrakaki and Vargo 1986). Part of this confusion stems from the high comorbidity shared between these two disorders. It has been estimated that two-thirds of patients with panic disorder will have an episode of major depression sometime during their life (Breier et al. 1986), and from 30 percent to 50 percent of patients develop a major depression after the onset of their panic disorder (secondary depression) (Lesser 1988).

A number of studies using discriminant function and principal component analyses (Gurney et al. 1972, Mountjoy and Roth 1982, Roth et al. 1972, Schapira et al. 1972) have indicated that it is possible to differentiate major depression and anxiety disorders by symptom picture. The symptoms that were best at discriminating between the two were diurnal variation, early morning awakening, and psychomotor retardation for depression, and panic attacks, agoraphobia, depersonalization, derealization, and perceptual distortions for anxiety disorders.

In clinical practice, it can be quite easy to make the distinction. Some patients are quite adamant that they are not depressed, and indeed, they have none of the typical symptoms we associate with depressive illness. Other patients who do admit to having depressive symptoms will state clearly, "I am depressed because I have these attacks, and I can't go places that I used to. If it weren't for the fears, I would not be depressed." These patients with secondary depressions may have a syndrome more akin to demoralization. On the other hand, differentiation in some patients may be very difficult if the patient sees the time course of panic and depressive symptoms as being the same or overlapping to such a degree that no temporal sequencing is possible. When the two co-exist, and the depression is severe, the patient may have a more severe and protracted course of the panic disorder (Clancy et al. 1978, Van Valkenberg et al. 1984). However, secondary depressions of moderate severity are not necessarily a poor prognostic sign for the successful pharmacologic treatment of the panic disorder (Lesser et al. 1988). Even if the diagnosis cannot be made with absolute certainty, it is of some comfort that the antidepressants used to treat major depressions also are effective in panic disorder, and data show that alprazolam is effective in treating panic disorder even when the patient has a secondary depression (Lesser et al. 1988).

Another interesting diagnostic consideration occurs when patients with anxiety disorders are viewed not from the perspective of episode-based pathology (Axis I), but from the perspective of long-term personality functioning (Axis II). Symptoms of anxiety, although not necessarily part of the diagnostic criteria for specific personality disorders, are certainly experienced by patients with personality disorders. For example, in patients with borderline personality disorders, anxiety of panic proportions may be at the core of their pathology, and their symptom picture often includes multiple phobias. Yet there is little specificity of a particular anxiety disorder with borderline personality disorder, or any other personality disorder for that matter. The exception to this statement is the considerable overlap between avoidant personality disorder and generalized social phobia.

Careful and systematic study of the personality styles or disorders associated with anxiety disorders has begun only recently (Starcevic 1992, Stein et al. 1993). As is the case in studying personality in depression, it has been shown that in patients with PD and agoraphobia a broad range of personality measures are influenced by the presence of state anxiety (Reich et al. 1986). This makes it difficult to discuss pre-morbid personality styles assessed during an active phase of illness. Nevertheless, studies have reported that among PD patients with phobic avoidance, dependent personality disorders were more prevalent (approximately 40 percent) than in patients with PD and no avoidance (Reich et al. 1987). The investigators correctly note that it was not possible to state whether the dependent behavior preceded the PD or was a result of it, though they cite the earlier work of others, which suggests that dependent traits do predispose to the development of anxiety disorders.

A theoretical model of personality, describing personality and temperamental dimensions of novelty seeking, harm avoidance, and reward dependence has been postulated by Cloninger (1986). In a model with great heuristic value, he uses this theory, which has neurobiological correlates as well, to understand the development of a variety of anxiety states. At present, this has more theoretical than diagnostic utility, but is an interesting approach to understanding psychopathology.

DIFFERENTIATION FROM MEDICAL DISORDERS

It should be obvious from what has been said above that the multitude of physical symptoms that are an integral part of anxiety disorders, particularly PD, make distinctions from actual physical disease a necessary and potentially difficult component of the total work-up of these patients. Indeed, the typical patient with PD will make many visits to emergency rooms and to his or her primary care physician prior to seeking help in the mental health sector. Since the symptoms of anxiety mimic those seen in many medical diseases, some of which are quite serious (Hall 1980), patients often undergo many repeated diagnostic tests. The specific medical illnesses and suggested diagnostic work-ups have been detailed elsewhere (Ballenger 1987, National Institute of Mental Health 1993, Raj and Sheehan 1987) and will only be reviewed briefly here.

Some medical conditions actually cause symptoms of anxiety and panic; when treated, the panic attacks abate. This was officially recognized in *DSM-III-R* with the designation of organic anxiety disorder and now in *DSM-IV* as anxiety disorder due to a general medical disorder. This diagnosis should be used when either recurrent panic attacks and/or generalized anxiety occur in the context of an illness or of substance use that is known to be associated with anxiety. Examples of such illnesses are hyperthyroidism, Cushing's syndrome (excess production of the hormone cortisol), pheochromocytoma (a tumor of the adrenal glands producing adrenaline), and hypoglycemia. Stimulant drugs such as amphetamines, cocaine, and caffeine, when taken in excess, also can produce a picture of anxiety and panic attacks, now referred to as substance-induced anxiety disorder.

A large number of additional diseases cause isolated symptoms or clusters of symptoms which are prominent in PD. Symptoms referable to the cardiovascular system are probably most frequently reported by patients (Ballenger 1987, Beitman et al. 1989, Marks and Lader 1973). These symptoms include palpitations, rapid heart rate, heaviness in the chest, and chest pain, often radiating to the arms. Patients often think that they are having a heart attack or that their heart cannot possibly continue to beat in this manner for very long. Examples of cardiac illnesses which share some symptoms with panic attacks are numerous. Cardiac arrhythmias are disturbances in the rate and rhythm of the heartbeat that can present in a similar fashion to a panic attack. Episodes of chest pain on the basis of coronary artery dysfunction also can mimic an acute panic attack, especially since panic attacks can be precipitated by exercise.

The association between the mitral valve prolapse syndrome (MVPS) and PD has been complex and its status remains unresolved. MVPS is a disorder in which there is an anatomic abnormality of the mitral valve of the heart. It often is present and asymptomatic in many healthy individuals. However, when severe, it may cause a syndrome characterized by palpitations, rapid heart rate, chest pain, anxiety, and fatigue. The diagnosis is usually made after clinical examination and echocardiographic studies of the heart. Reviews of the many studies investigating the relationship between PD and MVPS suggest that there is a relationship between the two, although the nature of the relationship is difficult to state with certainty (Katerndahl 1993). Because MVPS may place patients at increased risk for several additional medical complications, it is important to evaluate patients for its presence. However, patients with PD respond to medications in a similar fashion whether or not they have MVPS (Gorman et al. 1981)

Complaints referable to the respiratory system, for example, shortness of breath, rapid breathing (hyperventilation), and a feeling of "air hunger," also are frequent in patients with panic attacks. An illness such as asthma, which presents in dramatic, episodic attacks and is associated with considerable anxiety, can be confused with a panic attack. Other respiratory conditions to be alert for are chronic obstructive lung disease, and recurrent pulmonary emboli, whereby small clot-like particles become lodged in lung tissue, thereby decreasing the ability of the lung to properly oxygenate the blood.

Because multiple hormones act on target organs, including the brain, there is a complex interplay between hormonal status and behavior. Dysregulations of the thyroid, parathyroid (important in the regulation of calcium), adrenal glands, and pancreas all have been associated with episodes of panic. However, in large studies of patients with PD, few abnormalities were found in thyroid function (Fishman et al. 1985, Lesser et al. 1987), and no cases were reported of hypoglycemia (Gorman et al. 1984, Uhde et al. 1984).

Neurologic symptoms also are commonly seen in panic attacks. Patients often have episodes of dizziness, lightheadedness or a giddy feeling, perceptual distortion, headache, and paresthesia (a feeling of pins and needles in the extremities). Some of these symptoms may be the result of hyperventilation, but others may be associated with actual neurologic disease, such as inner ear dysfunctions (Meniere's disease, acute labrynthitis) or brain tumors. Panic attacks may share some symptoms with epilepsy, especially partial complex seizures or temporal lobe seizures. However, as is the case with other illnesses mentioned above, this is not a common cause of panic attacks.

Because many of the illnesses discussed here are serious and require specific treatment, it is necessary that they be considered in the differential diagnosis. On the other hand, not every patient needs to have sophisticated medical investigations for each one. Indeed, the clinician must walk a fine line between conducting appropriate medical evaluations, and reinforcing the view that the patient has a medical illness and that further testing will ultimately lead to the "answer."

A minimum medical work-up should include a careful history, with emphasis upon use of medications, drugs, and caffeine; a physical examination; baseline laboratory studies to assess anemia, electrolyte and calcium disturbances, and thyroid function; and an electrocardiogram. If suspicions are aroused about specific disease processes, more specialized diagnostic tests, such as 24-hour cardiac monitoring, electroencephalograms, glucose tolerance tests, and so on, can be obtained.

CONCLUSIONS

Anxiety disorders as a group and panic disorders in particular are commonly seen in the general population, in medical practices, and in the mental health setting. They have been recognized and well described for years, though they have undergone extensive changes in nomenclature. According to Spitzer and Williams (1985), the purposes of classification in mental health are communication, control (the ability to either prevent the occurrence or modify the course of the disorder), and comprehension (understanding the causes of the disorder). When compared to previous systems, our current system certainly goes a long way towards reaching these goals. Whether the current separation of the remaining disorders successfully fulfills these expectations must await further findings from research and from clinical practice.

REFERENCES

Ballenger, J. C. (1987). Unrecognized prevalence of panic disorder in primary care, internal medicine and cardiology. *American Journal of Cardiology* 60:39J–47J.

Beitman, B. D., Mukerju, V., Lamberti, J. W., et al. (1989). Panic disorder in patients with chest pain and angiographically normal coronary arteries. *American Journal of Cardiology* 63:1399–1403.

Breier, A., Charney, D. S., and Heninger, G. R. (1986). Agoraphobia with panic attacks: development, diagnostic stability, and course of illness. *Archives of General Psychiatry* 43:1029–1036.

Burton, R. (1621). *The Anatomy of Melancholy.* London: Dent, 1932.

Clancy, J., Noyes, R., Hoenk, P. R., and Slymen, D. J. (1978). Secondary depression in anxiety neurosis. *Journal of Nervous and Mental Disease* 166:846–850.

Cloninger, C. R. (1986). A unified biosocial theory of personality and its role in the development of anxiety states. *Psychiatric Developments* 3:167–226.

Da Costa, J. M. (1871). On irritable heart: a clinical study of a form of functional cardiac disorder and its consequences. *American Journal of Medical Science* 61:17–52.

Diagnostic and Statistical Manual of Mental Disorders (1980). 3rd ed. Washington, DC: American Psychiatric Association.

———— (1987). 3rd ed., rev. Washington, DC: American Psychiatric Association.

———— (1994). 4th ed. Washington, DC: American Psychiatric Association.

Eisenberg, L. (1992). Treating depression and anxiety in primary care. *New England Journal of Medicine* 326:1080–1084.

Fishman, S. M., Sheehan, D. V., and Carr, D. B. (1985). Thyroid dysfunction in panic disorder. *Journal of Clinical Psychiatry* 46:422–423.

Freud, S. (1962). On the grounds for detaching a particular syndrome from neurasthenia under the description "anxiety neurosis." *Standard Edition* 3.

Gorman, J. M., Fyer, A. J., Glicklich, J., et al. (1981). Mitral valve prolapse and panic disorders: effect of imipramme. In *Anxiety: New Research and Changing Concepts*, ed. D. J. Klein and J. G. Rabkin. New York: Raven Press.

Gorman, J. M., Martinez, J. M., Liebowitz, M. R., et al. (1984). Hypoglycemia and panic attacks. *American Journal of Psychiatry* 141:101–102.

Gurney, C., Roth, M., Garside, R. F., et al. (1972). Studies in the classifi-
    cation of affective disorders: the relationship between anxiety states
    and depressive illness—II. *British Journal of Psychiatry* 121:162–166.
Hall, R. C. W. (1980). *Psychiatric Presentations of Medical Illnesses.* New York:
    SP Medical and Scientific Books.
Janet, P., and Raymon, F. (1898). *Les Nevroses et Idees Fixes.* 2 Vols. Paris:
    Felix Alcan.
Katerndahl, D. A. (1993). Panic and prolapse: meta-analysis. *Journal of
    Nervous and Mental Disease* 181:539–544.
Klein, D. F. (1964). Delineation of two drug-responsive anxiety syn-
    dromes. *Psychopharmacologia* 5:397–408.
——— (1980). Anxiety reconceptualized. *Comprehensive Psychiatry* 21:
    411–427.
Klein, D. F., Ross, D. C., and Cohen, P. (1987). Panic and avoidance in
    agoraphobia: application of path analysis to treatment studies.
    Archives of General Psychiatry 44:377–385.
Lesser, I. M. (1988). The relationship between panic disorder and
    depression. *Journal of Anxiety Disorders* 2:3–15.
Lesser, I. M., Rubin, R. T., Lydiard, R. B., et al. (1987). Past and cur-
    rent thyroid function in subjects with panic disorder. *Journal of Clini-
    cal Psychiatry* 48:473–476.
Lesser, I. M., Rubin, R. T., Pecknold, J. C., et al. (1988). Secondary
    depression in panic disorder and agoraphobia: frequency, severity,
    and response to treatment. *Archives of General Psychiatry* 45:437–443.
Marks, I., and Lader, M. (1973). Anxiety states (anxiety neurosis): a
    review. *Journal of Nervous Mental Disorder* 156:3–18.
Mountjoy, C. Q., and Roth, M. (1982). Studies in the relationship be-
    tween depressive disorders and anxiety states. Part 2. Clinical items.
    Journal of Affective Disorder 4:149–161.
National Institute of Mental Health. (1993). *Panic Disorder in the Medical Set-
    ting,* by W. Katon, NIH Publication No. 93-3482. Washington D.C.:
    Superintendent of Documents, U.S. Government Printing Office.

Nemiah, J. C. (1974). Anxiety, signal, symptom, and syndrome. In *American Handbook of Psychiatry*, 2nd ed., vol. 3, ed. S. Arieti and E. B. Brody. New York: Basic Books.

Raj, A., and Sheehan, D. V. (1987). Medical evaluation of panic attacks. *Journal of Clinical Psychiatry* 48:309–313.

Reich, J., Noyes, R., Coryell, W., and O'Gorman, T. W. (1986). The effect of state anxiety on personality measurement. *American Journal of Psychiatry* 143:760–763.

Reich, J., Noyes, R., and Troughton, E. (1987). Dependent personality disorder associated with phobic avoidance in patients with panic disorder. *American Journal of Psychiatry* 144:323–326.

Robins, L. N., and Regier, D. A. (1991). *Psychiatric Disorders in America: The Epidemiologic Catchment Area Study*. New York: Free Press.

Roth, M., Gurney, C., Garside, R. F., and Kerr, T. A. (1972). Studies in the classification of affective disorders: the relationship between anxiety states and depressive illness—I. *British Journal of Psychiatry* 121:147–161.

Schapira, K., Roth, M., Kerr, T. A., and Gurney, C. (1972). The prognosis of affective disorders: the differentiation of anxiety states from depressive illnesses. *British Journal of Psychiatry* 121:175–181.

Spitzer, R. L., and Williams, J. B. W. (1985). Classification of mental disorders. In *Comprehensive Textbook of Psychiatry/IV*, vol 1, ed. H. I. Kaplan and B J. Sadock, 4th ed., pp. 591–613. Baltimore: Williams & Wilkins.

Starcevic, V. (1992): Comorbidity models of panic disorder/agoraphobia and personality disturbance. *Journal of Personality Disorders* 6:213–225.

Stavrakaki, C., and Vargo, B. (1986). The relationship of anxiety and depression: a review of the literature. *British Journal of Psychiatry* 149:7–16.

Stein, D. J., Hollander E., and Skodol, A. E. (1993). Anxiety disorders and personality disorders: a review. *Journal of Personality Disorders* 7:87–104.

Uhde, T. W., and Nemiah, J. C. (1989). Panic and generalized anxiety disorders. In *Comprehensive Textbook of Psychiatry*, vol. V, ed. H. I. Kaplan and B. Sadok, p. 453. Baltimore: Williams & Wilkins.

Uhde, T. W., Vittone, B. J., and Post, R. M. (1984). Glucose tolerance testing in panic disorder. *American Journal of Psychiatry* 141:1461–1463.

Van Valkenburg, C., Akiskal, H. S., Puzantian, V., and Rosenthal, T. (1984). Anxious depressions: clinical, family history, and naturalistic outcome—comparisons with panic and major depressive disorders. *Journal of Affective Disorder* 6:67–82.

CHAPTER THREE

Cognitive-Behavioral Treatment of Agoraphobia

———◆———

Agoraphobia is the most dramatic of the phobias, often resulting in the sufferer's becoming completely housebound.

Until the recent revolution in treatment, this debilitating disorder was considered virtually untreatable. The turning point of effectiveness in the new treatment was addressing patients' perceived fear, whether rational or irrational, that certain situations cause anxiety or even panic, and that they are to be avoided. While this seems obvious now, twenty years ago the idea of an anxiety disorder was itself controversial because the implications ran counter to the psychodynamic understanding of agoraphobia.

This chapter describes Drs. Carmin and Pollard's effective cognitive-behavioral treatment program developed at St. Louis University. It provides an introduction to the concepts and treatment techniques that are developed further throughout the book and emphasizes careful assessment and understanding of the patient in the treatment process.

———◆———

Cognitive-Behavioral Treatment of Agoraphobia

CHERYL N. CARMIN
C. ALEC POLLARD

INTRODUCTION

The syndrome of agoraphobia has been alluded to in the psychiatric literature since the late 1800s, when it was first described by Benedikt as "place dizziness" or *platzschwindel* (Benedikt 1870). Shortly after, the term agoraphobia was formally coined by Westphal to describe a fear of the marketplace (Westphal 1888). Despite having been given a variety of names with differing emphases on specific symptoms, agoraphobia has been described with remarkable consistency over the years. Two components of agoraphobic fear have been repeatedly mentioned as defining characteristics. First, unlike those who suffer from specific phobias, agoraphobics often avoid a spectrum of seemingly unrelated situations. What unites these various situations is the fear that escape or access to safety might be difficult or somehow impeded. Examples of situations which agoraphobics typically avoid include traveling distances from home, crowds, public transportation, being alone, or being in places such as elevators or the middle of auditoriums from where it may be difficult to depart (Chambless et al. 1984). In addition to avoiding situations perceived as dangerous, agoraphobics actively seek situations where they feel safe (Rachman 1984). For example, many feel the need to have a safe or trusted person accompany them. In the most severe cases, an individual may become housebound.

The concept of agoraphobia, however, has evolved into more than just a fear of external situations. The second defining characteristic of this disorder is fear of physical sensations (interoception) and heightened somatic concern. Agoraphobics are not only afraid of specific situations per se, but of experiencing an attack of symptoms in those situations. Thus, individuals with agoraphobia avoid or try to control interoceptive as well as exteroceptive stimuli.

These two fundamental fears, of external situations and internal sensations, are integral to the current definition of agoraphobia and are reflected in diagnostic criteria. The *Diagnostic and Statistical Manual, DSM-IV* (1994), defines agoraphobia as:

> A. Anxiety about being in places or situations from which escape might be difficult (or embarrassing) or in which help may not be available in the event of having an unexpected or situationally predisposed Panic Attack or panic-like symptoms. Agoraphobic fears typically involve characteristic clusters of situations that include being outside the home alone, being in a crowd or standing in a line, being on a bridge, and traveling in a bus, train, or automobile.
>
> B. The situations are avoided (e.g., travel is restricted) or else are endured with marked distress or with anxiety about having a Panic Attack or panic-like symptoms, or require the presence of a companion. [p. 396]

The disorder may be classified either as panic disorder with agoraphobia or as agoraphobia without history of panic disorder, depending on the nature of the feared symptom attack. With the former diagnosis, agoraphobic avoidance is associated with unexpected panic attacks, whereas the latter diagnosis involves a fear of symptom attacks (e.g., dizziness, loss of bowel control, headache) other than panic.

Anxiety disorders, including agoraphobia, are prevalent and potentially chronic conditions, more so than either affective or substance abuse disorders (Kessler et al. 1994). Agoraphobia alone affects up to 6 percent of the population, according to data from the Epidemiologic Catchment Area survey (Myers et al. 1984) and the more recent National Comorbidity Study (Kessler et al. 1994). At least twice as many women as men are affected by the disorder and onset typically occurs in young adulthood (Joyce et al. 1989). Individuals suffering from this disorder tend to experience a markedly diminished quality of life and make frequent use of medical services (Klerman et al. 1991, Pollard et al. 1989). They also experience more chronic anxiety than patients with panic disorder alone (Dukman-Caes and De Vries 1991). In addition, agoraphobics are at risk for alcohol abuse (Thyer et al. 1985), depression (Lesser 1990), other anxiety disorders (Stein et al. 1989), and personality disorders (Brooks et al. 1989), particularly avoidant, dependent, and histrionic types (Chambless et al. 1992).

Over the years, a variety of approaches has been used to treat agoraphobia. Certain drugs, for example, have been beneficial in reducing panic attacks and, to a lesser extent, apprehension and avoidance. Medications available for agoraphobia are briefly discussed later in this chapter (see also Chapter 15). Several different psychological approaches have been tried as well, including psychodynamic psychotherapy (Shear et al. 1993), hypnosis and subliminal therapy (Yager 1988), behavioral treatments (Wolpe 1990), and newer cognitive behavioral therapies (Beck et al. 1985, Clark 1988, Klosko et al. 1990). However, based on the results of controlled outcome studies, behavioral and cognitive-behavioral therapies have most clearly demonstrated their effectiveness as treatments for agoraphobia. (See Chambless and Gillis 1993, McNally 1994, Shapiro et al. 1993 for comprehensive reviews.)

The purpose of this chapter is to describe the cognitive-behavioral treatment of agoraphobia. Because almost all of the treatment research on agoraphobia involves panic disorder with agoraphobia, this chapter primarily addresses this more common form of the disorder. However, we briefly discuss issues relevant to the treatment of agoraphobia without history of panic disorder in a special section of this chapter. Although we describe the panic treatment portion of the therapy, the reader is referred to Klosko and Barlow's chapter for a more thorough discussion of the treatment of panic disorder.

AN INTEGRATED COGNITIVE-BEHAVIORAL MODEL OF AGORAPHOBIA

There are several different compelling explanations in the cognitive-behavioral literature for how agoraphobia develops and a number of contributing factors have been identified. Until the relative utility of the various models and factors has been more clearly demonstrated, we believe it is useful to draw from several theories. Based on our model, a variety of factors are proposed to contribute either to the etiology or to the maintenance of agoraphobia. Factors that contribute to agoraphobia can be divided into three categories: predisposing factors, precipitants, and maintenance factors. Figure 3–1 outlines our model of the way in which these factors influence agoraphobia.

Predisposing Factors

Predisposing factors refer to factors which increase the likelihood an individual will experience or react maladaptively to panic attacks at some point in life. Both biological and psychological predispositions may contribute to panic onset or influence the course of panic and its complications.

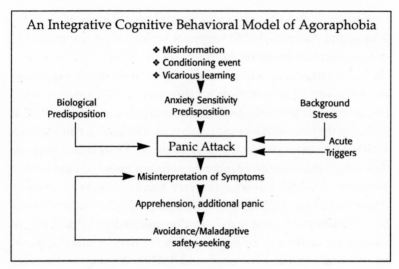

Figure 3–1

ANXIETY SENSITIVITY

Anxiety sensitivity is a trait that may predispose an individual to experience panic attacks. People with high anxiety sensitivity fear their anxiety symptoms due to a belief that these symptoms have harmful consequences (McNally 1989). Any symptom associated with anxiety, even if triggered by other emotions or physical processes, can be misperceived as potentially catastrophic. Thus, high anxiety sensitivity is one risk factor for the development of panic disorder and agoraphobia (McNally and Lorenz 1987). High levels of anxiety sensitivity can be acquired through misinformation, vicarious learning, or conditioning experiences (McNally 1994).

BIOLOGICAL VULNERABILITY

Several biological factors have been implicated in the etiology of panic (Maser and Woods 1990). Continuing family linkage and twin research into the genetics of agoraphobia (Crowe et al. 1983, Morau and Andrews 1985) suggest a biological predisposition to the disorder can be inherited. Based on the results of biochemical challenge studies, it is believed that some individuals experience dysregulation in one or more of their neurotransmitter systems. Dysfunction in the norepinephrine system (Charney et al. 1990) as well as in the serotonin system (Lesch et al. 1992, Maser and Woods 1990) has been suggested as a cause of panic. There is also evidence that some panic-disordered individuals have a carbon dioxide (Klein 1993) or a GABA-minergic receptor benzodiazepine sensitivity (Nutt and Lawson 1992). It has been proposed that more than one neurotransmitter system may in fact be involved and that different areas of the brain may be implicated in the development of panic, anxiety, and avoidance (Gorman et al. 1989). We suggest that some individuals have a biological vulnerability to panic and agoraphobia; however, other psychological or environmental factors are required for the disorder to develop (Barlow 1988).

Precipitants

Precipitants are factors that elicit panic attacks in predisposed individuals. Someone with a biological predisposition to panic and high anxiety sensitivity will not experience panic onset until exposed to a precipitant. There are two categories of precipitants: background stressors and acute triggers.

BACKGROUND STRESSORS

Panic onset usually occurs at a time of major life change or stress (Pollard et al. 1989). The impact of background stress is often cumulative and not necessarily immediate; an individual may have been dealing with a major life event for several months before having a panic attack. It is this cumulative effect that appears to prime the predisposed individual for panic.

ACUTE TRIGGERS

A predisposed individual undergoing a major life event is highly vulnerable to acute triggers that elicit panic. Although patients often report their first panic attack seemed to come "out of the blue," our model suggests there is often an acute interoceptive or exteroceptive trigger for the attack. Some triggers are obvious, such as the acute psychological and physiological effects of smoking marijuana. However, triggers can also be subtle, for example, the cognitive and somatic stimuli associated with worrying about life problems. Psychophysiological arousal induced by situations like standing in a slow line at the grocery store or driving in rush hour traffic can be acute triggers of panic as well. Because the situational trigger has not historically been associated with such an extreme fear response, the panic attack is perceived by the individual as uncued or spontaneous.

Maintenance Factors

The experience of a panic attack does not inevitably lead to agoraphobia. Although predisposing and precipitating factors are responsible for panic onset, specific maintenance factors are necessary to perpetuate panic and shape the development of agoraphobia. Identification of maintenance factors is crucial to a cognitive behavioral approach because they are the target of most cognitive and behavioral interventions.

Most contemporary cognitive-behavioral models of agoraphobia have been influenced in one way or another by the "fear of fear" concept. Goldstein and Chambless (1978) posit that fear of fear is central to agoraphobia and results from Pavlovian interoceptive conditioning. After the first panic attack (unconditioned stimulus), individuals with agoraphobia become hypervigilant to the physical sensations of being anxious (conditioned stimuli associated with panic) and thereafter respond with fear (conditioned response) to these anxiety-related sensations, which are perceived as the harbingers of panic. A conditioned fear reaction to sensations associated with panic is established, thus setting a cycle in motion that inevitably results in a panic in response to certain interoceptive cues.

In contrast to the earlier work of Goldstein and Chambless (1978), more cognitively oriented theorists hold that panic results from the catastrophic misinterpretation of anxiety-related physical sensations or other strong affective responses (Clark 1988). In this model, catastrophic cognitions create a positive feedback loop since they intensify anxiety, which increases physiologic reactivity. Thus, for the agoraphobic who has just climbed a flight of stairs, rapid heart rate is misinterpreted as an impending heart attack. This misinterpretation creates anxiety, which accelerates heart rate further, and the cycle continues to repeat and escalate. Agoraphobia develops when the individual becomes increasingly fearful of and avoids those situations in which panic symptoms are perceived as being particularly likely or catastrophic. By avoiding situations associated with panic, agoraphobics are unable to test the accuracy of their catastrophic beliefs about these symptoms (Salkovskis 1988). It is the failure to test, and presumably to invalidate, these maladaptive beliefs that maintains the phobic behavior.

Beck's cognitive formulation of agoraphobia emphasizes the agoraphobia sufferer's cognitive vulnerability set (Beck et al. 1985). Though similar, Beck's model differs from Clark's (1988) in that the belief system regarding vulnerability to physical threat is already in place prior to a panic attack and serves to predispose certain individuals to panic. For example, an agoraphobic may believe that when alone, he or she is vulnerable to physical or psychological threat and that this situation can be remedied by having unrestricted access to a safe place or person. If assistance or escape is in some way prevented, physical symptoms may not be able to be ignored. These symptoms are then interpreted as indications of impending disaster, which then further escalates anxiety. Once again, a vicious cycle begins that culminates in panic and subsequent avoidance.

Cognitive-attentional models of agoraphobia attempt to integrate interoceptive sensitivity and cognitive misinterpretations (Belfer and Glass 1992). Such models suggest that agoraphobics are excessively aware of and selectively attend to physiologic arousal (MacLeod et al. 1986). This information-processing model also suggests that agoraphobics are predisposed to catastrophically misinterpret the meaning of their symptoms. The attentional bias inherent in agoraphobic anxiety is part of an encoding process whereby certain cues are attended to selectively and mislabeled as threatening.

Taking into account many of these ideas, our model suggests agoraphobia is maintained by a vicious cycle of misinterpretations of internal sensations, panic attacks, apprehension about future attacks, and maladaptive avoidance and safety-seeking behavior. The way in which individuals respond to initial and subsequent panic attacks over time determines whether agoraphobia develops. If the individual misinterprets the physical sensations of the first attack as harmful, this misinterpretation will lead to apprehension about and a desire to avoid future attacks. The individual avoids or tries to control internal sensations associated with panic and any external situation viewed as increasing the probability or dangerousness of those sensations. Likewise, the individual seeks "safe" situations (e.g., home, a trusted companion) believed to reduce the probability or danger of the sensations. This pattern perpetuates agoraphobia by preventing the individual from finding out that the feared catastrophic outcomes of panic do not occur, thus reinforcing the patient's cognitive distortions and perpetuating the tendency to respond to certain interoceptive and exteroceptive cues maladaptively.

ASSESSMENT

The assessment of agoraphobia has become increasingly precise over the years. Typically, the purpose of assessment is to establish proper diagnosis, measure symptom severity and disability, identify factors that contribute to the development of the disorder (e.g., background stressors, learning history), delineate factors currently maintaining the problem (e.g., maladaptive coping strategies such as avoidance, cognitive distortions), and rule out other conditions that might mimic or exacerbate the symptoms of agoraphobia. Despite the fact that most cognitive-behavioral clinicians examine these factors, there is still a great deal of variability in the specific assessment instruments used (Shear et al. 1994). Thus, we present one set of procedures as a model. Specific instruments or procedures can of course be modified to suit the individual clinician's preferences.

Prior to beginning the assessment, and especially before beginning treatment, patients are encouraged to see their physicians if they have not had a recent medical examination. Since there are several physical conditions with symptoms that are similar to or mimic anxiety symptoms, it is important to ensure a patient is not suffering from an undiagnosed medical problem. It is also important to determine that the patient can participate in therapy safely. Medical clearance is particularly important for cognitive-behavioral therapy since anxiety symptoms are often provoked during treatment. For a more thorough discussion of the medical assessment of agoraphobic patients, the reader is referred to Goldberg (1988), Pollard and Lewis (1989), and Raj and Sheehan (1987).

Cognitive-behavioral assessment of agoraphobia typically includes a clinical interview, self-report instruments, self-monitoring of symptoms, a behavioral test, and a medical examination (Craske and Barlow 1993). Less frequently, psychophysiologic assessment (e.g., heart rate, muscle tension) may be included as well.

Clinical Interview and Diagnosis

There are several clinician-administered structured interviews which have been developed to diagnose anxiety disorders. These instruments include the Anxiety Disorders Interview Schedule–Revised

(ADIS-R) (DiNardo and Barlow 1988), the Schizophrenia and Affective Disorders Schedule–Life Time Version (Anxiety Modified) (SADS-LA) (Manuzza et al. 1989) and the Structured Clinical Interview for *DSM-III-R* (SCID) (Spitzer and Williams 1992). Revised versions of each of these instruments based on *DSM-IV* (1994) were being developed or studied at the time this chapter was written. For the most part, all of these instruments provide reliable and valid diagnoses; however, interviewers must be trained to use the instruments and each takes a considerable amount of time to administer. For these reasons, some clinicians may elect not to use these instruments.

In our clinical setting, we rely on a semi-structured interview, which addresses current symptoms, the history of these symptoms, and past psychiatric, medical, family, and social histories. In addition, we use a self-report diagnostic instrument, the Anxiety Symptoms Interview–IV (ASI–IV) (Pollard and Carmin 1995). The ASI–IV can be administered by a clinician but can be completed by the patient in about 15 to 20 minutes. Therefore, the ASI–IV is practical for use in most clinical settings. Unlike the more extensive structured diagnostic instruments, however, the ASI–IV is primarily used as an adjunct to a clinical interview.

Self-Report Questionnaires

There are several self-report measures available to assess symptom severity and degree of avoidance, and to identify factors contributing to the agoraphobia. The self-report instruments developed at our clinic include a History Questionnaire, Life Events Questionnaire, Worry about Panic Scale, Phobic Severity Rating Scale, Panic Cognitions Questionnaire, Physical Symptoms During Panic Questionnaire, Panic Appraisal Form, and Panic and Avoidance Questionnaire. Instruments included in our packet developed by other clinicians include the Mobility Inventory (Chambless et al.

1985), Anxiety Sensitivity Index (Peterson and Reiss 1992), and the Fear Survey Schedule (Wolpe and Lang 1969). Each instrument and its primary purpose is outlined in Table 3–1.

Self-Monitoring

Because self-report instruments require recall of past symptoms, they are vulnerable to distortion such as under- or over-reporting symptoms. Thus, our patients also complete instruments which require them to monitor panic symptoms (Panic Diary) and anxiety (Anxiety Rating Scale) as they occur over the course of a day or week (see Table 3–1). One difficulty with self-monitoring procedures, however, is nonadherence. Self-monitoring takes more effort and requires patients to focus on symptoms they might prefer to forget or avoid. If the value of this source of information is explained, however, most patients with agoraphobia comply fully with the assessment process.

Behavioral Tests

Another valuable source of information is behavioral tests such as the Behavioral Approach Test (BAT). The BAT asks patients to attempt to perform a challenging task related to their agoraphobia. First, patients identify a difficult task they are currently unable to perform because of agoraphobic fear. For example, the task might be spending 3 hours at the mall alone or driving 30 miles unaccompanied to visit a relative. The task should be one that, if performed, both the clinician and patient agree would indicate significant clinical improvement. Patients are then asked to perform as much of the task as they can: stay as long as they can at the mall alone or drive as far as they can toward a target destination before deciding to stop. Some clinics have a course for patients to follow as part of a stan-

Table 3–1. Panic Disorder with Agoraphobia Assessment Packet: Questionnaires

Instrument	Purpose
History Questionnaire*	Historical data and background information
Life Events Questionnaire*	History of major life events/ stressors
Phobic Severity Rating Scale*	Self-rating of fear and avoidance
Panic Cognitions Questionnaire*	Self-report of catastrophic thoughts during panic
Physical Symptoms During Panic*	Self-rating of severity of physical symptoms during panic attacks
Panic Appraisal Form*	Probability and self-efficacy estimates
Mobility Inventory	Self-rating of situational avoidance
Panic and Avoidance Questionnaire*	Details about coping/ avoidance
Fear Survey Schedule	Ratings of specific fears
Anxiety Sensitivity Index	Self-rating of anxiety sensitivity
Worry About Panic Estimate*	Self-rating of anticipatory, panic-related anxiety

*Questionnaires developed by the authors and available upon request.

dardized BAT, but such courses may not be relevant to the fears of every patient. Performance on the BAT provides information about the patient's level of avoidance at baseline and at various assessment points in treatment. The BAT can also be the basis for in vivo exposure once therapy has been initiated.

Interoceptive assessment (IA) measures a patient's sensitivity to various internal sensations associated with panic. During this procedure, sensations (increased heart rate, dizziness, difficulty breathing, etc.) are provoked under the therapist's supervision by one of several procedures (e.g., running in place or stair-stepping, spinning, deliberate hyperventilation). For each provocation procedure, patients are asked to report their level of anxiety and the extent to which the provoked sensations resemble those associated with panic. Sensations that elicit high anxiety and are perceived as being similar to panic sensations typically become the focus of interoceptive exposure, a procedure described in the treatment section of this chapter and also in Chapter 9 of this book.

TREATMENT OF AGORAPHOBIA

A number of studies suggest that cognitive behavioral treatment of agoraphobia takes between eight and fifteen sessions (e.g., Craske and Barlow 1993). However, while many individuals obtain substantial improvement in a relatively short time, this is not always the case. Comorbid anxiety disorders, depression, personality disorders, and abuse of alcohol or drugs abuse, not being ready to engage in treatment, and a chaotic family situation are among those factors that can complicate and extend the duration of treatment. Therefore, although we will be describing a fourteen-session model, it is with the understanding that the model is for the typical treatment of uncomplicated agoraphobia. An individual patient may need more or less treatment, modification of the sequence of treatment components, or the addition of adjunctive interventions.

Primary Treatment Components

Treatment of agoraphobia involves education, symptom management, cognitive restructuring, and exposure to interoceptive and exteroceptive fear cues. Specific cases may require other treatments as well, such as medication or family therapy. These adjunctive treatments will be discussed in the next section. In this section we will focus on the primary components of the cognitive-behavioral treatment of agoraphobia. For a session-by-session model of how these interventions can be applied, see the appendix to this chapter.

EDUCATION

The first step in the treatment process is providing information about agoraphobia. Educating patients and their families about agoraphobia helps dispel fears of being crazy or out of control, clarify that the symptoms are real and treatable, and provide reassurance that other people suffer from this disorder.

Education about agoraphobia can be provided in several ways. Once the initial evaluation is completed, there should be sufficient history and assessment data to allow the therapist to adapt the cognitive-behavioral model to each patient. From the outset, the therapist is building a cognitive-behavioral case formulation which incorporates and explains both etiologic and maintenance factors unique to each patient. By apprising the patient of the formulation, the therapist is, at the same time, educating the patient about the therapist's model so both can share a common language and base of understanding.

In addition to the therapist's providing information, other resources are available to educate patients about agoraphobia. There are several informative books (e.g., Clum 1989, Craske and Barlow 1994, Wilson 1986) available to consumers that discuss agoraphobia largely from a cognitive-behavioral perspective. In addition, there are films, such as *Stories of Hope* (National Institute of Mental Health 1994), made specifically to provide consumers with an overview of agoraphobia and its treatment.

ANXIETY MANAGEMENT SKILLS

Once patients have a good understanding of agoraphobia, it is then helpful for them to develop skills that should allow them to cope effectively with the physical symptoms of anxiety and panic. Although the specific contributions of coping strategies have yet to be established, some form of anxiety management is usually part of cognitive-behavioral treatment and many patients prefer to have an identified procedure for managing anxiety symptoms before they begin the exposure components of therapy. No single type of coping strategy has been demonstrated to be superior, although certain strategies are used more commonly than others (Clark et al. 1985).

From the standpoint of clinical utility, training patients in the use of paced diaphragmatic breathing is easier and less time consuming than teaching relaxation skills. We typically rely on the use of breathing as an intervention that addresses the management of acute anxiety symptoms, whereas relaxation training is better suited for reducing overall levels of generalized anxiety and stress. The two approaches can, however, be used in concert without difficulty.

There are a number of different instructions for breathing retraining procedures. We tend to keep instructions as simple as possible. Patients are encouraged to slow their rate of respiration to a comfortable pace and continue to focus on maintaining slowed respiration. The other key element is instructing patients to inhale and exhale through their nose in order to prevent inadvertent hyperventilation. Some patients find it useful to place one hand below their collarbone and one hand slightly above their belt line as a means of monitoring whether their breathing is shifting from thorax to diaphragm.

It is important that use of breathing skills be periodically monitored to ensure patients are not hyperventilating, holding their breath, or otherwise breathing incorrectly. The symptoms of hyperventilation closely resemble those of panic. Some authors (e.g., Ley 1989) believe hyperventilation is one cause of panic attacks. Thus, it is important that patients not train themselves to hyperventilate under the mistaken impression they are breathing diaphragmatically.

Once patients have mastered paced breathing or another anxiety management strategy, they can practice using the techniques in situations that provoke anxiety. Anxiety management skills may be used in two types of situations. One situation occurs when anxiety is still at a low level and beginning to creep upward. Implementing anxiety management at this point may prevent anxiety from increasing further, thus reinforcing the patient's ability to exert some control over his or her symptoms.

Alternatively, when in a high anxiety-producing situation, patients can use anxiety management once anxiety levels plateau or have begun to diminish spontaneously. By approaching anxiety provoking situations and using anxiety management skills in this manner, the patient is able to challenge the notion that anxiety will remain at high levels forever and that they are unable to tolerate the symptoms. In addition, utilizing anxiety management skills in this way helps circumvent use of these skills as a means to avoid the experience of feared internal sensations.

COGNITIVE RESTRUCTURING AND COPING

Once the patient has learned a procedure to manage the physical aspects of anxiety, the focus of therapy can turn to cognitive restructuring. This component of treatment is designed to modify the patient's specific misappraisals of threat and to challenge maladaptive beliefs which contribute to escalating levels of anxiety. A first step in this process involves increasing patients' awareness of the thoughts they experience when anxious. While some individuals easily identify their thoughts, others find this task difficult. Some mechanism for provoking typical threat-related cognitions may be needed. This can be accomplished by test exposures or behavioral experiments. Once in an anxiety-arousing situation, patients are asked to keep a first-person account of their automatic thoughts. The therapist reviews the thought record later with the patient to better understand the nature of the fears and to discern clues about related cognitive distortions. For example, an agoraphobic might report being unwilling to stand in a line. Avoidance of standing in line could be related to a variety of fears, including feeling dizzy, not being able to breathe, fainting or dying, or being humiliated. Understanding a patient's basic fears and anxiety-related thoughts is necessary to identify the patient's cognitive distortions.

Cognitive distortions are the threat appraisal errors that lead to phobic responses. They tend to fall into one of two general categories: probability distortions and severity distortions. Distortions of probability are misappraisals of the likelihood of some feared catastrophic event occurring. Agoraphobics tend to exaggerate the probability that panic will occur. They are often surprised they do not experience attacks as frequently as they predicted when they start exposing themselves to feared sensations and situations.

Severity distortions involve exaggerations of the consequences of panic attacks. Some individuals perceive the probability of panic to be relatively low but remain fearful because they believe panic outcome, or their inability to deal with the outcome, will be catastrophic.

Understanding the nature of cognitive distortions can determine the kind of exposure necessary and what cognitive coping strategies might be helpful. When discussing coping strategies with patients, we introduce the idea that anxiety has both mental and physical aspects. To manage the mental aspects, automatic thoughts related to the threat of panic, patients are assisted in developing cognitive coping statements. These statements are phrases that patients repeat to themselves when in anxiety provoking situations. They are designed to counter the cognitive distortions that contribute to anxiety.

There are several steps involved in developing an individualized coping statement. First, the patient's feared catastrophe needs to be identified (e.g., physical harm vs. loss of control vs. humiliation). Next, the patient needs to describe the series of events he or she fears will occur between the initial panic sensation and the ultimate feared catastrophe. Third, based on an analysis of this series of events, the clinician determines what cognitive distortions the patient is making (i.e., is the patient exaggerating the probability or severity of panic outcome). Finally, a coping statement that specifically corrects the identified cognitive distortion is developed. Unlike the patient's cognitive distortions, the statement should accurately reflect the probability and severity of panic-related danger. The coping statement thus provides the patient with a healthy alternative to the maladaptive automatic thoughts typically generated in the presence of panic sensations. Examples of coping statements and the fear thoughts they counteract are provided in Table 3–2.

Some agoraphobic patients may find it difficult to concentrate on their coping statements when in anxiety-producing situations. They often need to practice using their statements in less difficult situations first. They may also find it beneficial to write their coping statements on a card and carry it with them for a while. Sometimes coping statements are recorded on an audiotape and played on portable tape players when both patient and therapist have decided that constant coaching would be beneficial.

A few comments about the use of coping statements are in order. First, it is important that the statements not reflect unrealistic reassurance (e.g., "I'm not going to panic, no matter what."). Unrealistic reassurance is maladaptive since it is inaccurate and does

Table 3–2. Coping Statements for Fearful Thoughts

Patient's Fear	Coping Statement
If my heart races, then I will have a heart attack and die.	My heart rate is up because I'm anxious. The sensation will pass. I'm safe.
If I panic here, I will do something out of control. Others will know I'm loony. I will never be able to face them again.	Most people won't care if I'm anxious. I can deal with those who do.

not challenge the distortion. Further, a coping statement should not be a distraction from the exposure. If patients are focused on repeating their coping statements rather than engaging in the situation, they may be avoiding some aspect of the exposure necessary to disprove their maladaptive beliefs. The coping statement should, instead, be assisting in the disputation of anxiety-arousing thoughts. A useful coping statement should be accurate, relatively brief, in a language the patient understands, and a correction of the patient's cognitive distortion. Further, since a patient may have more than one cognitive distortion, several coping statements may need to be developed. One statement may not address all of the patient's fears.

INTEROCEPTIVE EXPOSURE

Having learned coping strategies, patients are ready to begin the process of exposing themselves to the things they fear. We typically begin with exposure to interoceptive stimuli. The fear of fear concept of agoraphobia has brought greater attention to the fact that agoraphobics fear interoceptive as well as exteroceptive cues. Thus, interoceptive exposure is the process by which patients are exposed to bodily sensations they fear and associate with panic. With repeated exposure to these sensations, patients have the opportunity to practice coping effectively and to discover that the catastrophic outcomes they expect from these sensations do not occur.

The first step of interoceptive exposure is selecting which bodily sensation or sensations will be provoked. Sensations that elicit anxiety and are most similar to sensations associated with panic should be targeted. Data from the interoceptive assessment, the Physical Symptoms of Panic Questionnaire, and the clinical interview are all useful sources of information in selecting sensations for interoceptive exposure.

Once a sensation is selected, a provocation procedure should be chosen that will duplicate the target sensation. Three of the most commonly reported feared sensations are rapid heartbeat or palpitations, dizziness or light-headedness, and difficulty breathing. Increased heart rate and palpitations can usually be produced by having the patient engage in stair-stepping, running in place, or some other form of aerobic exercise. Patients can create dizzy or light-headed sensations by spinning in a rotating chair or by turning in circles. Respiratory discomfort can be created by intentional hyperventilation, breath holding, or breathing through a straw. A variety of other provocation procedures can be used to create other feared sensations, such as staring in a mirror (depersonalization), compression of a limb to reduce circulation (numbness or tingling), and tightening muscles (tension, shaking, trembling). We would like to emphasize again, however, the necessity of having patients evaluated by a physician prior to beginning the procedure.

Typically, we begin interoceptive exposure in the therapist's office and with a relatively low level of intensity. For example, a patient afraid of dizzy sensations might begin with a single spin in a rotating chair. At first, the therapist may provide coping assistance. Eventually, though, it is essential that patients learn to cope with their sensations independently. When the patient can experience a single chair spin with little or no anxiety, the therapist then suggests trying two spins. Before moving on to the next provocation (e.g., another set of spins), the patient should report reduced anxiety and feel ready to experience additional exposure. There is no preferred number of provocations per session, but the greater the number of exposures the patient can tolerate, the more opportunities there will be for progress. Patients should be instructed to practice the same procedure daily at home between sessions. They should be encouraged to tolerate as much exposure as possible, but the pace of therapy is determined by the patient.

Patients vary greatly in their reactivity to interoceptive exposure procedures. Most patients panic or at least become anxious despite the fact that they are in a healthcare setting and accompanied by a therapist. Others will have little or no response as long as the therapist is in the room. In such cases, the therapist may need to leave the office while the patient is experiencing the provocation procedure. In other instances, only interoceptive exposure experienced at home or in another setting will be able to provoke anxiety. The therapist must work collaboratively with each patient to determine the most relevant procedure and setting for interoceptive exposure.

The amount of time spent on interoceptive exposure also varies among patients. A few patients show remarkable progress within a couple of weeks while others may require months of exposure. The decision to terminate interoceptive exposure is based on clinical judgment. Generally speaking, however, interoceptive exposure sessions are discontinued once the patient can tolerate all previously feared sensations at moderately high levels of intensity with little or no anxiety.

In Vivo Exposure

Once less reactive to internal sensations, patients can begin exposure to feared situations. This process, known as *in vivo* exposure, has long been a centerpiece of the behavioral treatment of phobias and remains an integral part of current cognitive-behavioral approaches to agoraphobia.

The first step of in vivo exposure is to create a list of situations, cues, or tasks the individual avoids because of a fear of experiencing panic. In addition to the clinical interview, the Phobic Severity Rating Scale and the Mobility Inventory are useful instruments to assess situational avoidance.

As is most common today, we use a graded approach to exposure: patients at first expose themselves to situations associated with lower levels of fear and gradually take on more difficult exposures as they progress. In order to facilitate selection for exposure, phobic situations can be listed in a hierarchical fashion according to how much they are feared by the individual. Patients then expose themselves to situations at the lower end of the hierarchy and gradually work their way up.

An alternative way to structure graded exposures, however, involves use of the Behavioral Approach Test (BAT). With this approach, the patient is asked to identify a task (e.g., driving a car unaccompanied to visit an aunt 30 miles away, or spending 3 hours in a crowded shopping mall) that would be very difficult or impossible to perform specifically because of the agoraphobic fear. Preferably, the task is one that can be graded along a single dimension (e.g., time or distance). Once a target task has been established, patients are instructed to approximate the task to the best of their ability. For example, if the patient's target task is to drive 30 miles to visit a relative, he or she is instructed to get into the car and drive as far along the route to the relative's home as possible. Patients are instructed to do as much as they can during each exposure but are allowed to quit at any time if necessary. A patient whose target task is to spend three hours in a crowded mall, would be instructed to go to the mall and spend as much time there as possible before returning home. Progress is marked by distance or time achieved on each trial. Patients are asked to practice their exposures as frequently as possible. A BAT is considered completed once a patient has been able to achieve the entire target task consistently with relative comfort. At that point, the patient's avoidance and mobility can be reassessed and additional exposures can be set up to address any remaining situational avoidance.

Additional Treatment Options

Although education, anxiety management skills, cognitive restructuring and coping, and interoceptive and in vivo exposure represent the primary components of cognitive-behavioral treatment, a number of other interventions may be indicated in specific cases. Couples therapy, for example, has been found to have a positive impact on the treatment of agoraphobia (Cerny et al. 1987). At the very least, key family members should be educated about agoraphobia and how to be supportive of recovery.

It is sometimes helpful to provide skills training to address performance deficits that contribute to a patient's stress or disability. For example, assertion skills training may help some patients deal more effectively with background stress exacerbated by their inability to set limits or say no to others. For patients experiencing problems related to child rearing, parenting skills training may help reduce stress and induce a greater sense of control. The type of skills training used depends of course upon the patient's needs.

Another effective treatment option is medication. Drugs like alprazolam, clonazepam, phenelzine, and imipramine have been found to be more effective than placebo in reducing one or more of the primary symptoms of agoraphobia. Although drug treatments are sometimes used as an alternative to cognitive-behavioral treatment, the two forms of therapy can be integrated effectively (Mavissakalian and Michelson 1986). (See Chapter 15 for a further discussion of medication.)

Agoraphobia without History of Panic Disorder

Although most cases of agoraphobia appear to be panic-related, there is a second category of this syndrome known as agoraphobia without history of panic disorder (AWHPD) in *DSM-IV* (1994). Usually, this second type of agoraphobia involves a fear of symptom attacks other than panic, such as headache, loss of bladder or bowel control, vomiting, cardiac-related symptoms (e.g., chest pain), or dizziness. Like panic attacks, other symptom attacks associated with agoraphobia are also aversive and tend to have a sudden and unpredictable onset. The cognitive distortions and the types of situations (e.g., being alone, crowds, traveling from home) feared by individuals with AWHPD are also similar to those feared by agoraphobics with panic (Pollard et al., in press). Because of these similarities, until there are more controlled outcome studies specifically addressing agoraphobia without panic, it is reasonable to apply relevant interventions effective with panic-based agoraphobia to the treatment of AWHPD.

All of the primary treatment components discussed in this chapter are potentially useful for the treatment of agoraphobia without panic, with the possible exception of interoceptive exposure. Use of interoceptive exposure will depend on the type of symptom attack feared. Exposure to dizzy sensations is reasonable, for example, but it is not feasible to expose patients to vomiting or headaches. From a cognitive-behavioral perspective, however, successful treatment will depend on finding alternative ways to help patients with AWHPD modify their cognitive distortions regarding the threat potential of symptom attacks.

Marks (1987) has also reported cases of agoraphobia that did not involve a fear of symptom attacks. In these cases, the primary fear appears to be related to the external situations they avoid. In vivo exposure alone has been an effective intervention for these patients and education and training in symptom management strategies may also be helpful.

APPENDIX:
A SESSION-BY-SESSION MODEL
OF THE TREATMENT OF AGORAPHOBIA.

Session #	Procedure
1	• Administer a diagnostic instrument (e.g., ASI-IV) • Clinical interview: assess presenting problem, additional medical and psychological problems, and current level of functioning • Hand out assessment packet, which is completed by the patient at home and returned at the next appointment
2	• Collect assessment packet and review briefly to insure it has been completed • Continue clinical interview: assess history of problem and patient's personal, medical, and family history • Ask patient to complete any incomplete assessment forms by the next session [Review and interpret assessment forms between the 2nd and 3rd sessions]
3	• Ask any remaining assessment questions • Provide patient with conclusions of assessment, including diagnosis and treatment recommendations • Outline a general cognitive behavioral model of agoraphobia and the patient's responsibility in treatment • Secure patient's commitment to therapy (or ask that she or he consider options and inform therapist of his or her decision at the next session) • Assign any relevant reading

4
- Reassess patient's commitment to treatment and establish mutually agreed upon goals
- Begin psychoeducation: Provide facts about agoraphobia, debunk negative stereotypes, outline the specific factors you believe have contributed to the patient's problem and how CBT will address them (allow for biological contributions, even if medication is not used)
- Assess the patient's intellectual understanding of the CBT model and stress the importance of this before proceeding
- Ask patient to self-monitor anxiety and panic episodes and attempt to identify the triggers that elicit each episode

5
- Review patient's anxiety and panic log and use it to illustrate CBT model
- Introduce the concept of anxiety and panic management
- Explain the role of hyperventilation in panic attacks
- Teach paced breathing technique
- Assign daily practice of paced breathing

6
- Review patient's experience with paced breathing and refine any deficiencies
- Introduce the concept of cognitive coping statements as another tool for anxiety and panic management
- Discuss cognitive contributions to panic, in particular the role of threat appraisals that exaggerate the probability and/or severity of panic
- Develop with the patient a coping statement that attempts to correct the patient's distortion of panic's threat potential
- Teach the patient how to use the coping statement and ask him or her to practice daily, using it at first in low threat situations

7 • Review patient's experience using coping statements and make any needed adjustments
• Conduct interoceptive assessment and decide on provocation procedure to be used in interoceptive exposure (IE)
• Explain rationale for IE and begin procedure in your office
• Ask patient to practice procedure at home daily

8–10 • Continue interoceptive exposure until patient is able to experience all sensations associated with panic with little or no anxiety
• Ask patient to complete a situational fear hierarchy for the next session

11–14 • Using situational fear hierarchy as your guide, begin at low end of hierarchy and ask patient to enter and remain in feared situations. Therapist may accompany patient at first but should encourage independent exposure as much and as soon as possible (Alternatively, use BAT format and instruct patient to perform as much of the targeted task as possible each exposure trial)
• Patient may enter increasingly difficult situations as he or she masters less anxiety provoking situations

REFERENCES

Barlow, D. H. (1988). *Anxiety and Its Disorders: The Nature and Treatment of Anxiety and Panic.* New York: Guilford.
Beck, A. T., Emery, G., and Greenberg, R. L. (1985). *Anxiety Disorders and Phobias: A Cognitive Perspective.* New York: Basic Books.
Belfer, P. L., and Glass, C. R. (1992). Agoraphobic anxiety and fear of fear: test of a cognitive attentional model. *Journal of Anxiety Disorders* 6:133–146.

Benedikt, M. (1870). Uber platschwindel. *Allegemeine Wiener Medizinsche Zeitung* 15:488.

Brooks, R. B., Baltazar, P. L., and Munjack, D. J. (1989). Co-occurrence of personality disorders with panic disorder, social phobia, and generalized anxiety disorder: a review of the literature. *Journal of Anxiety Disorders* 3:259–285.

Cerny, J. A., Barlow, D. H., Craske, M. G., and Himadi, W. G. (1987). Couples treatment of agoraphobia: a two-year follow-up. *Behavior Therapy* 18:401–415.

Chambless, D. L., Caputo, G. C., Bright, P., and Gallagher, R. (1984). Assessment of fear in agoraphobics: the body sensations questionnaire and the agoraphobic cognitions questionnaire. *Journal of Consulting and Clinical Psychology* 52:1090–1097.

Chambless, D. L., Caputo, G., Gracely, S., et al. (1985). The Mobility Inventory for agoraphobia. *Behavior Research and Therapy* 23:35–44.

Chambless, D. L., and Gillis, M. M. (1993). Cognitive therapy of anxiety disorders. *Journal of Consulting and Clinical Psychology* 61:248–260.

Chambless, D. L., Renneberg, B., Goldstein, A., and Gracely, E. J. (1992). MCMI diagnosed personality disorders among agoraphobic outpatients: prevalence and relationship to severity and treatment outcome. *Journal of Anxiety Disorders* 6:193–211.

Charney, D. S., Woods, S. W., Price, L. H., et al. (1990). Noradrenergic dysregulation in panic disorder. In *Neurobiology of Panic Disorder*, ed. J. C. Ballenger, pp. 92–105. New York: Wiley-Liss.

Clark, D. M. (1988). A cognitive model of panic attacks. In *Panic: Psychological Perspectives*, ed. S. Rachman and J. D. Maser, pp. 362–385. Hillsdale, NJ: Erlbaum.

Clark, D. M., Salkovskis, P. M., and Chalkley, A. J. (1985). Respiratory control as a treatment for panic attacks. *Journal of Behavior Therapy and Experimental Psychiatry* 16:23–30.

Clum, G. A. (1989). Psychological interventions vs. drugs in the treatment of panic. *Behavior Therapy* 20:429–457.

———— (1990). *Coping with panic.* Pacific Grove, CA: Brooks/Cole Publishing.

Craske, M. G., and Barlow, D. H. (1993). Panic and agoraphobia. In *Clinical Handbook of Psychological Disorders,* ed. D. H. Barlow, pp. 1–47. NY: Guilford.

———— (1994). *Mastering Anxiety and Panic.* Albany, NY: Graywind Publications.

Crowe, R. R., Noyes, R., Pauls, D. L., and Slymen, D. (1983). A family study of panic disorder. *Archives of General Psychiatry* 40:1065–1069.

Diagnostic and Statistical Manual (1994). 4th ed. Washington, DC: American Psychiatric Association.

DiNardo, P., and Barlow, D. H. (1988). Anxiety Disorders Interview Schedule–Revised (ADIS-R). Albany, NY: Graywind Publications.

Dukman-Caes, C. I. M., and De Vries, M. W. (1991). Daily life situations and anxiety in panic disorder and agoraphobia. *Journal of Anxiety Disorders* 5:343–357.

Evans, L., Kenardy, J., Schneider, P., and Hoey, H. (1986). Effect of a selective serotonin uptake inhibitor in agoraphobia with panic attacks: a double-blind comparison of zimelidine, imipramine, and placebo. *Acta Psychiatrica Scandinavia* 73:49–53.

Goldberg, R. J. (1988). Clinical presentations of panic-related disorders. *Journal of Anxiety Disorders* 2:61–75.

Goldstein, A. J., and Chambless, D. L. (1978). A reanalysis of agoraphobia. *Behavior Therapy* 9:47–59.

Gorman, J. M., Liebowitz, M. R., Fyer, A. J., and Stein, J. (1989). A neuroanatomical hypothesis for panic disorder. *American Journal of Psychiatry* 146:148–161.

Joyce, P. R., Bushnell, J. A., Oakley-Browne, M. A., et al. (1989). The epidemiology of panic symptomatology and agoraphobic avoidance. *Comprehensive Psychiatry* 30:303–312.

Kessler, R. C., McGonagle, K. A., Zhao, S., et al. (1994). Lifetime and 12-month prevalence of *DSM-III-R* psychiatric disorders in the United States: results from the National Comorbidity Survey. *Archives of General Psychiatry* 51:8–19.

Klein, D. F. (1981). Anxiety reconceptualized. In *Anxiety: New Research and Changing Concepts*, ed. D. F. Klein and J. G. Rabkin, pp. 235–263. New York: Raven.

Klein, D. G. (1993). False suffocation alarms, spontaneous panics, and related conditions: an integrative hypothesis. *Archives of General Psychiatry* 50:306–317.

Klerman, G. L., Weissman, M. M., Oulette, R., et al. (1991). Panic attacks in the community: social morbidity and health care utilization. *Journal of the American Medical Association* 265:742–746.

Klosko, J. S., Barlow, D. H., Tassinari, R., and Cerny, J. A. (1990). A comparison of alprazolam and behavior therapy in treatment of panic disorder. *Journal of Consulting and Clinical Psychology* 58:77–84.

Lesch, K. P., Wiesmann, M., Hoh, A., et al. (1992). 5-HT receptor-effector system responsitivity in panic disorder. *Psychopharmacology* 106:111–117.

Lesser, I. M. (1990). Panic disorder and depression: co-occurence and treatment. In *Clinical aspects of panic disorder*, ed. J. C. Ballenger, pp. 181–191. New York: Wiley-Liss.

Ley, R. (1989). Dyspneic-fear and catastrophic cognitions in hyperventilatory panic attacks. *Behavior Research and Therapy* 27:549– 554.

MacLeod, C., Mathews, A., and Tata, P. (1986). Attentional bias in emotional disorders. *Journal of Abnormal Psychology* 95:15–20.

Manuzza, S., Fyer, A. J., Martin, L. Y., et al. (1989). Reliability of anxiety assessment: 1. Diagnostic agreement. *Archives of General Psychiatry* 46:1093–1101.

Marks, I. M. (1987). Behavioral aspects of panic disorder. *American Journal of Psychiatry* 144:1160–1165.

Marks, I. M., Gray, S., Cohen, D., et al. (1983). Imipramine and brief therapist-aided exposure in agoraphobics having self-exposure homework. *Archives of General Psychiatry* 40:153–162.

Maser, J. D., and Woods, S. W. (1990). The biological basis of panic: psychological interactions. *Psychiatric Medicine* 8:121–147.

Matuzas, W., Uhlenhuth, E. H., Glass, R. M., et al. (1986). *Alprazolam and imipramine in panic disorder—A life table analysis.* Paper presented at the 25th Annual Meeting of American College of Neuropsycho-pharmacology, Washington, DC, December.

Mavissakalian, M., and Michelson, L. (1986). Agoraphobia: relative and combined efforts of therapist-assisted in vivo exposure and imipramine. *Journal of Clinical Psychiatry* 47:117–122.

McNally, R. J. (1989). Is anxiety sensitivity distinguishable from trait anxiety? A reply to Ulenfeld, Jacob, and Turner (1989). *Journal of Abnormal Psychology* 98:193–194.

———— (1994). *Panic disorder: A Critical Analysis.* New York: Guilford.

McNally, R. J., and Lorenz, M. (1987). Anxiety sensitivity in agoraphobics. *Journal of Behavior Therapy and Experimental Psychiatry* 18:3–11.

Morau, C., and Andrews, G. (1985). The familial occurrence of agoraphobia. *British Journal of Psychiatry* 146:262–267.

Myers, J. K., Weissman, M. M., Tischler, G. L., et al. (1984). The prevalence of psychiatric disorders in three communities. *Archives of General Psychiatry* 41:959–970.

National Institute of Mental Health (1994). *Panic Disorder: Stories of Hope.* Washington, DC: National Institute of Mental Health.

Nutt, D., and Lawson, C. (1992). Panic attacks: a neurochemical overview of models and mechanisms. *British Journal of Psychiatry* 160:165–178.

Peterson, R. A., and Russ, S. (1987). *Treatment Manual for the Anxiety Disorders Index.* Worthington, OH: IDS Publishing Company.

Pollard, C. A., and Carmin, C. N. (1995). *The Anxiety Symptoms Interview—IV.* St. Louis: St. Louis University Press.

Pollard, C. A., Henderson, J. G., Frank, M., and Margolis, R. B. (1989). Help-seeking patterns of anxiety-disordered individuals in the general population. *Journal of Anxiety Disorders* 3:131–138.

Pollard, C. A., and Lewis, L. (1989). Managing panic attacks in emergency patients. *Journal of Emergency Medicine* 7:547–552.

Pollard, C. A., Pollard, H. J., and Corn, K. J. (1989). Panic onset and major events in the lives of agoraphobics: a test of contiguity. *Journal of Abnormal Psychology* 98:318–321.

Pollard, C. A., Tait, R. C., Meldrum, P., et al. (in press). Agoraphobia without panic: case illustrations of an overlooked syndrome. *Journal of Nervous and Mental Disease.*

Rachman, S. (1984). Agoraphobia: a safety-signal perspective. *Behavior Research and Therapy* 22:59–70.

Raj, A., and Sheehan, D. V. (1987). Medical evaluation of panic attacks. *Journal of Clinical Psychologists* 48:309–313.

Salkovskis, P. M. (1988). Phenomenology, assessment, and the cognitive model of panic. In *Panic: Psychological Perspectives*, ed. S. Rachman and J. D. Maser, pp. 111–136. Hillsdale, NJ: Lawrence Erlbaum.

Shapiro, L. E., Pollard, C. A., and Carmin, C. N. (1993). Treatment of agoraphobia. In *Handbook of Effective Psychotherapy*, ed. T. R. Giles, pp. 171–194. New York: Plenum.

Shear, M. K., Cooper, A. M., Klerman, G. K., et al. (1993). A psychodynamic model of panic disorder. *American Journal of Psychiatry* 150: 859–866.

Shear, M. K., Leon, A., and Spielman, L. (1994). Panic disorder: directions for future research. In *Treatment of Panic Disorder: A Consensus Development Conference*, ed. B. E. Wolfe and J. D. Maser, pp. 227–236. Washington, DC: American Psychiatric Press.

Sheehan, D. V., and Sheehan, K. H. (1982). The classification of phobic disorders. *International Journal of Psychiatry in Medicine* 12:243–266.

Sheehan, D. V., Ballenger, J., and Jacobson, G. (1980). Treatment of endogenous anxiety with phobic hysterical and hypochondriacal symptoms. *Archives of General Psychiatry* 37:51–59.

Spitzer, R. L., and Williams, J. B. W. (1992). *Structured Clinical Interview for DSM-III-R (SCID): User's Guide.* Washington, DC: American Psychiatric Press.

Stein, M. B., Shea, C. A., and Uhde, T. W. (1989). Social phobic symptoms in patients with panic disorder: practical and theoretical implications. *American Journal of Psychiatry* 146:235–238.

Thyer, B. A., Himle, J., Curtis, G. C., et al. (1985). A comparison of panic disorder and agoraphobia with panic attacks. *Comprehensive Psychiatry* 26:208–214.

Westphal, C. (1888). *Agoraphobia, A Monopathic Phenomenon.* (T. J. Knapp and M. T. Schumaker, Trans.) Lahnan, ME: University Press of America. (Original work published 1871).

Wilson, R. (1986). *Don't Panic.* New York: Harper and Row.

Wolpe, J. (1990). *The Practice of Behavior Therapy.* 4th ed. New York: Pergamon.

Wolpe, J., and Lang, P. J. (1969) *Fear Survey Schedule.* San Diego, CA: Educational and Industrial Testing Service.

Yager, E. T. (1988). Treating agoraphobia with hypnosis, subliminal therapy and paradoxical intention. *Medical Hypnoanalysis Journal* 3:156–160.

Zitrin, C. M., Klein, D. F., and Woerner, M. G. (1980). Treatment of agoraphobia with group exposure in vivo and imipramine. *Archives of General Psychiatry* 37:63–72.

Zitrin, C. M., Klein, D. F., Woerner, M. G., and Ross, D. C. (1983). Treatment of phobias: I. Comparison of imipramine hydrochloride and placebo. *Archives of General Psychiatry* 40:125–138.

CHAPTER FOUR

Generalized Anxiety Disorder

Generalized anxiety disorder (GAD) may be the most common of the anxiety disorders, as it includes such concepts as "free-floating anxiety" and the chronic worrier. In this chapter the current diagnostic view of the syndrome is delineated, along with the emerging treatment implications. GAD often presents one of the most difficult syndromes to treat, even for those experienced in the treatment of phobias. Since there is no overt phobic avoidance in GAD, new solutions have been pioneered by Dr. Borkovec and his group, who have amassed and carefully researched an eclectic group of treatment strategies. Other ideas of interest presented in this chapter are the possible value of worrying, and the application of therapeutic flexibility in cognitive-behavioral programs.

Generalized Anxiety Disorder*

T. D. BORKOVEC
LIZABETH ROEMER

DESCRIPTION OF THE DISORDER

Generalized anxiety disorder (GAD) has undergone numerous transitions in definition. It was separated from panic disorder in *DSM-III* but remained a residual category until *DSM-III-R*, wherein worry became its defining feature. Although research on the disorder has been limited, considerable empirical investigation has occurred in the last few years and a better understanding of its nature, functions, and effective treatment is emerging.

Clinical Features

Generalized anxiety disorder is a chronic condition centrally defined in *DSM-IV* (1994) as excessive anxiety and worry about a number of events or activities unrelated to other Axis I disorders and

* Preparation of this chapter was supported in part by Grant MH-39172 from the National Institute of Mental Health to the senior author.

occurring more days than not over a six-month minimum period of time. The presence of three out of six associated features (restlessness or feeling keyed up, being easily fatigued, difficulty concentrating, irritability, muscle tension, and trouble sleeping) is also required. Thus, the generally anxious individual experiences more or less constant cognitive and somatic anxiety throughout the day. Unlike phobic disorders, this anxiety is not triggered by easily identifiable or discrete environmental stimuli, nor is it due to panic attacks.

Associated Features

Eighty-two percent of GAD cases meet criteria for other anxiety and depression disorders, the highest comorbidity rate among the anxiety disorders, and GAD is the most common additional diagnosis associated with other principal anxiety disorders (23 percent; Brown and Barlow 1992). The most common additional diagnoses among GAD clients (social and simple phobias) (Sanderson and Wetzler 1991) share few of the GAD features, however, and co-occurrence of GAD and the anxiety disorder most similar to it in some ways (obsessive-compulsive disorder) is very rare (Brown et al. 1993). Although additional diagnoses of depression occur among 29 percent of GAD patients, dysthymia and major depression are more common in both principal panic disorder with severe avoidance and obsessive-compulsive disorder (Brown and Barlow 1992). Finally, some authors (e.g., Tollefson et al. 1991) have noted frequent comorbidity of irritable bowel syndrome and GAD.

Whereas earlier research suggested an absence of familial aggregation for GAD (e.g., Torgerson 1983), more recent studies have found greater frequency of GAD and lower frequency of panic disorder among relatives of GAD probands than among relatives of panic disorder probands (e.g., Noyes et al. 1992).

Basic research has revealed distinctive features associated with GAD. Clients have a preattentive bias to diverse threat cues, especially those associated with their worries (Mathews 1990), are more likely to interpret ambiguous material in a threatening way, and predict negative, low-probability events to be more likely (Butler and Mathews 1983). Moreover, worrying about one topic increases the accessibility of worries related to other topics (Montalvo et al. 1989).

Worrying functions as a cognitive avoidance of perceived threat and is negatively reinforced in two ways. First, worry about low-probability events is usually followed by their nonoccurrence, leading to a superstitious engagement in worry. GAD subjects acknowledge such a possible function to a greater degree than control subjects (Roemer et al. 1991). Second, worry just prior to phobic images eliminates cardiovascular response to the images (Borkovec and Hu 1990). Thus, GAD clients can escape or avoid somatic anxiety to fear material by worrying, giving meaning to their common report that worry helps them prepare for the worst. By doing so, however, they avoid complete functional exposure, prevent the processing of emotional material (Foa and Kozak 1986), and thus perpetuate anxious meanings. The nature of worry provides clues to how it may function in this way. Worry is composed primarily of negative thoughts (as opposed to images), and GAD clients show greater negative thinking and less imagery than nonanxious individuals even during relaxation (Borkovec and Inz 1990). Verbal articulation of emotional material does not produce the same degree of cardiovascular response that imagery of the same material does (Vrana et al. 1986). Indeed, it is the thought element of worry that suppresses physiologic response to phobic material (Borkovec et al. 1993). In fact, although muscle tension tends to be high, GAD clients display a *restriction* in variability of skin conductance and heart rate both during rest and in response to challenge (cf. Hoehn-Saric and McLeod 1988), suggesting a deficiency in vagal tone and an autonomic inflexibility.

Because the perceived threats exist only in the future, thus precluding motoric avoidance, GAD clients have learned to use abstract worry for *cognitive* avoidance of their anxiety-provoking environments and anxious experience, a method that guarantees maintenance of their anxiety disorder. Worry breeds more worry; habit is continually strengthened so that clients become increasingly stuck in a worrisome pattern of responding. The resultant cognitive rigidity and associated autonomic rigidity are evident in the clients' constant predictions of negative events, reports that they always expect the worst, and such cognitive distortions as dichotomous thinking, personalization, mind reading, and overgeneralization.

Epidemiology

No adequate information on the prevalence of GAD as defined by *DSM-III-R* is available. Breslau and Davis (1985) and the NIMH Epidemiological Catchment Area investigation for its second wave (Blazer et al. 1991) both used the *DSM-III* definition and found lifetime prevalence of 9 and 5.8 percent, respectively. In the latter study, GAD tended to be more frequent among women, blacks, young adults, and persons with low income or occupational status. Such estimates led Rapee (1991) to argue that GAD may be one of the most common anxiety disorders, even though those affected make up only about 10 percent of people seeking treatment for anxiety of depression problems (Brown and Barlow 1992).

In ten therapy outcome studies of GAD, 65 percent of the clients were women, and the average age was 36 years (Borkovec and Whisman, in press). Age at onset ranges widely (Noyes, in press), tending on the average to be in the mid-teens to early twenties (Rapee 1991). GAD occurs at an earlier age and with a more gradual onset than panic disorder (e.g., Noyes et al. 1992).

Etiology

Given the gradual onset of GAD, it is not surprising that 80 percent of patients are unable to recall specifically the onset of their problems (Rapee 1985). The chronic nature of the disorder presents difficulties, then, to researchers interested in its precursors. Two studies have suggested historical contributors to the development of GAD. Torgerson (1986) found that GAD clients report experiencing the death of a parent before the age of 16 more often than panic disorder clients, and Blazer and colleagues (1987) determined that a GAD diagnosis was more common among subjects who had experienced at least one unexpected negative life event. More recently, college students meeting *DSM-III-R* criteria for GAD reported a greater number of traumatic events than nonanxious subjects (Roemer et al. 1991). Traumatic events would reasonably lead to a view of the world as a dangerous, unpredictable, or uncontrollable place with which one may not be able to cope. However, retrospective data are suspect. Anxious individuals may be more likely to recall negative events or interpret an event as traumatic at the time of its occurrence. The latter possibility suggests that the origins of the disorder may arise even earlier in childhood. The child's attachment to a primary caregiver may play a crucial role. Bowlby (1973) proposed that an insecurely attached child will develop a working model of the world as a threatening place. Both GAD clients (Cassidy 1992) and college students (Roemer et al. 1991) show signs of having been insecurely attached as children on self-report measure of attachment. Of course, difficulties remain with the possible unreliability of retrospective report, and it has yet to be determined whether such attachment patterns are distinctive of GAD or are common across anxiety disorders.

DIFFERENTIAL DIAGNOSIS AND ASSESSMENT

DSM-III-R *and* DSM-IV *Categorization*

Changes in *DSM-IV* from *DSM-III-R* include: (a) retention of worry as the cardinal feature with its minimum six-month duration; (b) elimination of the "unrealistic" criterion; (c) requirement that the worry be pervasive, i.e., be about a number of events or activities unrelated to a single Axis I disorder, and not be part of posttraumatic stress disorder; (d) simplification of the 18-item list of somatic symptoms to the 6-item list; and (e) requirement that the worry be difficult to control and that the anxiety, worry, or physical symptoms significantly interfere with normal routine or cause marked distress. The diagnosis is excluded if the generalized anxiety is due to substance-induced or secondary anxiety disorder, or if the symptoms are present only during a mood disorder, psychotic disorder, or a pervasive developmental disorder. Several of these suggested changes are specifically based on empirical information generated in the last five years, some of which is summarized below.

GAD clients score higher on a trait measure of worry than do individuals with any other anxiety disorder (Brown et al. 1992), and trait-worry is statistically independent of other measures of anxiety and depression within GAD samples (Brown et al. 1992, Meyer et al. 1990). Assessors have found uncontrollability of worry and its interference with functioning to be present in 100 percent of GAD clients (Borkovec 1992), and ratings of the severity of that interference distinguish GAD from other anxiety disorders (Borkovec et al. 1991). The pervasiveness of GAD worry is revealed by clients' report of a greater number of worry topics than nonanxious controls (5.2 vs. 1.2; Borkovec et al. 1991), by their greater likelihood of reporting excessive worry about minor things (92.5 percent vs. 32–71 percent for those with other anxiety disorders and 0 percent for controls) (Barlow 1988, Borkovec et al. 1991), and by the fact that, unlike nonanxious people, nearly one-third of their worry topics are not easily categorized into major themes (Shadick et al. 1991). Finally, GAD is characterized more by central nervous system (CNS) arousal (excessive muscle tension and vigilance and scanning) than by autonomic hyperactivity (Noyes et al. 1992). Thus, only three of the six most commonly found CNS-related symptoms (restlessness or feeling keyed up, being easily fatigued, difficulty concentrating, irritability, muscle tension, and trouble sleeping) will be required for diagnosis.

Differential Diagnosis

Because of high comorbidity rates for GAD, several disorders (especially social and simple phobia) need to be considered carefully to accurately diagnose a principal GAD case. Because GAD is associated with low interrator reliability (kappa = 0.57) (Brown and Barlow 1992), use of established structured interviews is highly recommended, and in research it is imperative that independent diagnostic interviews be conducted by two separate assessors to reduce the likelihood of false-positive cases.

One of the most important factors to consider in differential diagnosis is the focus of the client's worries (Rapee 1991). If the worry clearly relates to another diagnosable Axis I disorder (e.g., panic attacks, weight gain), then that worry does not contribute to a GAD diagnostic decision. Given the diffuse nature of GAD worry, however, GAD clients frequently report worrying about phobic situations (particularly social ones) in addition to several other areas of life. The crucial distinction, then, is whether the worrying is truly pervasive and covers many life circumstances, in which case a GAD diagnosis would be appropriate.

GAD clients often report earlier periods of major depression or background dysthymia. It seems that their pattern of catastrophizing leads them at times to feel helpless and hopeless. To distinguish clients for whom GAD is principal, it is useful to obtain a history of the course of both the anxiety and the depression symptomatology. If GAD symptoms are present only during a depressive episode, diagnosis of GAD is inappropriate. In deciding whether GAD is the principal diagnosis, consider whether the anxiety preceded the onset of the depression, whether the depression occurs only when the anxiety is present, and whether the anxiety is currently more severe than the depression. GAD clients frequently indicate that their anxiety has always been present or that it precedes the emergence of depressive episodes. Some clients report that the depression has at times been worse than the anxiety but that it occurs less frequently and that it is the anxiety that they most want to change.

An additional diagnostic issue relates to post-traumatic stress disorder (PTSD). The possible role of past trauma in the etiology of some cases of GAD was mentioned earlier. Decisions rest on whether PTSD is diagnosable, and if so, what its severity level is relative to that of GAD. It is also useful to know whether the GAD symptoms were present prior to the occurrence of the traumatic event.

Clients often present with GAD symptoms when undergoing significantly stressful life experiences, and the anxiety and worry are reasonable reactions to these. Although the six-month duration criterion reduces the likelihood of misdiagnosis, severe life conditions can persist even longer without adequate adjustment. Such cases, if diagnosed at all, are more properly placed under adjustment reactions, with reevaluation after the stressor has been removed. A few cases present greater difficulty; the assessor may remain uncertain whether the life events are severe enough to account for the disturbance or whether the worry and anxiety are truly excessive in their context. The presence of GAD symptoms prior to the event would lean toward principal GAD diagnosis.

Assessment Strategies

Our program uses the revised Anxiety Disorders Interview Schedule (ADIS-R) (DiNardo and Barlow 1988), a structured diagnostic interview covering the anxiety and mood disorders in detail and screening for such other disorders as psychosis and substance abuse. Other structured interviews that cover GAD include the Structured Clinical Interview for *DSM-III-R* (Spitzer et al. 1990) and the

Schedule for Affective Disorders and Schizophrenia (Endicott and Spitzer 1978). The Hamilton Rating Scale for Anxiety (HARS) and the Hamilton Depression Rating Scale (HDRS) (Hamilton 1959, 1960) can be included to provide assistance in distinguishing the severities of anxiety and depression symptoms and to generate assessor-determined measures for evaluating pre-therapy to post-therapy change for clinical or research purposes.

Commonly used self-report instruments with GAD include the trait version of the State-Trait Anxiety Inventory (STAI) (Spielberger et al. 1983) and the Beck Depression Inventory (BDI) (Beck et al. 1978). The Penn State Worry Questionnaire (PSWQ) (Meyer et al. 1990) is becoming increasingly popular because of its very good psychometric properties and its focus on the central defining feature of GAD. Finally, some measure of dysfunctional beliefs (e.g., the Dysfunctional Attitudes Scale) (Weissman and Beck 1978) is well recommended if cognitive therapy is likely to be one of the interventions used.

In order to assess fluctuations in daily anxiety level for functional analytic use in therapy, clients can complete a daily diary in which they rate four times a day their average level of anxious experience over the preceding few hours. They also monitor any acute episodes of anxiety and record details about the internal and external circumstances that surrounded the event to provide information on situations and responses contributing to their anxiety.

TREATMENT

Evidence for Prescriptive Treatments

BEHAVIOR THERAPY

Early research in the treatment of GAD emphasized relaxation techniques, targeting the somatic aspects of anxious experience. The absence of clear and discrete fear-producing stimuli in the environment precluded the deployment of the exposure methods so effec-

tive in the treatment of phobias. Thus, the establishment of a generalized coping response that could be used any time anxiety was
detected and the choice of relaxation as such a portable skill made
sense. Subsequent basic research and clinical experience led to several developments. Recognition of the central role of cognitive and
somatic anxiety cues resulted in increasing use of these internal
stimuli in self-monitoring and imaginal exposure techniques. The
latter tended toward a family of methods that included self-control
desensitization (Goldfried 1971), anxiety management training
(Suinn and Richardson 1971), and stress inoculation (Meichenbaum and Turk 1973). All emphasized the rehearsal of coping
strategies in response to in-session initiation of anxious experience
and their application to naturally occurring anxiety, including in vivo
exposures to problematic situations to facilitate extinction and to
increase generalization of the strategies. Second, more thorough
methods of applied relaxation were employed (e.g., Ost 1987),
including differential relaxation, cue-controlled relaxation, and systematic training in application of relaxation to incipient anxiety cues.
Third, given increasing evidence of the special role that conceptual
activity plays in maintaining GAD, cognitive therapy (Beck and
Emery 1985) was incorporated to focus on self-statements and
underlying dysfunctional beliefs that demonstrate a view of the
world as a dangerous place and the client as an individual ineffective at coping with it.

  This resulting package of behavioral and cognitive techniques
is the most effective approach for GAD treatment based on existing empirical evidence (cf. Borkovec and Whisman, in press,
Chambless and Gillis 1993) The results of eleven outcome investigations on *DSM*-defined GAD indicate that the package consistently produces clinically significant improvements in both anxiety
and depression, is associated with low dropout rates, and yields
change clearly maintained at long-term follow-up. Although differences in outcome have not always appeared between cognitive-

behavioral therapy and elements of the total package or nonspecific factors alone, comparisons of effect size, degree of within-group change, and frequency of clients' meeting criteria for clinically significant change all favor the integrated package approach. In the most recent investigation (Borkovec and Costello 1993), for example, the percentage of clients reaching high end-state functioning by 1-year follow-up was greatest for cognitive-behavioral therapy (58 percent), followed by applied relaxation (37.5 percent) and nondirective therapy (26.7 percent). Such figures also indicate that, despite progress in the development of treatment methods for GAD, not all clients are returned to normal levels, and further technique development is required.

Pharmacotherapy

Three types of medication have been evaluated in the pharmacologic treatment of GAD: benzodiazepines, azaspirones (mostly buspirone), and antidepressants (mostly imipramine), and existing empirical information documents some usefulness for each drug in acute (4- to 12-week) treatment. By far, the benzodiazepines have been the most thoroughly researched. Although these three classes differ in a number of ways (e.g., site of effect, mechanism of action, type and severity of side effects), research has yet to reveal differential efficacy or optimal matching of client characteristics to type of medication. A recent review by Schweizer and Rickels (in press) tentatively suggests that benzodiazepines may be favored for somatic symptoms, whereas buspirone or imipramine may be better for cognitive symptoms or when depression is part of the clinical picture.

One of the greatest general limitations of pharmacologic intervention for GAD is that anxiety symptoms very frequently return once medication is discontinued. For example, in two of the few drug studies that have evaluated long-term (1-year) follow-up after acute benzodiazepine treatment, relapse rates were found to be 63 percent (Rickels et al. 1986) and 81 percent (Rickels et al. 1980). These rates contrast vividly with the routine maintenance of improvement demonstrated for cognitive-behavioral therapies.

A second major limitation has to do with associated effects of medications. Side effects are common, resulting in frequent unacceptability by clients and high dropout rates in outcome trials. And although current evidence suggests that benzodiazepines and buspirone continue to have anxiolytic effects without dose escalation among those clients who continue to take them over considerable periods of time, physical dependence and withdrawal are nearly inevitable among clients chronically taking benzodiazepines. Consequently, there is need for careful, gradual tapering of medication to achieve discontinuation (Schweizer and Rickels, in press).

Because of these overall characteristics of pharmacologic interventions for GAD, Barlow (1988) has suggested that drug treatment be limited to very brief use during times of intense anxiety caused by environmental stressors, whereas Schweizer and Rickels (in press) have recommended that maintenance drug therapy for chronic GAD involve intermittent rather than continuous medication use, with buspisone preferred to benzodiazepines because of its greater safety, the lack of physical dependence, and the likely presence of antidepressant effects. So little adequate research exists, however, on the long-term efficacy of any medication for GAD that considerably more empirical information will be needed before confident assertions about drug intervention can be made.

ALTERNATIVE TREATMENTS

Two outcome investigations included nondirective (simple reflective listening) therapy alone as a comparison condition. In one (Blowers et al. 1987), this condition was superior to no treatment on a few measures, inferior to anxiety management training on some measures, and equivalent to the latter condition on several other assessments. In the Borkovec and Costello (1993) study, nondirective therapy was inferior to the other two conditions at posttherapy and 1-year follow-up, and many of its immediate treatment effects disappeared by follow-up. Even so, one-fourth of those in the nondirective group still met criteria for high end-state functioning a year after therapy, so the intervention may be specifically effective for a subset of clients. Whether a more thorough version of experiential therapy, with its focus on the allowance and acceptance of previously denied or suppressed emotional experience (Greenberg and Safran 1987), might circumvent the apparent avoidance of affect demonstrated by GAD clients and thus facilitate emotional processing to yield significant change remains an as yet unresearched question.

The cognitive-behavioral package described above focuses primarily on learning to cope with the symptoms of anxiety via cognitive and relaxation strategies. The favorable outcomes of controlled protocol evaluations represent the degree of change possible with the use of a fairly rigid treatment; therapists in such trials are not allowed to use additional methods, even behavioral or cognitive ones, if those techniques are not specifically prescribed by the protocol manual. Demonstrated efficacy is thus likely to be a conservative estimate of what can be accomplished by the less restricted use of the various cognitive-behavioral methods available to the therapist and potentially very relevant to particular clients and their circumstances. For example, the use of assertion training, problem-solving training, marital therapy, parent management training, time management strategies, and study skill counseling might have made good clinical sense from a functional analytic point of view with some specific clients involved in our protocol studies. These methods could reasonably contribute to reducing the degree of worry and stress in daily living and should be incorporated into a general cognitive-behavioral treatment for GAD whenever appropriate.

Selecting Optimal Treatment Strategies

While keeping in mind the addition of tailored treatment elements for specific cases, we will describe the basic cognitive-behavioral package that we believe is currently the best available core therapy for GAD. Our description is a summary of the protocol treatment currently being evaluated in an experimental trial and is the second generation of the manual (Borkovec and Costello 1993).

The degree of operational definition contained in protocol manuals notwithstanding, the therapeutic alliance is crucial for maximizing client motivation to change and willingness to expend the effort required. Our clients are told in Session 1 that the work will always be a collaborative effort, wherein we have expertise in the general principles of change and they are the experts about themselves and their own experience. Our role is to provide the techniques known nomothetically to be useful, and it is their role to discover through observation and experimentation how to translate those methods and their underlying metaphors into applications effective for their unique personalities and circumstances. Listening carefully to what the clients are communicating and adjusting interventions in response to their feedback represent therapist behaviors important to ensuring successful outcome.

SELF-MONITORING AND EARLY CUE DETECTION

Self-monitoring is basic to all else that follows in treatment. The rationale provided to the client emphasizes that anxiety is not just present or absent; it is a process over time that tends to spiral in response to detected threat and is self-reinforcing upon each occurrence. It is not our reactions that are problematic; our reactions to our reactions perpetuate the problem and are the targets for solution. The spiral occurs on the basis of both between-system and within-system interactions. A between-system interaction might involve, for example, an initial catastrophic image of a possible bad event, which leads to increased muscle tension, which produces restricted range of autonomic activity, which validates that something bad is actually going to happen, which activates worrisome thinking in an effort to escape somatic anxiety and avoid the occurrence of the future catastrophe. An example of within-system process is the chain of negative thinking that defines a worrisome episode. The longer one engages in worry, the more related and unrelated worry material is primed, the more this chain of association is strengthened in memory, and the more readily accessible it is upon next detection of threat. Over time, reinforced storage of these spirals yields stuck habits of responding any time an external or internal anxiety cue is detected, and they are increasingly organized to support dysfunctional beliefs about self, the world, and the future that predispose the individual to perceive threat in an increasing number of situations. Monitoring the spiral and its individual elements—images, worrisome thoughts, somatic reactions, affective experiences, possible behavioral reactions (such as subtle avoidance behavior, rushing, or procrastination), and the environments often associated with their initiation—and learning to catch them earlier and earlier in the sequence represent the very first goals of therapy. Coping responses will then be applied to cues detected early, with several advantages. At an early stage of the spiral, anxiety is less intense, and so coping responses are more effective. Short-circuiting of the spiral at an early stage also precludes further strengthening in memory of the entire habitual sequence. New associations, in contrast, are being strengthened. Early cues no longer mean only danger; they increasingly come to mean that it is time to deploy a coping response. Training in early cue detection uses imagery recall, role playing, periodic and frequent cueing of the client during the session whenever the therapist detects rising tension or anxiety, and encouragement to self-monitor during the week, looking for even earlier cues.

Emphasis on Flexibility in Coping

Another general concept crucial in the treatment of GAD is the notion of flexibility. Because the client engages in stuck habits of thinking and rigid autonomic activity, the higher-order goal of therapy is to establish playful, experimental, and multiple coping responses. Thus, several types of methods will be incorporated into relaxation training, and during cognitive therapy multiple self-statements and alternative beliefs and perspectives will be encouraged for any given situation. In all instances the therapist asks the client to focus attention back on present-moment sensation or the task at hand after deploying coping responses, emphasizing that anxious experience is elicited largely by illusory images and thoughts about a future that does not now exist.

Applied Relaxation

In the first session we provide an easily learned and rapidly effective relaxation method, so that the client has a coping response immediately available for rehearsal and application during the very first week. It involves diaphragmatic breathing, wherein the client learns to engage in slowed, paced breathing from the abdomen rather than the thorax. This technique not only provides a quick parasympathetic elicitor that targets somatic aspects of anxious responding, but also gives the client an attention-focusing device useful for terminating anxiety-provoking images and worrisome thoughts. Frequency of its application is emphasized, making use of temporal and behavioral reminders throughout the day and, of course, applying it in response to any detected early anxiety cues. Systematic training in progressive muscular relaxation as a means of increasing parasympathetic tone and strengthening the depth of the relaxation response begins in the second session and proceeds over sessions through combinations of major muscle groups and recall training (cf. Bernstein and Borkovec 1973). It is accompanied by instructions to practice twice daily and eventually includes training in differential relaxation and cue-controlled relaxation. Later in therapy, clients are also introduced to guided imagery and meditational techniques and experiments to discover which methods work best under which circumstances and for which of the interacting systems involved in their particular spiral sequence. Distinctions are also made among the various moments when the usefulness of relaxation responses can be anticipated: just before, during, and in recovery just after a stressful event. Behavioral approach assignments are made whenever motoric avoidance is in evidence and as engineered opportunities to practice the developing coping responses. Throughout therapy, emphasis is placed on the concept of "moving toward" a deeply relaxed state (especially during daily applications) rather than achieving some ultimate, ideal state, and unique words that best represent a particular client's experience are used as metaphors to describe the adaptive state (e.g., "tranquility," "peace," "centered").

Eventually, the above methods are subsumed under the generic concept of "letting go" that will be applied metaphorically to other aspects of client experience later in therapy. Clients will be asked to begin letting go of anxious images, worrisome thoughts, and negative affect in a manner analogous to the releasing of muscle tension during the tensing phase of progressive relaxation training. They are told that this process involves first recognizing the internal event (to preclude automatic avoidance of it) and then detaching from it, allowing it to merely pass through their experience (in contrast to suppressing the experience, distracting oneself from it, or attaching to and dwelling on it). The latter is emphasized because of research indicating the difficulty of suppressing material (Wegner et al. 1987) and the increase in negative affect associated with suppressed material (Roemer and Borkovec, in press).

SELF-CONTROL DESENSITIZATION

A further general concept is the importance of the systematic use of imagery methods. GAD clients use worry to suppress affect and physiological reactivity. Thus, imagery is an important vehicle for accessing affective meaning and for providing exposures to and processing of emotional material that is otherwise avoided. Second, establishing new, adaptive habits requires the frequent application of coping responses, particularly to earlier and earlier spiral cues.

Self-control desensitization (SCD) provides repeated opportunities to rehearse the deployment of the "letting go" reaction. It allows for the presentation of various internal cognitive (especially worry) and somatic anxiety cues to initiate anxious experience in the therapeutic setting, establishes their alternate meaning as cues for coping rather than for further spiraling, and increases the general habit strength of the various coping responses through practice. Numerous environmental situations commonly associated with stress or worry are used as the external context of the images, and various cognitive and somatic cues identified in assessment to be a frequent part of the client's anxious sequences are introduced into each image. As soon as the client begins to experience actual anxiety, the imagery proceeds to having the client imagine relaxing himself or herself while remaining in the situation, letting go of the anxiety, and engaging in alternate self-talk and shifts in perspective that have been developed during previous cognitive therapy portions of the session (see below). After eliminating the anxious experience, the client continues to imagine successfully coping with the situation for a while and then turns off the images altogether and focuses solely on deep relaxation in the office.

Repetitions of the same image continue until the client no longer feels anxiety in response to the anxiety-provoking image or is able to terminate anxiety rapidly with his or her coping responses, at which time new combinations of external and internal cues are presented. There is no attempt to exhaust possible situations or internal cues; rather, the goal is to provide a representative sampling of commonly encountered experiences. Images early in therapy are often taken from events that were problematic during the previous week, whereas anticipated events predominate in the content of images later in therapy. Clients also conduct their own SCD after each relaxation practice session at home, making use of images treated in prior sessions at first and later creating their own images that are more directly relevant to their current or upcoming circumstances. There are also times with particular clients when systematic desensitization may be useful. If a client is having difficulty eliminating anxiety to an imagined situation in SCD, or if the products of cognitive restructuring continue to not "feel true" for a particular situation, straightforward extinction through systematic desensitization can often break through the difficulty.

COGNITIVE THERAPY

In cognitive therapy, we largely follow Beck and Emery's (1985) recommendations: (a) demonstrations of the causal role of perspectives, thoughts, and images in eliciting emotion; (b) identification of automatic thoughts, thought styles, and underlying beliefs; (c) viewing predictions and beliefs as hypotheses rather than as facts; (d) logical analysis of thoughts and beliefs and the use of probability, evidence, and behavioral experiments to test them; (e) use of decatastrophizing methods; (f) development of alternative (and especially multiple and flexible) thoughts and beliefs; and (g) therapist's dependence on Socratic method in each of the above steps to facilitate client confidence and competence. Particular emphasis is placed on worries; they reflect the major themes and negative predictions so characteristic of the disorder. Clients are often asked to stream their worries out loud so that we can examine their content and processes.

Characteristic worry streams are also used to initiate worry process in SCD. Furthermore, from the first or second session onward, clients are given a worry diary in which they identify each worry that occurs during the day and specify what outcomes they fear might happen. Once the actual outcome occurs, they provide scale ratings to reflect whether the outcome was worse or better than predicted and how well they coped. The purpose of this monitoring is multifold: (a) to facilitate the self-monitoring and detection of incipient worry processes; (b) to focus attention on actual outcomes and their discrepancy from predicted, feared outcomes; (c) to begin establishing a clear history of evidence about the world undistorted by dysfunctional styles such as negative filtering; and (d) to obtain evidence as to whether they can cope well with life, despite their overgeneralized belief that they are incapable of doing so.

Although any number of distorted beliefs may be revealed, our experience with GAD suggests that some styles are particularly salient: perfectionism, personalization, catastrophization, negative filtering, mind reading, and overgeneralization. And it is a rare GAD client for whom the word "should" does not make up a substantial percentage of his or her vocabulary. Very early in therapy, before conducting a full logical analysis of "shoulds" and other sources of potentially arbitrary rules, we highlight this tendency and suggest that the word can routinely be replaced with the word "could." Such substitution reminds clients about the all-important notions of choice and multiple possibilities (rather than singular necessity) and flexibility (rather than rigidity and stuck habit), and it removes much of the pressure that they often place on themselves.

Problems in Carrying Out Interventions

Because GAD is a chronic condition characterized by a general cognitive style of negative predictions, clients are often demoralized when they enter therapy and have difficulty believing that they can change. Many clients are also time-urgent, and adding tasks to an already busy schedule can result in compliance problems. The most useful approach to these potential problems is to provide as soon as possible strategies whose use yields some noticeable, even if small, effects both in the session and during daily life. Relaxation training usually produces a pleasant state; diaphragmatic breathing, quickly learned and applied, often results in reports by the second session that some success was achieved with its application. SCD is a good method for showing the client small but systematic changes: the time necessary to generate anxiety via imaginal threat cues routinely increases with repetition, and the time to eliminate the anxiety decreases. Early cognitive therapy would wisely aim at small cognitive distortions associated with mildly anxiety-provoking situations so that the client experiences a clear and convincing perspective shift and resulting anxiety reduction. If the therapist continues to emphasize that change will be gradual as habit strength grows and as applications are transferred to more situations, and if the daily diaries are systematically tracking small gains in process and outcome, then client motivation is likely to be increased and maintained. Most clients come to realize with therapist guidance and experiments outside of therapy that the time they invest now in learning to reduce their anxiety will pay off in greater productivity in their important life tasks in addition to greater tranquility.

Although the above problems can result in poor adherence to homework and practice, on the whole GAD clients are very compliant. In fact, successful therapy aims ultimately at reducing their frequent fear of negative evaluation by the therapist, and such issues are explicitly raised for intervention. Clients who, toward the end of therapy, are reporting failure to carry out assigned tasks without feeling guilty or are engineering their own tasks because they think them to be more useful than what the therapist recommended provide us with special joy.

Not all the interventions described earlier will have direct relevance for every client. It is important for the therapist to be sensitive to client feedback, to emphasize methods that are proving useful and not to insist on those that are not, and to work with the client to develop individualized meanings and applications from the available generic strategies. Insisting on the continued use of methods that the client finds of little value will only produce a poor therapeutic relationship. Given the variety of techniques available and our emphasis on flexibility, to do so is completely unnecessary.

Two subsets of GAD clients have a poor prognosis in this protocol therapy. The first group consists of those experiencing significant, realistic stress whose effects are superimposed on a GAD style of reacting. These stressors either enter the client's life after therapy has begun, or their significance becomes apparent only during the course of therapy. Our anecdotal observation in some cases is that clients do often seem to come up with methods such as greater assertion, more effective problem solving, or better parenting or spousal relationship behaviors on their own as they become more relaxed and realistic in their thinking. The restrictions of protocol therapy, however, do not allow us to implement such methods, nor can we directly help the client with significant life decisions aimed at producing more adaptive external circumstances to relieve the stress. Although our cognitive-behavioral interventions can provide some relief, there are limits to their effectiveness when severe, realistic stress exists.

The second subgroup is even more difficult. We have called this small minority of clients the "entitlement" group. Several sessions of therapy are required before we recognize their characteristics. Tension, anxiety, and worry are indeed the predominating emotional experiences, but their source is an underlying anger and frustration usually aimed at other people or the "system" in general. From their perspective, their stress is due to others who will not behave the way they wish them to behave or to a system (e.g., school or work institutions) that is not set up to meet their needs. No motivation to change themselves in any way derives from this perspective, and none of their thought styles is seen as distorted or maladaptive. Thus far, we have observed virtually no clinical improvement in this group of clients. Clearly, neither the underlying assumptions of our protocol therapy nor the rationale offered to these clients for it is conducive to creating a strong therapeutic alliance.

Relapse Prevention

Maintenance issues are addressed explicitly toward the end of therapy, but they also emerge throughout treatment. It is a rare client who does not experience a return of severe anxiety during the course of therapy, an event that is often viewed as a setback or is taken as evidence that he or she will never change. The therapist reminds the client that anxiety is a common and natural response, that novel events will always pull toward a reemergence of old habits, that the client already has evidence from prior weeks that what he or she is learning has been having an effect, and that he or she is always able to reengage his or her new coping strategies and develop his or her strength and effectiveness further. The hypothesis that he or she has lost all gains can be tested during the upcoming week.

Toward the end of therapy, images of future anxiety episodes and worries about relapse can be employed in SCD, and the therapist reminds the client that he or she now knows how to use SCD for any newly encountered situations. The therapist also uses reverse role plays and devil's advocate positions to reinforce independent use of generic cognitive strategies. Finally, one or two booster/fading sessions are held during the month after post-treatment assessment. Maintenance and relapse issues are once again covered, and clients are given an individually tailored handout that summarizes the specific steps of each intervention that was useful for them so that they can reinstitute at a future time any of the methods they have learned. The empirical literature regarding the durability of the effects of cognitive behavioral therapy with GAD is quite clear: immediate gains are routinely maintained and at times even further augmented by long-term follow-up (cf. Borkovec and Whisman, in press).

CASE ILLUSTRATION

Case Description

Susan, a 24-year-old unmarried woman, was in her last year of college, pursuing a degree in engineering. Excessive worry and anxiety had been a serious problem for the past four and a half years and were accompanied by several distressing physical symptoms, particularly muscle tension and abdominal distress ("pit in my stomach"). She complained of constant difficulties coping with the stress of responsibilities at both school and work. Susan described experiencing intense worry regarding her perceived inability to cope in a variety of school-related situations that interfered with her performance (particularly by causing procrastination) such that she had had several failures, which in turn reinforced her lack of faith in her abilities. Her father had died two years previously, and this additional stressor had led to such difficulty completing her schoolwork that she withdrew from school after failing several classes. She was currently enrolled in school again but continued to experience constant worry and great difficulty in completing her work.

Differential Diagnosis and Assessment

Two independent assessors conducted the ADIS-R and agreed on a principal GAD diagnosis. Susan also received an additional diagnosis of social phobia, because many of her worries focused on social-evaluative concerns. GAD was considered principal because Susan worried about a broad range of topics, of which social situations were one subset. Excessive worry topics included getting her school work done, living up to her own sense of her potential, money, her job procrastination, and many minor daily hassles. Assessment revealed a severity rating for GAD of 5.0 (between "definitely" and "markedly disturbing/disabling" on the 0- to 8-point assessor rating) and 4.0 for social phobia. Questionnaire scores included a HARS of 20.5, HDRS of 15, STAI of 57, BDI of 15, and PSWQ of 65.

Treatment Selection

Susan was a client in our current outcome study. Random assignment placed her in the group receiving cognitive-behavioral treatment, which included applied relaxation, SCD, and in-depth cognitive therapy. By protocol specification she received a total of 14 sessions prior to posttreatment assessment (four 2-hour and ten 90-minute sessions).

Treatment Course and Problems in Carrying Out Interventions

Session 1 was spent presenting our conceptualization of generalized anxiety and the rationale for the tripartite treatment package in the context of this conceptualization. The presentation was tied into what the therapist specifically knew about Susan's history and symptoms derived from the assessments. It was important for Susan to begin to see the way the spiral of anxiety worked in her daily functioning, with thoughts, images, affect, somatic sensations. and behaviors each contributing to her anxiety process over time. The therapist also emphasized specific, crucial habits that Susan had—for example, perceiving school assignments as representing a threat of failure, which led to images of professors confronting her about missed assignments, causing somatic sensations such as muscle tension and abdominal pain, which confirmed her initial perception of threat and interfered with her ability to concentrate on the task at hand.

The therapist described ways of changing these habits, emphasizing the importance of recognizing early cues in each system and targeting each system with a particular technique. The notions of flexibility and experimentation were stressed, with therapy providing many different alternative responses to change the overall habitual pattern of anxiety.

Within this framework of flexibly altering anxious patterns, the specific components of therapy were discussed. Susan and the therapist began identifying anxious automatic thoughts and styles and generating multiple alternative, less anxiety-provoking thoughts through logical analysis. Susan was also told that therapy would involve identifying somatic and imaginal cues and learning a variety of forms of relaxation to provide several coping responses to these cues. In addition, SCD was presented as a way to practice applying new cognitive and relaxation coping methods to identified cues in order to weaken previous anxious habits and strengthen newly developed habits of coping.

After being certain that Susan understood the rationale and answering her questions, the therapist introduced the first relaxation technique, diaphragmatic breathing. Susan noticed a difference in her anxiety level as soon as she tried the method.

At the end of session, Susan mentioned some of her anticipatory anxiety about therapy. She had been afraid she would have nothing to say or not be able to understand what the therapist was saying. She reported feeling better at this point, having made some conceptual connections and having recognized some anxiety cues already. This was explored as one example of how negative predictions are often unsubstantiated.

Session 2 included a review of the week, further training in thought identification, and presentation of progressive muscular relaxation. Susan indicated that she had noticed the whole cycle of anxiety for the first time during the previous week. In so doing, she recognized that her anticipatory fear was worse than the actual situation and began saying to herself, "This is not as bad as I think it's going to be," which she found calmed her down. In addition, she found that focusing on her breathing in stressful situations helped her think more clearly and stopped her habitual anxious spiral from increasing.

At the beginning of Session 3, a difficulty in complying with the homework was discussed. When Susan reported that she had not kept the daily diary, she stated that she knew that was "bad." Through imagery recall, Susan was able to identify that once she had missed one or two times of recording, every thought of the diary became associated with negative predictions that she would never be able to keep the diary well, and with negative thoughts about herself and her inability to get things done. This caused her to avoid any reminder of the diary and therefore to write entries less often, further strengthening negative associations to the diary. Describing this pattern in session led Susan to come up with some ways of changing it on her own. She decided to make the diary more a part of her schedule so she would be less likely to forget about it initially, and to remember that even if she did not complete her diary entries every day, she could still get many days completed instead of worsening the situation by giving up altogether. The therapist chose to address Susan's implicit fear of his disapproval in a later cognitive therapy session.

Later in the session, Susan and the therapist reviewed a printed list describing maladaptive thought styles and discussed the ones that seemed most relevant to her. She recognized her tendencies toward catastrophizing, negative filtering, overgeneralization, dichotomous thinking, and thinking in terms of "shoulds." In response to the therapist's Socratic questioning regarding catastrophizing, Susan recognized a primary pattern to her anxiety: her fear that things would go badly kept her from doing things, so that in the end things did go badly. This pattern occurred in several situations, such as completing the daily diary, getting schoolwork done, and meeting her professors when she was having problems in classes. She expressed excitement and relief at this realization:

> *Susan:* I never really realized how it all tied in to that. I never really saw how I didn't get things started as a result of being so anxious of what the outcome would be.
> *Therapist:* How does that make you feel?
> *Susan:* I'm seeing where it's coming from. That if this is what's causing it, then now I can focus on how to change that, so that it won't be that way anymore. It makes me feel a lot better, more optimistic about getting through the semester. I'm feeling this way now, but if I start doing this other thing, I'm going to be able to deal with it better, start predicting the other way as opposed to the catastrophe thing.

Susan developed alternative thoughts to reflect this perspective shift and continued to explore this pattern during the next several sessions. Each session involved identifying maladaptive thoughts she had identified in situations during the week, treating these thoughts as hypotheses, and developing alternative hypotheses to apply in similar situations during the next week. She responded to predictions that she would never get any work done by saying to herself, "I'll just do a little bit at a time." This change was made at several levels. She would use the alternative thoughts while planning work, making more realistic plans, and realizing that if she did what she could she often did more than when she tried to do everything. Moreover, she would feel better while doing it. She also used this change in perspective moment to moment, taking many breaks while working on a particular project and thinking about how many pages she had read instead of how many remained.

These changes were enhanced by the continued relaxation training and its daily application, which were reducing Susan's general stress level. Susan experienced particular success with diaphragmatic breathing, which she began to find herself applying more automatically any time her anxiety level increased. Her ability to relax was leading her to think more clearly and therefore complete more work. This strengthened the validity of her alternative thought that she could get work done as opposed to the old predictions of never getting anything done. Self-control desensitization was used at the end of relaxation training on images of external and internal cues relevant to her anxious experience to further strengthen her relaxation applications.

During later sessions, Susan was periodically stopped and asked to rate her present anxiety level and then to let go of and relax away existing tension or anxiety in whatever way she chose. This encouraged early cue detection and provided multiple opportunities to rehearse applied relaxation. Susan used the metaphor of "letting go" of anxious thoughts and images in her applied relaxation, and in Session 5 described that this worked better for her than "pushing" thoughts away: "not so much worrying about putting this off and forgetting about it but just letting the anxiety go so that I can concentrate on something else. It's different. I'm not so worried then about how much more I'm going to have to do. I'm not worrying so much about that. It's actually easier to let it go than to push it aside."

As Susan found that her new strategies of letting go, practicing relaxation twice a day to strengthen the response, and generating alternative thoughts (particularly in response to her overgeneralized, catastrophic predictions of failure) were helping her to reduce her anxiety level and to get more work done, she began to choose more intensely anxiety-provoking images in SCD. In Session 7, for example, she used a scene of giving an upcoming class presentation, focusing on her fear that she would be unable to answer questions the teacher might ask. She coped with this anxiety in imagery by focusing on her breathing, letting go, and reminding herself that she knew a lot about the topic and could use her knowledge to come up with an answer as she had in previous presentations. She was also able, following decatastrophization of the fear, to generate alternative thoughts such as "Even if I fail this, I won't fail the class." At the beginning of Session 8, Susan was pleased to report that the presentation had gone very well and that she had not experienced the customary "pit" in her stomach.

By Session 9, Susan was coping well, generalizing her coping skills to a variety of situations. She found that in stressful situations she automatically looked for alternatives to her thoughts, focused on her breathing and letting go of anxiety, or both. She reported looking forward to the upcoming semester as an opportunity to try out her new way of being from the beginning of the term rather than from a position of being already behind, as she had been when she began therapy. Therapy at this point began to focus more on potential new situations. The anticipation of job interviews was approached at first using decatastrophization methods. As her fears at each level were identified, Susan quickly generated alternative perspectives (e.g., "I won't know an answer"—"I'll be able to come up with one or they'll learn what I don't know"; "I won't get the job"—"There are other jobs"; "I won't get any job"—"I'll go back to school"). Susan applied her new strategy of taking work a little at a time to the upcoming project of putting together her résumé.

During Session 10, attention was paid to issues of maintenance and relapse prevention, because Susan was continuing to feel relaxed, calm, and hopeful about the future. When asked what would happen if she felt anxious again in a situation, Susan said that she would still be able to use her new coping responses even if she exceeded her preferred level of anxiety. The therapist pointed out that given the strength and automatic nature of her new habits, it was unlikely old habits would reemerge even if the spirals started again. Susan enjoyed trying to imagine how she could work up her anxiety (e.g., in SCD) and realizing that coping statements and coping responses came to mind quickly and automatically.

Before Session 11 Susan missed several appointments. When she did arrive for the session, she was somewhat anxious and reported that she had found out that she might not be able to graduate, had to write a petition, and needed several professors to sign it. She felt anxious and jumpy when she first found out about this and felt the "pit" in her stomach again. However, that night she had actually sat down and started writing a draft of the petition, doing a little bit at a time. She was pleased to realize that although initially she had reacted in her old way, she had been able to cope later and reinstitute the new habits. The therapist reminded Susan that one can cope before, during, or after an anxious situation (or all three), another flexible aspect of this approach to anxiety.

As Susan continued to discuss the past several weeks she recognized the cycle she had experienced before finding out about the graduation problem. She had been leaving some tasks until the last minute and was therefore choosing to miss her therapy sessions. She found herself thinking that she *should* have gone to therapy, that she wasn't working hard enough in therapy, and that now therapy wouldn't work. However, she also had responded to these thoughts by generating alternative perspectives, such as "I *could* have gone, but I made a choice to do my homework." She was pleased to notice later that not only did the products of therapy continue to work effectively even though she had missed sessions, but she actually demonstrated to herself her continued improvement in her coping quite well with the extremely unpredictable, anxiety-provoking situation of not graduating.

Susan was able in the session to identify the fears she had that her therapist would think less of her because of the missed sessions and to respond to this thought with the alternative perspective that what her therapist thought of her was less important than what she thought of herself and that she knew she was still working on coping with her anxiety even if her therapist might not think so. This internalized sense of herself was a very important shift in perspec-

tive for Susan, because much of her social-evaluative concern originated from her previous core belief that if people thought badly of
her, they must be right.

The next three sessions were spent continuing maintenance
and generalization training. Susan's feelings about leaving therapy
were also discussed. She would miss the support of the therapeutic
relationship, but she was feeling confident now in her ability to
continue the progress she had made and knew it was time to fly on
her own.

Outcome and Termination

At post-treatment assessment Susan no longer met diagnostic criteria for GAD and received a GAD symptom severity rating of 2.5
("mild anxiety"). The severity rating of social phobia was 1.5 (less
than "mild"). Her other scores included 5.5 on the HARS, 3. 5 on
the HDRS, 36 on the STAI, 3 on the BDI, and 46 on the PSWQ.
All of these scores were within nonanxious norms and indicated high
end-state functioning.

Following the assessment Susan had one more session to
finalize termination and maintenance issues. Susan was feeling very
pleased with the changes she had made and optimistic about her
future. Although she still did not know whether she would graduate, she felt comfortable with that uncertainty and confident that
she would be all right either way.

Follow-Up and Maintenance

Susan let our staff know several months later that she had in fact
graduated and was doing well. At her six-month follow-up, her
GAD severity rating had further decreased, to 2.0. The severity rat-
ing of social phobia was 1.5. She had a HARS rating of 2.0, a
HDRS rating of 3.0, a STAI score of 34, a BDI score of 3, and a
PSWQ score of 45.

SUMMARY

Our understanding of the nature of generalized anxiety has increased greatly over the past few years. GAD clients are characterized by a rigid perception of the world as a threatening place, leading to a habitual response of verbal-linguistic worry that avoids imaginal activity, suppresses somatic experience, and results in autonomic rigidity. In this context, cognitive-behavioral treatment characterized by flexibility and the targeting of cognitive, imaginal, somatic, and behavioral systems with multiple relaxation and cognitive coping strategies is quite effective in providing anxiety and worry relief that is maintained at long-term follow-up. However, because many clients continue to experience residual anxiety after treatment, it is clear that further progress remains to be made.

REFERENCES

Barlow, D. H. (1988). *Anxiety and Its Disorders.* New York: Guilford.

Beck, A. T., and Emery, G. (1985). *Anxiety Disorders and Phobias: A Cognitive Perspective.* New York: Basic Books.

Beck, A. T., Rush, A. J., Shaw, B. F, and Emery, G. (1978). *Cognitive Therapy of Depression.* New York: Guilford.

Bernstein, D. A., and Borkovec, T. D. (1973). *Progressive Relaxation Training.* Champaign, IL: Research Press.

Blazer, D., Hughes, D., and George, L. K. (1987). Stressful life events and the onset of a generalized anxiety syndrome. *American Journal of Psychiatry* 144:1178–1183.

Blazer, D. G., Hughes, D., George, L. K., et al. (1991). Generalized anxiety disorder. In *Psychiatric disorders in America: The Epidemiological Catchment Area Study,* ed. L. N. Robins and D. A. Regier, pp. 180–203. New York: Free Press.

Blowers, C., Cobb, J., and Mathews, A. (1987). Generalized anxiety: a controlled treatment study. *Behaviour Research and Therapy,* 25, 493–502.

Borkovec, T. D. (1992). *Psychological processes in generalized anxiety disorder.* Paper presented at the annual meeting of the American College of Neuropsychopharmacology, San Juan, Puerto Rico, December.

Borkovec, T. D., and Costello, E. (1993). Efficacy of applied relaxation and cognitive behavioral therapy in the treatment of generalized anxiety disorder. *Journal of Consulting and Clinical Psychology* 61:611–619.

Borkovec, T. D., and Hu, S. (1990). The effect of worry on cardiovascular response to phobic imagery. *Behaviour Research and Therapy* 28:69–73.

Borkovec, T. D., and Inz, J. (1990). The nature of worry in generalized anxiety disorder: a predominance of thought activity. *Behaviour Research and Therapy* 28:153–158.

Borkovec, T. D., Lyonfields, J. D., Wiser, S., and Diehl, L. (1993). The role of worrisome thinking in suppression of cardiovascular response to phobic imagery. *Behaviour Research and Therapy* 31:321–324.

Borkovec, T. D., Shadick, R. N., and Hopkins, M. (1991). The nature of normal versus pathological worry. In *Chronic Anxiety and Generalized Anxiety Disorder,* ed. R. Rapee and D. H. Barlow, pp. 29–51. New York: Guilford.

Borkovec, T. D., and Whisman, M. A. (in press). Psychosocial treatment for generalized anxiety disorder. In *Anxiety Disorders: Psychosocial and Pharmacological Treatments,* ed. M. Mavissakalian and R. F. Prien. Washington, DC: American Psychiatric Association.

Bowlby, J. (1973). *Separation: Anxiety and Anger.* New York: Basic Books.

Breslau, N., and Davis, G. C. (1985). *DSM-III* generalised anxiety disorder: an empirical investigation of more stringent criteria. *Psychiatry Research* 14:231–238.

Brown, T. A., Antony, M. M., and Barlow, D. H. (1992). Psychometric properties of the Penn State Worry Questionnaire in a clinical anxiety disorders sample. *Behaviour Research and Therapy* 30:33–37.

Brown, T. A., and Barlow, D. H. (1992). Comorbidity among anxiety disorders: implications for treatment and *DSM-IV. Journal of Consulting and Clinical Psychology* 60:835–844.

Brown, T. A., Moras, K., Zinbarg, R. E., and Barlow, D. H. (1993). Diagnostic and symptom distinguishability of generalized anxiety disorder and obsessive-compulsive disorder. *Behavior Therapy* 24:227–241.

Butler, G., and Mathews, A. (1983). Anticipatory anxiety and risk perception. *Cognitive Therapy and Research* 11:551–565.

Cassidy, J. (1992). *Generalized anxiety disorder and attachment: emotion and cognition.* Paper presented at the Rochester Symposium on Developmental Psychopathology, Rochester, NY.

Chambless, D. L., and Gillis, M. M. (1993). Cognitive therapy of anxiety disorders. *Journal of Consulting and Clinical Psychology* 61:248–260.

Diagnostic and Statistical Manual of Mental Disorders. (1987). Washington, DC: American Psychiatric Association.

DSM-IV Draft Criteria. (1993). Washington, DC: American Psychiatric Association.

DiNardo, P. A., and Barlow, D. H. (1988). *Anxiety Disorders Interview Schedule—Revised (ADIS-R).* Albany, NY: Phobia and Anxiety Disorders Clinic, State University of New York.

Endicott, J., and Spitzer, R. L. (1978). A diagnostic interview: the schedule for affective disorders and schizophrenia. *Archives of General Psychiatry* 35:837–844.

Foa, E. B., and Kozak, M. J. (1986). Emotional processing of fear: exposure to corrective information. *Psychological Bulletin* 99:20–35.

Goldfried, M. R. (1971). Systematic desensitization as training in self-control. *Journal of Consulting and Clinical Psychology* 37:228–234.

Greenberg, L. S., and Safran, J. D. (1987). *Emotion in Psychotherapy.* New York: Guilford.

Hamilton, M. (1959). The assessment of anxiety states by rating. *British Journal of Medical Psychology* 32:50–55.

——— (1960). A rating scale for depression. *Journal of Neurology, Neurosurgery and Psychiatry* 23:56–62.

Hoehn-Saric, R., and McLeod, O. R. (1988). The peripheral sympathetic nervous system: its role in normal and pathologic anxiety. *Psychiatric Clinics of North America* 11:375–386.

Mathews, A. (1990). Why worry? The cognitive function of anxiety. *Behaviour Research and Therapy* 28: 455–468.

Meichenbaum, D. H., and Turk, D. (1973). *Stress Inoculation: A Skills Training Approach to Anxiety Management.* Unpublished manuscript, University of Waterloo, Ontario, Canada.

Meyer, T. J., Miller, M. L., Metzger, R. L., and Borkovec, T. D. (1990). Development and validation of the Penn State Worry Questionnaire. *Behaviour Research and Therapy* 28:487–496.

Montalvo, A., Metzger, R. L., and Noll, J. A. (1989). *The network structure of worry in memory.* Paper presented at the North Carolina Cognition Group, Davidson, NC, November.

Noyes, R. (in press). Natural course of anxiety disorders. In *Anxiety Disorders: Psychological and Pharmacological Treatments,* ed. M. R. Mavissakalian and R. F. Prien. Washington, DC: American Psychiatric Association.

Noyes, R., Woodman, C., Garvey, M. J., et al. (1992). Generalized anxiety disorder vs. panic disorder: distinguishing characteristics and patterns of co-morbidity. *Journal of Nervous and Mental Disease* 180:369–379.

Ost, L. (1987). Applied relaxation: description of a coping technique and review of controlled studies. *Behaviour Research and Therapy* 25:397–409.

Rapee, R. (1985). Distinctions between panic disorder and generalized anxiety disorder: clinical presentation. *Autralian and New Zealand Journal of Psychiatry* 19:227–232.

——— (1991). Generalized anxiety disorder: A review of clinical features and theoretical concepts. *Clinical Psychology Review* 11:419–440.

Rickels, K., Case, W. G., and Diamond, L. (1980). Relapse after short-term drug therapy in neurotic outpatients. *International Pharmacopsychiatry* 15:186–192.

Rickels, K., Case, W. G., Downing, R. W., and Fridman, R. (1986). One-year follow-up of anxious patients treated with diazepam. *Journal of Clinical Psychopharmacology* 6:32–36.

Roemer, L. Borkovec, M., Posa, S., and Lyonfields, J. D. (1991). *Generalized anxiety disorder in an analogue population: the role of past trauma.* Paper presented at the annual convention of the Association for Advancement of Behavior Therapy, New York, November.

Sanderson, W. C., and Wetzler, S. (1991). Chronic anxiety and generalized anxiety disorder: Issues in comorbidity. In *Chronic anxiety and generalized anxiety disorder*, ed. R. Rapee and D. H. Barlow, pp. 119–135. New York: Guilford.

Schweizer, E., and Rickels, K. (in press). Generalized anxiety disorder: pharmacological treatment. In *Anxiety Disorders: Psychological and Pharmacological Treatments*, ed. M. Mavissakalian & R. F. Prien. Washington, DC: American Psychiatric Association.

Shadick, R. N., Roemer, L., Hopkins, M., and Borkovec, T. D. (1991). *The nature of worrisome thoughts.* Paper presented at the annual convention of the Association for Advancement of Behavior Therapy, New York, November.

Spielberger, C. D., Gorsuch, R. L., Lushene, R., et al. (1983). *Manual for the State-Trait Anxiety Inventory (Form Y).* Palo Alto, CA: Consulting Psychologists Press.

Spitzer, R. L., Williams, J. B. W., Gibbon, M., and First, M. B. (1990). *Structured Clinical Interview for DSM-III-R–Patient Edition (SCID-P, Version 1.0).* Washington DC: American Psychiatric Press.

Suinn, R. M., and Richardson, R. (1971). Anxiety management training: a nonspecific behavior therapy program for anxiety control. *Behavior Therapy* 2:498–510.

Tollefson, G. D., Luxenberg, M., Valentine, R., et al. (1991). An open label trial of alprazolam in comorbid irritable bowel syndrome and generalized anxiety disorder. *Journal of Clinical Psychiatry* 52:502–508.

Torgerson, S. (1983). Genetic factors in anxiety disorders. *Archives of General Psychiatry* 40:1085–1089.

———— (1986). Childhood and family characteristics in panic and generalized anxiety disorders. *American Journal of Psychiatry* 143:630–632.

Vrana, S. R., Cuthbert, B. N., and Lang, P. J. (1986). Fear imagery and text processing. *Psychophysiology* 23:247–253.

Wegner, D. M., Schneider, D. J., Carter, S. R., and White, T. L. (1987). Paradoxical effects of thought suppression. *Journal of Personality and Social Psychology* 53:5–13.

Weissman, A. N., and Beck, A. T. (1978). *Development and validation of the dysfunctional attitudes scale: a preliminary investigation.* Paper presented at the annual meeting of the American Education Association, Toronto, November.

CHAPTER FIVE

Integrated Treatment of Social Phobia

Social phobia is a diagnostic category that was separated from other phobias for the first time in 1980. Perhaps for this reason there is less public awareness of this phobia than there is of others, such as agoraphobia. Since its identification, however, it has become increasingly clear that it is far more prevalent, and often much more disabling, than was originally thought.

In this chapter, Dr. Marshall updates information on social phobia, especially with regard to treatment issues. He provides an excellent summary of the use of medication with social phobias, a neglected topic until recently. In addition to cognitive-behavioral and group treatment, he emphasizes ways of interacting with and attitudes toward this particular diagnostic subgroup of people that integrate psychotherapy technique to enhance the effectiveness of treatment.

Integrated Treatment of Social Phobia

John N. Marshall

We have made substantial progress in our understanding and treatment of social phobia. Since its identification and delineation from other disorders in *DSM-III* (1980), professional levels of recognition have substantially risen. Understanding and awareness for the general public, however, have not followed suit. Most patients we see have not sought help for their social anxiety or it has been lost among other symptoms, not identified or complained of to someone who could provide treatment.

We have begun to realize that social phobia is much more prevalent than originally believed. Initial studies suggested a lifetime prevalence of 1.8–3.2 percent (Regier et al. 1988) but more recent surveys with improved diagnostic methods suggest a 7.9 percent one-year prevalence and a lifetime prevalence as high as 13.3 percent (Kessler et al. 1994). If accurate, this means that social phobia is the second most common mental disorder in the United States.

We are now able to describe other characteristics of this disorder as it affects the general population. Having a female-to-male ratio of approximately 2.5 to 1, the mean onset of social phobia is early: 11–15 years of age with onset after 25 being uncommon (Burke et al. 1990, Schneier et al. 1992). Because social phobia does tend to strike at this critical time of life (i.e., adolescence and young adulthood), this may explain the surprisingly high rates of disability and the unrelenting chronicity of this disorder. We know that socially phobic patients can be disabled in virtually all areas of their life. Scholastic endeavors are aborted; the ability to complete school and the abandonment of higher education goals are common sequelae. More than 70 percent of social phobics are in the lowest two quartiles of social economic status and, in one study, 22.3 percent of patients with pure social phobia were currently on welfare (Schneier et al. 1992). We also know there is a dramatic effect on one's human relationships. Over half of social phobics are single, divorced, or separated. Suicide attempts may be 15.7 percent higher than the general population (Schneier et al. 1992).

Research promising to tease apart the etiologic components of social phobia is continuing. One promising area is the search to characterize the neurobiology. Progress has been made in delineating social phobia from certain other disorders, especially panic disorder. We also know certain physiologic and hormonal systems do not appear to be affected, such as the hypothalamic-pituitary-adrenal axis or the hypothalamic-pituitary-thyroid axis, but we are less sure about where abnormalities may occur (Tancer 1993). Preliminary studies suggest possible disregulation in both dopaminergic and serotonergic systems (Davidson et al. 1993). Tancer (1993) suggests post-synaptic receptor supersensitivity may exist. Newly developed technologies such as magnetic resonance imaging and magnetic resonance spectroscopy are being brought to bear but at this time, findings remain non-specific (Davidson et al. 1993, Potts et al. 1993).

Progress has also been made in the establishment of broader models of etiology. Original studies of inhibited children by Kagan and colleagues (1988), expanded by Rosenbaum and colleagues (1994) to include parents, suggest a diathesis of anxiety-proneness, possibly representing an inherited physiologic predisposition to the development of severe social anxiety. The ultimate manifestation of this proneness might then depend on the extent of the disregulation or on the interaction of this predisposition with environmental factors including parental psychopathology (Rosenbaum et al. 1994).

THE PHARMACOLOGIC TREATMENT OF SOCIAL PHOBIA

There is little question but that social phobia, disabling as it is, is deserving of aggressive treatment. Although clinical practice seems to be improving in terms of consideration of psychopharmacologic interventions in the treatment of social phobia, the usual reasons, such as not recognizing the disorder, considering social phobia only a behaviorally responsive condition, and believing that it may be substantially a personality trait and therefore not responsive to medications, continue to prevail. Most of the socially phobic patients in our anxiety clinic have not been previously treated or appro-priately treated and often are seeking treatment after years of suffering severe symptoms. Advances in the use of pharmacologic agents are not about recently developed new agents but rather of an increased appreciation of the substantial comorbidity associated with social phobia and a more careful selection of the particularly appropriate drug. The selection of a medication efficacious for both (or all) disorders can be critical to successful amelioration of symptoms with fewer agents and/or side effects.

Beta-Adrenergic Blockers

The clinical use of beta-adrenergic blockers for social phobia appears to have been stimulated by psychological theories suggesting that anxiety is at least in part a response to perceived somatic sensations. These specific symptoms include dry mouth, palpitations, sweating, blushing and tremor, that is, hyperactivity of the beta-adrenergic nervous system. Clinical use was also reinforced by the observation that for years professional performers, including singers and instrumentalists, have been relying substantially on beta-blockers to overcome stage fright (performance anxiety) (Fishbein et al. 1988). This use has been largely without medical supervision and the performers strongly believe that the drugs are effective. Indeed, controlled studies of actual performance including blind ratings have shown beneficial effects on various types of performance (Brantigen et al. 1982). Initial open studies of social phobia with these drugs suggested clinical usefulness; however, in a larger and well-controlled study, beta-blockers were found not to be effective in generalized forms of social phobia. (Liebowitz et al. 1985, Liebowitz et al. 1986). This study confirmed our own experience, suggesting that beta-blockers are most effective when the required performance situation is circumscribed and where patients have generally low social anxiety in other situations. The positive effects of beta-blockers appear related to the suppression of autonomic cues but the lack of effectiveness for generalized social phobia likely occurs because cognitive anxiety levels are only indirectly and modestly altered. (Studies have shown that specific social phobics demonstrate higher heart rates in performance situations than do generalized social phobics) (Heimburg et al. 1990). The drugs most commonly used in these situations include propranolol and atenolol. The latter may be preferable as there appears to be less likelihood of adverse central nervous system side effects and the effective action of the drug is of longer duration.

Monoamine Oxidase Inhibitors

The MAOIs, appear to have the greatest efficacy in the treatment of social phobia, although few direct comparison studies exist.

Liebowitz first suggested the use of this class of drugs, in part because of experiences with atypical depressive patients who demonstrated excessive interpersonal sensitivity, a characteristic of socially phobic patients (Liebowitz et al. 1985). The initial open trial and subsequent controlled trials documented the efficacy of phenelzine. (Gelernter et al. 1991, Liebowitz et al. 1986, Liebowitz et al. 1992). Other studies showed tranylcypromine to be similarly effective (Versiani et al. 1988). This class of drugs is often avoided by practitioners because of common side effects and the possibility of a hypertensive crisis, which necessitates a low-tyramine diet. Two new MAOIs, moclobemide and brofaromine, have been developed, which appear to have the advantages of fewer side effects, a lowered risk of hypertensive crisis, and consequently less need for dietary restriction. Though presently marketed in Europe for depression, they are not available in the United States, and it does not appear that they will be in the near future.

MAOIs may be the first drug consideration when several commonly found comorbid conditions are present. Substantial numbers of socially phobic patients also suffer from panic disorder (Rosenbaum and Pollack 1994). Some studies place this comorbidity rate as high as 48 percent. (Starcevic et al. 1992). Panic disorder both with and without agoraphobia has been shown to respond to MAOIs. There has also been observation that another anxiety disorder, obsessive-compulsive disorder, when present with social phobia, may be preferentially treated with MAOIs (Carrasco et al. 1992). While generalized anxiety disorder is commonly found with social phobia, studies on the effectiveness of MAOIs for this disorder are lacking at this time. The MAOIs are, of course, antidepressants and therefore a likely choice when comorbid depression is present. Common practice, given the dietary restrictions and high levels of side effects, is for most clinicians to prefer a trial of SSRIs as a first-line treatment (perhaps in association with a benzodiazapine). If the depression were of the atypical type, beginning with a MAOI might be preferable. (Tricyclics have not been proven to be effective for social phobia.) There is also at least one case study reporting the successful treatment of social phobia and avoidant personality disorder with MAOIs (Deltito and Perugi 1986). We continue to debate where to draw the line between social phobia and avoidant personality disorder. Our positive experiences in this area reflect the need to not "write off" persons with personality disorder diagnoses, particularly avoidant personality, as being non-responsive to pharmacologic interventions.

Selective Serotonin Reuptake Inhibitors

There are now five open trials describing the potential usefulness of selective serotonin reuptake inhibitors (SSRIs) in the treatment of social phobia (Davidson 1994). These reports seem to indicate moderately positive results using fluoxetine. It should be kept in mind that direct comparison of effectiveness with other classes of medications, as well as with other SSRIs, are lacking. Successful treatment of social phobia with other SSRIs has not been reported. As noted, although the SSRIs in our experience appear to be slightly less effective for the treatment of core social phobia, this class of drugs might be a first-line treatment when comorbid depression exists to possibly provide treatment without additional agents. If needed, benzodiazepines can be safely used with SSRIs.

Social phobia is the anxiety disorder which presents with the highest comorbid alcohol abuse. This suggests the SSRIs as a first choice in the presence of a past history of drug or alcohol abuse or a questionable state of ongoing abuse.

It is also important to note that there are several other conditions that are found to have a high incidence of comorbidity with social phobia. This includes eating disorders, both bulimia and anorexia, as there is evidence that the SSRIs are useful in the treatment of these conditions (Brewerton et al. 1993, Halmi et al. 1991). Less commonly, body dysmorphic disorder and certain paraphilias are disorders for which there has been some speculation about the role of social phobia (Golwoyn and Sevlie 1992). Both of these conditions have been reported as occasionally having successful treatment with SSRIs. An interesting and useful side effect of the SSRIs in socially anxious young males is the inhibition of premature ejaculation by this class of medications.

Benzodiazepines

The benzodiazepines have been a valuable addition to the treatment of social phobia. Their implementation for this use is a natural follow-up to their recognized effectiveness in the treatment of other anxiety disorders. There have been five open trials and two controlled studies. Davidson's study of clonazepam was the largest, with substantial improvement occurring rapidly and with maximal improvement at eight weeks (Davidson et al. 1994). The mean dosage was 2.1 mg per day.

The effectiveness of the high-potency benzodiazepines in panic disorder suggests their suitability as a first choice of treatment in the common clinical situation of the co-occurrence of panic disorder and social phobia. For comorbid depression, a combination of either the SSRIs or MAOIs with a benzodiazepine can be used. The well-known high incidence of alcohol abuse among social phobics warrants careful investigation of patients' drinking patterns prior to the use of benzodiazepines. However, in my view, the absolute contraindication of this class of drugs, particularly if the patient has abstained from alcohol for a substantial period, is unwarranted (Marshall 1994a). There are patients for whom the SSRIs and MAOIs are not effective or, for some reason, not tolerated. We need to remind ourselves that the benzodiazepines, compared to multiple other agents often used for anxiety, are not as highly addicting as commonly believed. One needs to weigh the potential "theoretical" impact of the benzodiazepine on the drinking behavior versus the overall morbidity and disability associated with the combined condition. Also, it appears that for social phobia, the common pattern of its onset prior to alcohol abuse, as well as patients' descriptions of their drinking behaviors, suggests a strong self-medication pattern. Frequently, if the anxiety is adequately treated, this pattern can be interrupted and alcohol consumption reduced or abstained from as is needed.

A side effect not commonly mentioned in the literature but occasionally seen in anxiety clinics is the disinhibition of social behaviors associated with higher level doses of clonazepam. The situation may come to one's attention via complaints of the spouse, perhaps noting that the patient appears irritable, talks back, tells people off easily, or is otherwise unduly assertive. Sometimes it is difficult to sort out appropriate social behavior that is so markedly different from the patient's usual baseline behavior that it is believed pathologic. Usually a simple lowering of the dose, discussions, and education of the concerned individuals suffice in the amelioration of this problem.

Other Medications

Several other medications have been identified as potentially useful in the treatment of social phobia. Buspirone has been looked at in two open trials, with some success in the amelioration of social phobic symptoms (Clark and Agras 1991, Schneier et al. 1993). A few patients were described as having rather significant responses; most improvement is modest. One case report describes clonodine as being successful in the treatment of blushing, and another reports success with bupropion (Emmanuel et al. 1991, Goldstein 1987).

PSYCHOTHERAPEUTIC INTERVENTIONS

There are many reasons to include appropriate psychotherapeutic interventions as part of the integrated treatment of social phobia.

Some patients prefer not to use medications, others are unable to tolerate them for various reasons, and certain highly specific social phobias lend themselves primarily to behavioral interventions, for example, difficulty urinating in public restrooms. We also do not know how long medications should be used, and relapse rates are high when patients are treated only with medications. In our clinic, for moderately to severely distressed socially phobic patients, we recommend psychotherapy in conjunction with drug treatment. It should be noted, however, that thus far there are no studies to support the intuitively attractive notion that both modalities are superior to either alone. There are recent studies that suggest for some patients treated with certain highly specific psychotherapies, the two approaches may be comparable (Heimberg and Juster 1994).

The lead in the psychotherapies of social phobia has clearly been taken by those with cognitive and/or behavioral interests. Techniques that have been studied include social skills training, in vivo exposure, applied relaxation, and various "packages" that have integrated cognitive and behavioral components (CBT) (Heimburg and Barlow 1991). Supporters of CBT argue long-term maintenance of gains. There is a paucity of studies of other psychotherapeutic modalities applied to social phobia, and I know of no studies specifically utilizing psychodynamic interventions.

CBT is based on the belief that certain cognitions play a role in the development and maintenance of social fears and phobias. Described by multiple investigators, these approaches emphasize the negative cognitions experienced in anticipation of or during social situations, the expectation of negative consequences as a result of actual or feared behaviors, and overall cognitive biases regarding information that has an evaluative component to it (Heimburg 1993).

It has been our observation that the confrontation and eventual alteration of these beliefs and behaviors occurs most effectively in a group setting. With concepts borrowed substantially from treatments described by the Albany Social Phobia Program (Heimburg

and Juster 1994), our therapy groups meet for twelve weekly sessions, one-and-a-half hours in duration, and are comprised exclusively of social phobics. Although groups are time-limited, participants may repeat the group series and often do so. Components of
the therapy sessions include substantial education about social phobia with a cognitive-behavioral orientation, the production and subsequent identification of specific cognitions that commonly occur
in response to socially threatening situations, and exposure to the
anxiety-provoking situations in the context of the group interactions.
Initially the leaders, and eventually the group members, identify the
reoccurring negative cognitions which are produced in connection
with ongoing group exercises. Homework assignments are commonly used, with subsequent reporting of patients' experiences and
suggestions for alternations in both behavior and thought patterns.

THE ELEMENTS OF SUCCESSFUL THERAPY

Of course, most of us are not formally trained in cognitive-
behavioral techniques or may not have practical referral sources available. Unless he or she specializes in anxiety disorders, the practitioner may not have sufficient numbers of socially phobic patients
to enable the establishment of groups. There are, however, some
useful key elements and strategies that can be extrapolated from
more formal programs. Socially phobic patients, like other anxiety
patients, have an underlying fear of loss of control. They are often
ashamed of their symptoms, have never talked about them, and are
convinced that their own fears are strange and unique. Education
plays a major role in demystifying the condition, helping patients
to see that it is a disorder that is defined, that can be understood
and treated, and that substantial numbers of others suffer from the
same symptoms. Patients are also helped by understanding that all
of us respond to situations of being scrutinized or performance situations with some degree of anxiety or arousal and commonly expe-

rience similar symptoms. Beyond explanations occurring in therapy sessions, we suggest readings. *Social Phobia* (Marshall 1994b) is recommended for an overview of the disorder, or other books with more specific self-help advice are offered (e.g., Markway 1992).

A second major element that needs to be continually emphasized is the importance of exposure and the associated phenomenon of desensitization. It is common that patients, particularly when beginning a medication, will report that its efficacy is minimal or absent. However, in subsequent examinations of their behaviors, it becomes apparent that they have not exposed themselves to the feared situations. Once encouraged to do so, patients will often, with amazement, report dramatic diminishments of anxiety or significant social successes of which they had been unaware.

Other patients may insist they do not avoid feared social situations or that they are exposing themselves. However, upon careful exploration in the therapy session, it becomes clear that they are employing mechanisms to lessen the impact of the situation. Common mechanisms are distraction ("being somewhere else in my mind"), avoiding true participation in group settings, and generally keeping low profiles, such as speaking only with persons considered safe or avoiding other feared aspects of a situation. Careful review highlights these avoidant maneuvers. Mutual agreement on homework assignments and encouraging repetitive practice are cornerstones of therapy, even if the patient isn't receiving formal behavior therapy.

The continued focus in therapy sessions on specific encounters and responses leads naturally to the important element of identifying and discussing flawed cognitions. Gentle challenge, humor, mock exaggeration of consequences, and reinforcement for alternative interpretations are integral to the psychotherapy of social phobia. The therapist plays the role of a supportive coach dissecting, restructuring, and working through feared situations while encouraging, pushing gently, and reassuring.

Finally, but not least, a crucial element to successful treatment is the relationship. Common descriptions of behavioral approaches tend to portray images of the therapist as technician or mechanic, fixing something that is broken. As many have emphasized, change occurs best in the context of a therapeutic relationship in which there are trust and a subsequent feeling of safety. This is especially true of most anxiety patients, who are fearful, and of socially phobic patients, who may additionally suffer from poor or few relationships. A psychodynamic contribution to treatment can be useful in the examination of adverse countertransference ideas, such as "I'm anxious too in social situations but I got over it," leading to the minimizing of the patient's distress (Zerbe 1994). The active therapeutic stance does not obviate the need to listen. Reoccurring common themes are: perturbations in relationships, as the person grows and expands his or her horizons; guilt, shame, and grieving for what could have been; and the restructuring of self-image as repeated successes occur. Patients may feel disloyal to others as they begin to ask for more for themselves in life. Those of us originally trained in psychodynamic therapy should be ideally equipped to hear and understand those issues that arise as a result of more specific therapeutic interventions. Effective therapy for social phobia requires a thoughtful integration of multiple therapeutic frameworks.

REFERENCES

Brantigen, C. O., Brantigen, T. A., and Joseph, N. (1982). The effect of beta-blockade and beta stimulation on stage-fright. *American Journal of Medicine* 72:88–94.

Brewerton, T. D., Lydiard, R. B., and Herzog, D. B. (1993). Eating disorders and social phobia. *Archives of General Psychiatry* 50:70.

Burke, K. C., Burke, J. D., Regier, D. R., and Rae, D. S. (1990). Aged onset of selected mental disorders in five community populations. *Archives of General Psychiatry* 47:511–518.

Carrasco, J. L., Hollander, E., Schneier, F. R., and Liebowitz, R. R. (1992). Treatment outcome of obsessive-compulsive disorder with comorbid social phobia. *Journal of Clinical Psychiatry* 53:387–391.

Clark, D. B., and Agras, W. S. (1991). The assessment and treatment of performance anxiety in musicians. *American Journal of Psychiatry* 148:598–605.

Davidson, J. R. (1994) Social phobia: outlook for the '90s. *Journal of Clinical Psychiatry* 55 (11 suppl):509–514.

Davidson, J. R., Krishnan, K. R. R., Charles, H. C., et al. (1993) Magnetic resonance spectroscopy in social phobia: preliminary findings. *Journal of Clinical Psychiatry* 54 (12 suppl):19–25.

Deltito, J. A., and Perugi, G. (1986). A case of social phobia with avoidant personality disorder treated with MAOI. *Comprehensive Psychiatry* 27:225–258.

Emmanuel, N. P., Lydiard, B. R., and Ballenger, J. C. (1991). Treatment of social phobia with bupropron. *Journal of Clinical Psychopharmacology* 11:276–277.

Fishbein, M., Middlestadt, S. E., Ottati, V., et al. (1988). Medical problems among ICSOM musicians: overview of a national survey. *Medical Problems of Performing Artists* 3:1–8.

Gelernter, C. S., Uhde, W., Cimbolic, P., et al. (1991). Cognitive-behavioral and pharmacologic treatments of social phobia. *Archives of General Psychiatry* 48:938–945.

Goldstein, S. (1987). Treatment of social phobia with clonodine. *Biologic Psychiatry* 22:369–372.

Golwoyn, D. H., and Sevlie, C. P. (1992). Paraphilias, non-paraphilic sexual addictions, and social phobia. *Journal of Clinical Psychiatry* 53:330.

Halmi, K. A., Eckert, E., Marchi, P., et al. (1991). Comorbidity of psychiatric diagnosis in anorexia nervosa. *Archives of General Psychiatry* 48:712–718.

Heimburg, R. G. (1993). Specific issues in the cognitive-behavioral treatment of social phobia. *Journal of Clinical Psychiatry* 54:36–45.

Heimburg, R. G., and Barlow, D. H. (1991). New developments in cognitive-behavioral therapy for social phobia. *Journal of Clinical Psychiatry* 52 (11, suppl):21–30.

Heimburg, R. G., Hope, D. A., Dodge, C. S., and Becker, R. E. (1990). *DSM-III-R* subtypes of social phobia: comparison of generalized social phobics and public speaking phobics. *Journal of Nervous and Mental Disease* 178:172–179.

Heimburg, R. G., and Juster, H. R. (1994). Treatment of social phobia in cognitive-behavioral groups. *Journal of Clinical Psychiatry* 55 (suppl): 38–46.

Kagan, J., Reznick, J. S., and Snidman, N. (1988). Temperamental influences on reactions to unfamiliarity and challenge. *Advances in Experimental Medical Biology* 245:319–333.

Kessler, R. C., McGonagle, D. K., Zhao, S., et al. (1994). Lifetime and twelve month prevalence of *DSM-III-R* psychiatric disorders in the United States: results from the national comorbidity survey. *Archives of General Psychiatry* 51:8–19.

Liebowitz, M. R., Fyer, A. J., Gorman, J. M., et al. (1986). Phenelzine in social phobia. *Journal of Clinical Psychopharmacology* 6:93–98.

Liebowitz, M. R., Fyer, A. J., Gorman, J. M., and Kline, D. F. (1985). Social phobia: review of neglected anxiety disorder. *Archives of General Psychiatry* 42:729–736.

Liebowitz, M. R., Schneier, F., Campeas, R., et al. (1992). Phenelzine vs. atenolol in social phobia: a placebo-controlled comparison. *Archives of General Psychiatry* 49:290–300.

Markway, B. (1992). *Dying of Embarrassment.* New York: New Harbinger.

Marshall, J. R. (1994a). The diagnosis and treatment of social phobia and alcohol abuse. *Bulletin of the Menninger Clinic* 58 (2A):58–66.

——— (1994b). *Social Phobia: From Shyness to Stage-Fright.* New York: Basic Books.

Potts, N. L., Davidson, J. R., and Krishnan, K. R. (1993). The role of nuclear magnetic resonance imaging in psychiatric research. *Journal of Clinical Psychiatry* 54 (12, suppl):13–18.

Regier, D. A., Boyd, J. H., Burke, J. D., et al. (1988). Prevalence of mental disorders in the United States: based on five epidemiological catchment area sites. *Archives of General Psychiatry* 45:977–986.

Rosenbaum, J. F., Biederman, J., Pollack, R. A., and Hirshfield, D. R. (1994). The etiology of social phobia. *Journal of Clinical Psychiatry* 55 (6 suppl):10–16.

Rosenbaum, J. F., and Pollack, R. A. (1994) The psychopharmacology of social phobia and comorbid disorders. *Bulletin of the Menninger Clinic* 58 (2 Spring Suppl).

Schneier, F. R., Jilhod, B. S., Campeas, R., et al. (1993). Buspirone in social phobia. *Journal of Clinical Psychopharmacology* 13:251–256.

Schneier, F. R., Johnson, J., Hornig, C. D., et al. (1992). Social phobia: comorbidity and morbidity in an epidemiologic sample. *Archives of General Psychiatry* 49:282–288.

Starcevic V., Uhlenhuth, E. H., Kellner, R., and Pathak, D. (1992). Patterns of comorbidity in panic disorder and agoraphobia. *Psychiatric Research* 42:171–183.

Tancer, M. E. (1993). Neurology of social phobia. *Journal of Clinical Psychiatry* 54 (12, suppl): 26–30.

Versiani, M., Mondim, F. D., Nardi, A. E., and Liebowitz, M. R. (1988). Tranylcypromine in social phobia. *Journal of Clinical Psychopharmacology* 8:279–283.

Zerbe, K., (1994). Diagnosis in psychodynamic issues in social phobia. *Bulletin of the Menninger Clinic* 58 (2, suppl):A14.

CHAPTER SIX

Obsessive-Compulsive Disorder

Edna Foa and her colleagues at Temple University Medical Center have developed one of the best known and most effective programs in the treatment of obsessive-compulsive disorders. She was one of the first researchers who took ideas which were suggested in the literature as effective for obsessive-compulsive disorders and systematically tested them in a series of studies over the past thirty years. This chapter concisely reviews the main points of the treatment program that has been developed in accordance with these research findings and illuminates the points with case material.

Obsessive-compulsive disorder (OCD) has served as the model for an important step in treatment of mental disorders, that of redefining a disorder functionally through research and clinical observation. Previously, it was held that obsessions were thoughts and compulsions were acts. Experience with psychotherapy has favored a functional definition, that obsessions are what increase the anxiety and compulsions are what decrease it. For example, in the childhood rhyme "step on a crack, you break your mother's back," not stepping on a crack is a compulsive avoidance that reduces the anxiety of the obsessive thought of doing harm to mother. Another change in our understanding of OCD that Dr. Foa discusses involves the "strength of belief," "overvalued ideas," or "poor insight" as it is variously called, that is, the degree to which the person believes in the obsession or compulsion as reasonable rather than accepting it as pathological. It is a factor very difficult to change and perhaps the best predictor of treatment outcome.

Although phobias and obsessive-compulsive disorders are similar in many respects, the treatment of OCD is frequently more difficult and less successful than that of phobias. Before the development of these techniques, OCD was generally found to be quite refractory to any psychotherapeutic intervention. The treatment regimen described here is "exposure with response prevention." Anxiety is engendered by contact with the contaminant and gradually diminishes with exposure over time if the undoing response, the compulsive thought or act, is prevented. This goal is achieved in conjunction with effective new serotonin reuptake inhibitors and supportive psychotherapy.

Obsessive-Compulsive Disorder

EDNA P. FOA
MICHAEL J. KOZAK

DEFINITION OF OCD

According to the *DSM-IV* (1994) the essential features of obsessive-compulsive disorder (OCD) are recurrent obsessions or compulsions of significant severity. Obsessions are "persistent ideas, thoughts, impulses, or images that are experienced as intrusive and inappropriate and that cause marked anxiety or distress" (p. 418). Compulsions are "repetitive behaviors . . . or mental acts . . . the goal of which is to prevent or reduce anxiety or distress" (p. 418).

The view that obsessions and compulsions are functionally related has empirical support and is increasingly recognized (Rachman and Hodgson 1980). Foa and Tillmanns (1980), for example, proposed that obsessions and compulsions be *defined* on the basis of their functional relationship rather than on the modality in which they are expressed (mental or behavioral). Accordingly, obsessions are defined as thoughts, images, or impulses that *generate* anxiety or distress, and compulsions are defined as overt (behavioral) or covert (mental) actions that are performed in an attempt to *alleviate* the distress brought on by the obsessions. Behavioral rituals are equivalent to mental rituals (such as silently repeating numbers) in their functional relationship to distressing obsessions: both serve to reduce obsessional distress. In sum, both behavioral and mental rituals may be performed to prevent harm, restore safety, or reduce distress.

The functional view of the relationship of obsessions and compulsions is supported by findings that 90 percent of compulsions are viewed by OCD individuals as functionally related to obsessions and only 10 percent are perceived as unrelated to obsessions. Moreover, about 98 percent of obsessive-compulsives manifest both obsessions and rituals, either behavioral or mental (Foa et al. 1995).

There has been a growing consensus (Insel and Akiskal 1986, Kozak and Foa 1994, Lelliott et al. 1988) that a continuum of "insight" or "strength of belief" more accurately represents the clinical picture of OCD than the previously prevailing view that obsessive-compulsives recognize the senselessness of their obsessions. The *DSM-IV* has accommodated this recognition by including a subtype of OCD "with poor insight" into the senselessness of the obsessional ideas.

PREVALENCE AND COURSE OF OCD

Before the ECA (Epidemiological Catchment Area) studies OCD was considered rare, but is now known to be relatively common. OCD is estimated to occur in about 2.5 percent of the population (Karno et al. 1988). Slightly more than half of those suffering from OCD are female (Rasmussen and Tsuang 1986). Age of onset of the disorder ranges from early adolescence to young adulthood, with earlier onset in males (modal onset 13–15 years old) than in females (modal onset 20–24 years old) (Rasmussen and Eisen 1990). Development of the disorder is usually gradual, but acute onset has been reported in some cases. Chronic waxing and waning of symptoms is typical, but episodic and deteriorating courses have been observed in about 10 percent of patients (Rasmussen and Eisen 1989).

Table 6–1 summarizes the distribution of primary obsessions and compulsions identified in a sample of 425 individuals with obsessive-compulsive disorder. The most common obsessions involve contamination and various potential injuries to self or others from acts of commission or omission. Less frequent but still significant are obsessions with symmetry, physical health, religion, sex, hoarding, and unacceptable urges. Compulsions also take a variety of forms, of which the two most common are washing or cleaning and checking. Less common are repeating, mental rituals, ordering, hoarding, and counting.

Typically, individuals with OCD experience more than one type of obsession and compulsion. For example, a person can have contamination concerns as well as unacceptable urges to harm loved ones. This individual may wash excessively in response to the obsessions about contamination, and repeat special self-assurances in response to the unacceptable urges. The following case descriptions illustrate the most common obsessions and compulsions.

Table 6–1. Content of Primary Obsessions and Compulsions

Obsessions	Percentages of patients	Compulsions	Percentages of patients
Contamination	37.8	Checking	28.2
Fear of harm	23.6	Cleaning/Washing	26.6
Symmetry	10.0	Miscellaneous	11.8
Somatic	7.2	Repeating	11.1
Religious	5.9	Mental rituals	10.9
Sexual	5.5	Ordering	5.7
Hoarding	4.8	Hoarding/collecting	3.5
Unacceptable urges	4.3	Counting	2.1
Miscellaneous	1.0		

Case 1. Jane was a 30-year-old married woman with two children. She felt contaminated (a nonspecific feeling of being dirty, accompanied by extreme anxiety and discomfort) when in contact with her home town. Her symptoms began at age 16, when Jane felt contaminated by Christmas ornaments stored in her parents' attic. At first, only these ornaments were disturbing, but within a short period of time, everything that had been in direct or indirect contact with them led to anxiety and a concomitant urge to wash. In addition to feelings of contamination, the ornaments also produced strong feelings of sadness and depression. At the time she applied for treatment, Jane avoided anything associated with her home town, including family members. These elaborate avoidance efforts, however, proved inadequate to protect her. Jane continuously found herself confronted with items from her home town, such as chocolates manufactured there and sold in food stores, where they contaminated other groceries. Such encounters made it necessary for her to engage in extensive washing and cleaning rituals to restore a state of noncontamination. Jane was motivated to seek treatment when her grandmother, whom she loved and had not seen for seven years, became seriously ill. The fear of contamination prevented Jane from visiting her.

Case 2. Mike, a 32-year-old patient, engaged in checking rituals that were triggered by a fear of harming others. When driving he felt compelled to stop the car often to check whether he had run over people, particularly babies. Before flushing the toilet, Mike inspected the commode to be sure that a live insect had not fallen into the toilet—he did not want to be responsible for killing any live creature. In addition, he repeatedly checked the doors, stoves, lights, and windows, making sure that all were shut or turned off so that no harm, such as a fire or burglary, would befall his family as a result of his "irresponsible" behavior. In particular he worried about the safety of his 15-month-old daughter, repeatedly checking the gate to the basement to be sure that it was locked. He did not carry his daughter while walking on concrete floors in order to avoid killing her by accidentally dropping her. Mike performed these and many other checking rituals for an average of four hours a day. Checking behavior started several months after his marriage, six years before treatment. It increased two years later, when Mike's wife was pregnant with their first child, and continued to worsen over the years.

REVIEW OF TREATMENTS

OCD was formerly considered quite intractable: neither psychodynamic psychotherapy, nor a wide variety of pharmacotherapies, had been successful with it (Black 1974, Perse 1988). Now, however, there are two treatments of established efficacy: behavior therapy by prolonged exposure and pharmacotherapy with selective serotonin reuptake inhibitors (SSRIs).

Behavioral Treatments

EARLY BEHAVIORAL TREATMENTS

Despite initial claims of the efficacy of systematic desensitization with OCD, case reports indicated that it helped only 30 percent of patients (Beech and Vaughn 1978, Cooper et al. 1965). A number of other exposure-oriented procedures have also yielded generally unimpressive results (e.g., paradoxical intention, imaginal flooding, satiation, and aversion relief).

Other learning-based procedures aimed at blocking or punishing obsessions and compulsions, such as thought stopping, aversion therapy, and covert sensitization, have also been relatively unsuccessful with OCD. Thought stopping was found largely ineffective in several case studies and one controlled study (Emmelkamp and Kwee 1977, Stern 1978, Stern et al. 1975). Aversion procedures such as electric shocks, rubber-band snaps, and covert sensitization have fared somewhat better (Kenny et al. 1978, Kenny et al. 1973), but their long-term efficacy has not been determined.

EXPOSURE AND RESPONSE PREVENTION

Meyer (1966) successfully treated two cases of OCD with prolonged exposure to obsessional cues and strict prevention of rituals (response prevention), which was subsequently found highly successful in ten of fifteen cases and partly effective in the remainder; only two patients relapsed after 5 to 6 years (Meyer and Levy 1973, Meyer et al. 1974). Both uncontrolled and controlled studies of exposure and response prevention have been remarkably consistent: about 75 percent of patients are responders at post-treatment and follow-up (Foa and Kozak, in press).

This treatment entails repeated, prolonged (45 minutes to 2 hour) confrontation with situations that provoke discomfort and abstinence from rituals, despite strong urges to ritualize. Exposure is usually gradual, with situations provoking moderate distress encountered before more upsetting ones, and treatment sessions often include both imaginal and actual (in vivo) exposures. Many hours of additional exposure between treatment sessions are also prescribed. A manual that details the procedures of exposure treatment is available (Foa and Wilson 1991).

Exposure. The differential contributions of exposure and response prevention have been determined in a series of studies with obsessive-compulsive patients. The effects of exposure only, response prevention only, and their combination have been evaluated and the combination treatment was found to be more potent at both post-treatment and follow-up than were the two individual components. Moreover, the two components affect symptoms differently: exposure reduced obsessional distress, whereas response prevention reduced rituals (Foa et al. 1984, Foa et al. 1980; Steketee et al. 1982).

The combination of in vivo and imaginal exposure seems to afford no advantage over in vivo exposure immediately post-treatment, but does at follow-up, where there is somewhat less relapse after the combined procedure (Foa et al. 1980). In vivo exposure is sometimes impractical in addressing the feared catastrophes that characterize some obsessions (e.g., eternal hellfire) that can be better approached in imaginal exposure. Also, supplementing in vivo exposure with imagery exercises might circumvent the counterproductive defensive tactics of "cognitive avoiders."

In principle, fear reduction does not depend on whether anxiety-provoking stimuli are presented hierarchically beginning with the least distressing and proceeding to the most distressing, or if the most distressing stimulus is presented at the outset of treatment (Hodgson et al. 1972). However, in practice, it appears that patients prefer a gradual approach. Typically, situations of moderate difficulty are confronted first, followed by several intermediate steps before the most distressing exposure is accomplished. If a patient underestimates the difficulty of certain situations, additional intermediate steps can be interpolated. It is important, however, not to delay the most difficult exposures until the end of the treatment, lest insufficient time be available for habituation to these most distressing situations.

Duration of exposure definitely matters: prolonged continuous exposure is better than short interrupted exposure (Rabavilas et al. 1976). However, there is still the question of how much time is time enough. The simple answer is not some optimal time parameter, but rather that exposure should be long enough for a noticeable decrease in distress to occur. The required exposure time seems to differ among anxiety disorders as well as among individu-

als. For OCD, there is no fast rule about required exposure duration, but 90 minutes is a useful rule of thumb (Foa and Chambless
1978, Rachman et al. 1976).

Ideal frequency of exposure sessions has not been ascertained.
The intensive behavior therapy programs that have achieved the
most impressive results typically involve daily sessions, but favorable outcomes have also been achieved with more widely spaced
meetings.

Response Prevention. Perhaps in some inpatient facilities actions are
taken that actually prevent the patient from performing rituals
(e.g., turning off water supply in patient's room), but in outpatient
treatment, it is primarily the patient's responsibility to *choose* to ab-
stain from rituals. Although exposure reduces obsessional distress,
this does not in itself eliminate compulsions, which can develop
some independent habit strength. To reduce the urges to ritualize,
patients must practice refraining from ritualistic behavior. Self-
monitoring of both urges to ritualize and of violations of the abstinence rules can be used to enhance awareness of the processes
surrounding ritualization. In addition, a friend or family member
can be designated as a support person who can encourage the patient to resist urges to ritualize by offering reminders of its rationale (but not by coercion).

Short-Term Efficacy of Behavior Therapy

Meyer and colleagues' (1974) early reports of exposure and response
prevention were encouraging. Of fifteen patients treated by this
method, ten were rated much improved, and the remaining five,
moderately improved; only two patients had relapsed after 6 years.
These results prompted subsequent research that lent further support to the efficacy of the treatment. In a recent review of treatment

outcome studies, Steketee and Cleere (1990) described the results of nineteen studies that included both controlled trials and a series of case reports. Some of the studies specified the number of patients who improved and others reported group means. We have identified twelve studies of exposure and response prevention that included categorical data. The results of these studies are summarized in Table 6–2.

Of 330 patients studied, from 40 percent to 97 percent were improved to various degrees immediately after therapy (mean of fifteen sessions). The average percentage of improved patients in the twelve studies was 83 percent (weighted by number of patients per study).

Table 6–2. Short-Term Efficacy of Exposure Treatment

Study	Number of Patients	Number of Patients	Percent Responders
Marks et al. (1975)	20	15	75
Roper et al. (1975)	10	15	80
Boulougouris (1977)	15	11	60
Boersma et al. (1976)	13	15	85
Foa et al. (1983)	50	15	96
Julien et al. (1980)	18	20	95
Foa et al. (1992)	38	15	97
Hoogduin and Duivenvoorden (1988)	60	10	78
Hoogduin and Hoogduin (1984)	25	20	84
Cottraux et al. (1990)	15	25	40
Foa et al. (1984)	10	15	70
Emmelkamp et al. (1985)	42	10	81
Emmelkamp et al. (1989)	14	13	79
	Total = 330	M = 15	M = 83

Averages are weighted according to the number of patients in each study.

Some studies found greater improvement than others, but the causes of this variation cannot be ascertained because the studies differed from one another in several ways. First, they were conducted over a 20-year period, and in different countries, so sampling disparities may have contributed to variations in outcome. Second, in the earlier studies (e.g., Meyer et al. 1974, Marks et al. 1975), it was customary to hospitalize patients during treatment, whereas in later studies outpatient treatment became routine. Third, the number of treatment sessions varied from three to eighty, with many of the controlled studies using either ten or fifteen sessions. Other factors that also varied across studies included: duration of exposure, intervals between sessions, strictness of response prevention rules, degree of therapist involvement in exposure exercises, extent and nature of homework assignments, and inclusion of imaginal exposure. Fourth, and perhaps most importantly, the studies varied in how they defined responder status. Some studies determined responder status according to clinical global impression, and others according to percent reductions in particular symptom measures.

It should be noted that despite the high efficacy of exposure therapy with OCD, very few responders lose their symptoms completely. Patients in our clinic achieve an average symptom reduction of approximately 65 percent.

Long-Term Outcome of Behavior Therapy

Most of the treatment outcome studies of OCD reported both immediate and long-term follow-up data, but some reports focused especially on the long-term effects of treatment by reassessing patients for whom outcome data had already been published. Thus, different studies have referred to the same patients. For example, some of the patients included in the Marks and colleagues (1988) study were later reassessed and these data were reported by O'Sullivan and colleagues (1991). Ost (1992) identified a total of forty-nine reports of long-term results of behavioral treatment of OCD that described a variety of techniques, ranging from exposure and response prevention to satiation and aversion relief.

We focus here on sixteen studies that: a) used a variant of exposure and response prevention, and b) reported percent of patients improved at follow-up. Four of these studies involved designs in which some patients received behavior therapy in combination with drugs (Cottraux et al. 1990, Foa et al. 1992, Marks et al. 1980, Marks et al. 1988). All but one used crossover designs in which behavior therapy was given to all patients after drug effects were assessed. Because the drug effects were found to be either negligible or short-lasting, long-term outcome was attributed to behavior therapy, and therefore we are considering them here.

The long-term data described in the sixteen studies are summarized in Table 6–3, which presents the number of patients followed in each of sixteen studies, the percentage of patients rated improved, and the mean time to follow-up assessment. Inspection of the table reveals relatively large difference in long-term efficacy across studies, ranging from 100 percent to 50 percent responder rates. These differences probably stem from the procedural variations, such as number of sessions, strictness of response prevention, exposure length, and extent of therapist involvement, which parallel those noted above for short-term outcome.

To obtain an overall picture of the results of long-term outcome with behavior therapy, we computed weighted averages of percent responders and length of follow-up. Of the 376 patients who were included in the sixteen studies, 76 percent were treatment responders at follow-up. This result indicates substantial long-term maintenance of gains from exposure therapy. Our clinical impression is that the large majority of patients maintain their gains, but with minor attenuation of gains, and fluctuations around a point of partial improvement. Nevertheless, a significant minority (about 15 percent) relapse.

Table 6–3. Long-Term Efficacy of Exposure Treatment

Study	Number of Patients	Length of Follow-Up (in months)	Percent Responders
Meyer et al. (1974)	12	6–72	83%
Catts and McGonaghy (1975)	6	9–24	100%
Marks et al. (1975)	20	24	75%
Boulougouris (1977)	15	34	60%
Foa and Goldstein (1978)	19	15	84%
Emmelkamp and Rabbie (1981)	22	54	73%
Mawson et al. (1982)	37	24	83%
O'Sullivan et al. (1991)	34	72	74%
Bolton et al. (1983)	12	22	83%
Foa et al. (1983b)	37	12	76%
Foa et al. (1984)	11	12	80%
Hoogduin and Hoogduin (1984)	25	14.5	80%
Emmelkamp et al. (1985)	42	42	80%
Kasvikis and Marks (1988)	39	24	54%
Foa et al. (1992)	38	16	81%
Cottraux et al. (1990)	7	6	50%
	M = 376	M = 29.0	M = 76%

Averages are weighted according to the number of patients in each study.

Serotonergic Medications

Pharmacotherapy by selective serotonin reuptake inhibitors (SSRIs) has proven to be effective for OCD. The tricyclic antidepressant clomipramine (Anafranil) was the first FDA approved compound with an indication for OCD, and its usefulness has been documented in several double-blind controlled trials (DeVeaugh-Geiss et al. 1989, Marks et al., 1980, Thoren et al. 1980, Zohar and Insel, 1987). More recently, fluoxetine (Prozac) has also been established as an effective antiobsessive agent (Fontaine and Chouinard 1986, Jenike et al. 1989, Montgomery et al. 1993). Another SSRI, fluvoxamine (Luvox), has also been found effective (Goodman et al. 1989, Montgomery and Manceaux 1992, Perse et al. 1987, Price et al. 1987).

The various studies of SSRIs revealed responding rates of up to approximately 60 percent, but symptom reductions are quite modest. Conclusions about the relative efficacy of the different SSRIs are difficult in the absence of head-to-head comparisons. However, Greist and colleagues (1995) conducted a meta-analysis of large-scale double-blind controlled studies which suggests that clomipramine is superior to fluoxetine, fluvoxamine, and sertraline, and that the last three do not differ from one another in efficacy.

Improvements with SSRIs seem to depend heavily on continuation of the pharmacotherapy and relapse is evidence after discontinuation (Thoren et al. 1980). Ninety percent of a group who had improved with clomipramine were found to relapse within a few weeks after a blind drug withdrawal (Pato et al. 1988). Notwithstanding the somewhat lower relapse that has been found after withdrawal from fluoxetine (Fontaine and Chouinard 1989), the problem is substantial for this compound as well.

Combined Behavioral and Pharmacotherapies

The availability of two treatments that are partially effective individually has spawned a handful of investigations of their combined efficacy. Major improvement following behavior therapy, with a small additive effect of clomipramine was found immediately post treatment by Marks and colleagues (1980). However, the drug-only period was too short (four weeks) to allow optimal assessment of the efficacy of clomipramine alone. In a subsequent comparison of clomipramine and exposure treatment Marks and colleagues (1988) found that adjunctive medication had a small, transitory (eight week) additive effect: again, exposure was more potent than clomipramine. Although the design of the study did not allow evaluation of the long term effects of behavior therapy, a 6-year follow-up included in the above study revealed no drug effect and long-term improvement was associated with better compliance during exposure treatment (O'Sullivan et al. 1991).

Fluvoxamine and behavior therapy have been found to produce comparable reductions in OCD symptoms immediately after treatment and at 6-month follow-up, and behavior therapy plus fluvoxamine produced slightly greater improvement in depression than did behavior therapy alone (Cottraux et al. 1990). The superiority of the combined treatment for depression, however, was not evident at follow-up.

At the Medical College of Pennsylvania, an uncontrolled study examined the long-term effects (mean 1.5-years post-treatment) of intensive behavior therapy and fluvoxamine or clomipramine (Hembree et al. 1992). Patients had been treated with serotonergic drugs, intensive behavior therapy, or behavior therapy plus one of the two medications. Patients who were on medications at follow-up did equally well regardless of whether they had received behavior therapy in addition to medication or medication alone. However, patients who were medication-free at follow-up showed a different pattern: those who had received behavior therapy alone or behavior therapy plus medication were less symptomatic than those who had only received medication alone. Thus, patients treated with behavior therapy maintained their gains more than patients treated with serotonergic medication that was subsequently withdrawn.

The results of the studies described above lead to the conclusion that at present the treatment of choice for OCD is exposure and response prevention. It is more effective than medication, its efficacy is more lasting, and it has no continuing side effects. However, many patients are reluctant to accept this treatment because of their OCD-related fears. For those, pharmacotherapy should be considered with the hope that it will reduce the symptoms and thus enable them to accept exposure therapy.

IMPLEMENTING TREATMENT

The treatment program consists of three stages: treatment planning, intensive exposure/response-prevention, and a follow-up maintenance period. These are summarized below.

Treatment Planning Phase

The goals of the first interviews with the patient are twofold: establishing a diagnosis and collecting information pertinent to treatment planning. First the nature of the obsessions must be explored. The majority of obsessive-compulsives describe external cues that evoke distress. The therapist should solicit highly specific information about these cues in an attempt to identify the sources of concern. Such identification is important but often quite difficult, because patients are often unclear about the sources of their distress. For example, to understand the patient who fears touching leather items, animals, and men, one must recognize that all of these are associated with the concept of "maleness" (i.e., leather from male animals), and it is "maleness" that "contaminates." Identifying a concept that connects the various cues that trigger obsessions is important for determining the situations to which patients must be exposed. If treatment does not address the central concept, important triggers may be neglected, and there is increased risk for relapse.

Obsessional distress may arise from internal cues, including thoughts, images, or impulses that are disturbing, shameful, disgusting, or horrifying. Examples of these cues are impulses to stab one's child (triggered, in turn, by external cues such as knives or scissors), thoughts that one's spouse may have an auto accident on the way home, and images of having sex with Christ. Some patients are reluctant to disclose their obsessions, but they can usually be encouraged by direct questions, a matter-of-fact attitude, and assurances that most individuals have unwanted thoughts.

Often, the external and internal obsessional cues are associated with anticipated harm, which for some patients may constitute the primary cause for discomfort. Although the specific content of the feared disasters varies from patient to patient, most washers fear that contamination will result in disease, physical debilitation, or death to themselves or others. Most checkers fear being responsible for an error that will lead to physical harm (e.g., leaving the stove on and thereby burning the house down) or to psychological harm (e.g., setting the table incorrectly and being criticized by a significant other, writing "I am a homosexual" on a check and thereby losing others' respect). Those with repeating rituals are typically concerned that their upsetting thoughts will come to pass (e.g., an accident happening, losing control and stabbing someone, punishment from God). Information about external fear cues guides exposure in vivo; knowledge about internal cues and feared disasters guides imaginal exposure.

Both active and passive forms of avoidance are exhibited by obsessive-compulsives. Like phobics, they seek to circumvent situations that provoke discomfort. Usually, the targets of avoidance are straightforward (e.g., public toilets, shaking hands, garbage and trash, household appliances). However, the avoidance itself can take subtle form. For example, to avoid feces, an individual might side-step all brown spots on the sidewalk. To avoid contamination from "maleness," someone might refrain from sitting in waiting-room chairs that may have been used by males. It is important to identify such behavior and to proscribe it during treatment since even minor avoidances prevent full exposure to the fear cues. This failure would result in maintenance of obsessional fear. Continuing avoidance counters the exposure exercises because it prevents the patient from discovering that the feared situations are not harmful.

Common active forms of avoidance, that is, rituals, include washing, cleaning (including wiping with alcohol or spraying with Lysol), checking, repeating actions, placing objects in a precise order, and repeatedly requesting reassurance. They also include cognitive rituals, such as praying, thinking "good" thoughts, and listing events mentally. The function of rituals is to reduce distress associated with the obsessions. The relationship of each ritual to obsessional distress and to passive avoidance should be ascertained. When such a relationship is lacking, the diagnosis of obsessive-compulsive disorder becomes questionable.

On the basis of information about the internal and external fear cues, the feared harm, and the active and passive avoidance behaviors, a treatment program can be designed.

THE TREATMENT PROGRAM

Exposure

For obsessions triggered by external cues, in vivo exposure has been recommended over imaginal techniques (Emmelkamp and Wessels 1975, Rabavilas et al. 1976). For most patients, the rapidity with which the patient is introduced to the most anxiety-provoking situations seems not to affect outcome (Hodgson et al. 1972), but since patients prefer gradual exposure, we usually employ a five- or six-step hierarchy. For example, a patient who feared contamination from body secretions began with exposure to moderately difficult items such as doorknobs of public bathrooms. In the second session, discarded newspapers were added. In later sessions, he was introduced to sweat and toilet seats. By the sixth session, the patient confronted fecal material, which he feared most. The remaining nine treatment sessions were devoted to all of the above contaminants, with particular focus on the most disturbing ones. Although in the single study that investigated therapist modeling of exposure, it has not been demonstrated to enhance the efficacy of exposure (Rachman et al. 1973), clinical observations suggest that it is helpful for some patients.

The distress associated with internal cues and anticipated future disasters is addressed by imaginal exposure. The following is an example of an imaginal exposure scene for a patient with fears of contamination by "leukemia germs":

> Imagine that you are sitting in the waiting room at Mercy Hospital, waiting to see your brother, who had surgery. As you look around you, you notice a sign to the Oncology Department. You read it and start to feel the familiar sense of contamination. You know that leukemic patients have probably sat on the very chair you are sitting in now. You feel the contamination on your back and under your legs, spreading to your entire body. You wonder who sat on your chair in the past. You can visualize a man, balding and thin from chemotherapy. Just as you're sitting there you see a very thin woman, her hair with patches of baldness, who comes and sits next to you in the waiting room. . . .

Response Prevention

Fearful avoidance is directly addressed by deliberate exposure. However, exposure does not necessarily eliminate compulsions. As noted earlier, to maximize reduction of urges to ritualize, response prevention is required. The degree of strictness of the response prevention program has varied across studies, ranging from normal handwashing to total abstinence from washing for days. How strict response prevention should be is unknown. In our treatment program, washers are requested to refrain from all washing and cleaning except for one 10-minute shower every third day. To prevent "accidental" decontamination, dishwashing and other activities that normally necessitate contact with water are carried out with gloves or are assigned to someone else during treatment. Checkers are permitted at most a single check of items that are normally checked after use, such as stoves and door locks. Other objects judged not to require routine checking (e.g., unused electrical appliances, discarded envelopes) may not be checked.

In some treatment programs, patients have been supervised for 24 hours. In others no supervision is employed. Amount of supervision has not been demonstrated to affect outcome, perhaps because motivated patients will comply with treatment instructions without supervision and unmotivated ones will circumvent them. We typically request that patients have a designated supervisor whose task is to provide support and encouragement to resist urges to ritualize. We do not use physical force to prevent ritualistic behavior.

Although cognitive rituals may seem to be under less voluntary control than overt rituals, they may also be addressed by exposure techniques. Patients can be instructed to substitute confrontation with a relevant exposure situation for cognitive rituals. For example, a patient with urges to pray excessively when blasphemous thoughts arise can be instructed to entertain and exaggerate the blasphemous thought whenever an urge to pray occurs. It is important to distinguish between obsession and cognitive ritual, because, for example, it would be counterproductive to instruct the patient to engage in (i.e., confront) ritualized praying.

Schedule of Treatment Sessions

Intensive exposure at our clinic typically consists of fifteen 2-hour-long sessions conducted daily for three weeks. Clinical observations suggest that massed sessions are superior to spaced practice. The mechanism of any such superiority is unclear, especially in view of the likely efficacy of extensive daily self-exposure in the absence of sessions with the therapist. We suspect that frequent sessions help the patient to attend to the program requirements, and that they allow the therapist to discover errors that the patient is making and offer corrective instruction before the patient becomes demoralized.

Sessions customarily begin with an inspection of self-monitoring records and discussion of difficulties with self-exposure and ritual abstinence, including recommendations to circumvent them if they arise again. This is usually followed by a review of the planned exposures for the rest of the session. The remainder of the session consists of exposure, typically 45 minutes imaginal and 45 minutes in vivo. Toward the end of the session, new homework is assigned. Sometimes an in vivo exposure exercise requires that the therapist and patient travel outside the office, and an entire session will be devoted to this activity. Alternatively, an entire session might be devoted to imaginal exposure. Imaginal exposure procedures may be abandoned entirely if a script that evokes OCD-relevant affective images can not be developed.

Visits made by the therapist to the patient's home can be quite helpful, particularly when obsessive-compulsive habits are especially strong in the home. It is important that the learning that occurs in office sessions is generalized to the patient's home environment. Often, homework assignments are sufficient for this purpose, but a home visit by the therapist affords opportunities for direct observation of patient functioning in the home environment. A visit to the patient's place of employment can sometimes be important for the same reasons.

A typical home visit takes several hours on each of two consecutive days, usually at the end of a series of outpatient sessions. Additional exposures to feared situations are performed in and around the patient's home or workplace, and the therapist offers suggestions for further exposure. For example, the therapist might observe the patient contaminating or disordering the house, or the local grocery store. With the patient's explicit permission, the therapist can model the exposure exercises to be done. Many patients will report little or no discomfort when doing these exposures because of their similarity to previous exercises. Others, however, will find such exercises distressing. The therapist may discover some areas that the patient has not contaminated or disordered, either inadvertently or by systematic avoidance. The therapist's careful observation of the details of the patient's actions is a most important element of the home visit.

Follow-up sessions may help patients to maintain gains achieved during intensive therapy. We have found that one week of daily sessions devoted to relapse prevention followed by eight brief (10 minutes) weekly telephone contacts inhibited relapse (Hiss et al. 1994).

TREATMENT OF A WASHER: THE CASE OF JANE

We will now consider the application of the treatment procedures in the clinical setting using two cases: a checker and a washer.

The treatment of Jane (described earlier), who feared contamination from her home town, illustrates the application of exposure and response-prevention treatment for a patient with washing rituals. The preliminary interviews with Jane revealed that her obsessions were focused primarily on external objects. Because of the absence of anticipated harm, the treatment program did not include imaginal exposure. In preparation for treatment, we wrote to Jane's mother, who lived in the contaminated home town, and requested that she mail us objects from home, including clothing, books, and ornaments from the attic. These were stored by the therapist until the beginning of treatment.

In the first session, Jane and the therapist went into a supermarket that sold candy made in her home town, and purchased groceries located near the counter where the "contaminated" candy was displayed. When she touched the groceries to her face, hair, and clothing, anxiety increased to 50 SUDs (subjective units of disturbance, ranging from zero to 100) and declined to 20 SUDs after 90 minutes. Jane continued the exposure at home after the session, contaminating her entire house, including her bed, closets, drawers, and so on. On the second day she brought into the session books, kitchen utensils, and some clothes that she had been avoiding because of their indirect contact with her home town. On the third day, Jane handled and ate chocolates from her home town. In this session, her high level of anxiety necessitated some coaxing from the therapist; the patient started with brief contact by one finger and gradually increased it until she was able to touch the candy with her entire hand. During the next session, Jane changed into clothes sent from home. For the subsequent week, she wore her mother's clothes and handled ornaments that had come from the attic at her home. Anxiety to the latter contaminant increased to 90 SUDs and required 3 hours to habituate to a level of 40 SUDs. The remainder of treatment concentrated on contact with various items from home. In the last (fifteenth) session the therapist accompanied Jane to her home town, where they went to her attic to handle all of the objects that still provoked some discomfort. She brought some of them from her mother's attic back to her own home so that exposure to the source of contamination could continue.

Throughout this intensive 3-week program, Jane was instructed to refrain from washing her hands entirely and to limit her showering to 10 minutes every fifth day (our current practice is a shower every third day). To reinforce maintenance of her gains she was advised to return to her home town every 2 weeks over a period of 3 months. A follow-up 8 years later indicated that Jane's improvement had been maintained.

TREATMENT OF A CHECKER: THE CASE OF MIKE

Mike, the patient with the checking rituals described earlier, feared both external situations and the disasters that might ensue if he failed to ritualize. Treatment, therefore, included both imaginal and in vivo exposure, with the addition of response prevention. The first scene that Mike was asked to imagine was as follows: Mike was at school where he teaches. He failed to check the toilet bowl before flushing it. A school child came looking for his gerbil in the bathroom where the cage was kept. The cage was empty and the child cried, worrying that the gerbil fell into the toilet. Mike feared that he had indeed flushed the gerbil down the toilet, since he failed to check. During the image, his reported anxiety climbed to 80 SUDs, gradually diminishing to 30 SUDs. In vivo exposure during the first session involved flushing toilets in public restrooms with eyes closed. The homework assignment was to flush the toilet at home without prior checking.

In the second scene Mike imagined that he had forgotten to check the windows and doors, and a burglar entered and stole his wife's jewelry. She blamed him for the theft. In vivo, Mike was instructed to close doors and windows, checking briefly only once. Next, Mike was asked to imagine that he dropped his baby daughter on a concrete floor because he did not hold her properly and that she was hospitalized for injuries and both his wife and parents accused him of carelessness. In vivo exposure consisted of carrying his baby daughter while he walked on a concrete floor, until his anxiety decreased. In subsequent scenes Mike fantasized driving over a bump on the expressway, worrying that he had run over someone, and that the police pulled him over and charged him with a hit-and-run accident. His homework entailed city driving among pedestrians and potholes without stopping and without checking his rearview mirror or retracing his path.

At a 3-year follow-up, Mike reported 10 minutes of checking per day, compared to 4 hours per day before treatment. Most of the excessive checking was done in the classroom in an attempt to prevent papers from being mixed up; some brief unnecessary checking of doors and windows at home also persisted.

TREATMENT COMPLICATIONS

Noncompliance

When exposure/response prevention is described, about 25 percent of obsessive-compulsives decline to participate. This attrition process leaves in treatment only the motivated patients. Nevertheless, a few of them fail to abide by the agreed-upon rules, and a larger number try to bend them. Failure to resist rituals and persistence in avoidance patterns lead inevitably to a poor outcome.

It is unusual for an obsessive-compulsive patient to conceal ritualistic activity from the therapist. When this happens, the patient should be confronted with the implications for treatment outcome of the failure to comply. If noncompliance persists, therapy should be discontinued with the understanding that the patient may return when he or she is prepared to follow the treatment regimen. Continuance under conditions in which failure is likely to occur will leave the patient hopeless about future prospects for improvement.

Another motivational problem is posed by individuals who carry out exposure exercises without ritualizing but continue to engage in passive avoidance patterns. The persistence of such behaviors hinders habituation of anxiety to feared situations and may leave the patient with the erroneous belief that his avoidance protects him from harm. Failure to give up avoidance patterns also calls for a re-evaluation of continuation in treatment.

Familial Patterns

Family members have typically experienced intense frustration due to the patient's symptoms. It is not surprising that some are impatient, expecting treatment to result in rapid and complete symptom remission. Conversely, family members may continue to "protect" the patient from previously upsetting situations, thus reinforcing avoidance behaviors. Years of accommodation to the patient's peculiar requests have established familial habits that are difficult to break. Such patterns may hinder progress in treatment and interfere with maintenance of gains, thus requiring intervention.

Functioning without Symptoms

Many obsessive-compulsives have become socially and occupationally dysfunctional as their symptoms absorb an increasing proportion of their life. Successful treatment leaves them with a considerable void in their daily routine. Assistance in acquiring new skills and in planning both social and occupational activities should be the focus of follow-up therapy in such cases.

FAILURES AND RELAPSES

The interference of depression with treatment outcome has been widely noted (e.g., Foa et al. 1983a, Rachman and Hodgson 1980). However, depressed mood commonly co-occurs with OCD, and moderately depressed patients have been found to respond well to exposure-based treatment (Foa et al. 1992). Clinical observations suggest that severely depressed individuals benefit less from treatment and are particularly prone to relapse at follow-up. Antidepressant medication should be considered for these extremely depressed patients before they begin behavioral treatments.

A further stumbling block in treatment may be the patient's belief system regarding the likelihood that the feared consequences will in fact materialize. Foa (1979) observed that those who firmly believed that their worst fears would come to pass if they failed to protect themselves by ritualizing did not habituate to feared contaminants, whether within an exposure session or across sessions. Other investigators failed to find a linear relationship between strength of belief and outcome of exposure treatment (Lelliot et al. 1988). Perhaps only patients with the most strongly held obsessional beliefs are unresponsive to exposure treatment.

CONCLUSION

Exposure and response prevention have been established as a highly potent treatment for obsessive-compulsive disorder. It is notable, however, that many patients do not avail themselves of this treatment out of reluctance to confront their feared situations. Despite the potency of behavior therapy, good responders rarely find themselves entirely symptom free at the completion of this regimen. Most patients maintain their gains, but a small proportion do relapse (Foa et al. 1992). Relapse is most common among those patients who are only partially improved at the end of treatment. Pre-treatment with serotonergic antidepressants may prove useful for those who manifest severely depressed moods at the beginning of treatment, and for those who are reluctant to enter behavioral therapy.

REFERENCES

Beech, H. R., and Vaughn, M. (1978). *Behavioral Treatment of Obsessional States.* New York: Wiley.

Black, A. (1974). The natural history of obsessional neurosis. In *Obsessional States*, ed. H. R. Beech, pp. 19–54. London: Methuen.

Boersma, K., Den Hengst, A., Dekker, J., and Emmelkamp, P. M. G. (1976). Exposure and response prevention: a comparison with obsessive-compulsive patients. *Behaviour Research and Therapy* 14:19–24.

Bolton, D., Collins, S., and Steinberg, D. (1983). The treatment of obsessive-compulsive disorder in adolescence: a report of fifteen cases. *British Journal of Psychiatry* 142:456–464.

Boulougouris, J. C. (1977). Variables affecting the behavior modification of obsessive-compulsive patients treated by flooding. In *The Treatment of Phobic and Obsessive-Compulsive Disorders*, ed. J. C. Boulougouris and A. D. Rabavilas, pp. 73–84. Oxford: Pergamon.

Catts, S., and McConaghy, N. (1975). Ritual prevention in the treatment of obsessive-compulsive neurosis. *Australian and New Zealand Journal of Psychiatry* 9:37–41.

Cooper, J. E., Gelder, M. G., and Marks, I. M. (1965). Results of behaviour therapy in 77 psychiatric patients. *British Medical Journal* 1:1222–1225.

Cottraux, J., Mollard, E., Bouvard, M., et al. (1990). A controlled study of fluvoxamine and exposure in obsessive-compulsive disorder. *International Clinical Psychopharmacology* 5:17–30.

DeVeaugh-Geiss, J., Landau, P., and Katz, R. (1989). Treatment of OCD with clomipramine. *Psychiatric Annals* 19:97–101.

Diagnostic and Statistical Manual of Mental Disorders (1994). 4th ed. Washington, DC: American Psychiatric Association.

Emmelkamp, P. M. G., Hoekstra, R. J., and Visser, S. (1985). The behavioral treatment of obsessive-compulsive disorder: prediction of outcome at 3.5 years follow-up. In *Psychiatry: The State of the Art*, vol. 4, ed. P. Pichot, A. Brenner, R. Wolf, and K. Thau, pp. 265–270. New York: Plenum.

Emmelkamp, P. M. G., and Kwee, K. G. (1977). Obsessional ruminations: a comparison between thought-stopping and prolonged exposure in imagination. *Behaviour Research and Therapy* 15:441–444.

Emmelkamp. P. M. G., and Rabbie, D. M. (1981). Psychological treatment of obsessive-compulsive disorder: a follow-up four years after treatment. *Biological Psychiatry* 16:1095–1098.

Emmelkamp, P. M. G., van Linden van den Heuvell, C., Ruphan, M. and Sanderman, R. (1989). Home-based treatment of obsessive-compulsive patients: intersession interval and therapist involvement. *Behaviour Research and Therapy* 27:89–93

Emmelkamp, P. M. G., and Wessels, H. (1975). Flooding in imagination versus flooding in vivo. A comparison with agoraphobics. *Behaviour Research and Therapy* 13:7–15.

Foa, E. B. (1979). Failure in treating obsessive-compulsives. *Behaviour Research and Therapy* 16:391–399.

Foa, E. B., and Chambless, D. L. (1978). Habituation of subjective anxiety during flooding in imagery. *Behaviour Research and Therapy* 16: 391–399.

Foa, E. B., and Goldstein, A. (1978). Continuous exposure and complete response prevention of obsessive-compulsive neurosis. *Behavior Therapy* 9:821–829.

Foa, E. B., Grayson, J. B., Steketee, G. S., et al. (1983). Success and failure in the behavioral treatment of obsessive-compulsives. *Journal of Consulting and Clinical Psychology* 51:287–297.

Foa, E. B., Kozak, M. J., Goodman, W. K., et al. (1995). *DSM-IV* field trial: obsessive-compulsive disorder. *American Journal of Psychiatry* 152:90–96.

——— (in press). Obsessive-compulsive disorder: long-term outcome of psychological treatment. In *Long-term Treatments of Anxiety Disorders*, ed. M. Mavissakalian and R. Prien, Washington, DC: American Psychiatric Press.

Foa, E. B., Kozak, M. J., Steketee, G., and McCarthy, P. R. (1992). Treatment of depressive and obsessive-compulsive symptoms in OCD by imipramine and behavior therapy. *British Journal of Clinical Psychology* 31:279–292.

Foa, E. B., Steketee, G., Grayson, J. B., and Doppelt, H. G. (1983). Treatment of obsessive-compulsives: When do we fail? In *Failures in Behavior Therapy*, ed. E. B. Foa and P. M. G. Emmelkamp, pp. 10-34. New York: Wiley.

Foa, E. B., Steketee, G., Grayson, J. B., et al. (1984). Deliberate exposure and blocking of obsessive-compulsive rituals: immediate and long-term effects. *Behavior Therapy* 15:450–472.

Foa, E. B., Steketee, G., and Milby, J. B. (1980). Differential effects of exposure and response prevention in obsessive-compulsive washers. *Journal of Consulting and Clinical Psychology* 48:71–79.

Foa, E. B., Steketee, G., Turner, R. M., and Fischer, S. C. (1980). Effects of imaginal exposure to feared disasters in obsessive-compulsive checkers. *Behaviour Research and Therapy* 18:449–455.

Foa, E. B., and Tillmanns, A. (1980). The treatment of obsessive-compulsive neurosis. In *Handbook of Behavioral Interventions: A Clinical Guide*, ed. A. Goldstein and E. B. Foa, pp. 416–500. New York: Wiley.

Foa, E. B., and Wilson, R. (1991). *Stop Obsessing! How to Overcome Your Obsessions and Compulsions*. New York: Bantam Doubleday Dell.

Fontaine, R., and Chouinard, G. (1986). An open clinical trial of fluoxetine in the treatment of obsessive-compulsive disorder. *Journal of Clinical Psychopharmacology* 6:98–101.

——— (1989). Fluoxetine in the long-term maintenance treatment of OCD. *Psychiatric Annals* 19:88–91.

Goodman, W. K., Price, L. H., Rasmussen, S. A., et al. (1989). Efficacy of fluvoxamine in obsessive-compulsive disorder: a double blind comparison with placebo. *Archives of General Psychiatry* 46:36–44.

Greist, J. H., Jefferson, J. W., Kobak, K. A., et al. (1995). Efficacy and tolerability of serotonin transport inhibitors in obsessive compulsive disorder: a meta-analysis. *Archives of General Psychiatry*, 52:53–60.

Hembree, E. A., Cohen, A., Riggs, D., et al. (1992). *The long-term efficacy of behavior therapy and serotonergic medications in the treatment of obsessive-compulsive ritualizers*. Unpublished manuscript.

Hiss, H., Foa, E. B., and Kozak, M. J. (1994). Relapse prevention program for treatment of obsessive-compulsive disorder. *Journal of Consulting and Clinical Psychology* 62:801–808.

Hodgson, R. J., Rachman, S., and Marks, I. M. (1972). The treatment of chronic obsessive-compulsive neurosis: follow-up and further findings. *Behaviour Research and Therapy* 10:181–189.

Hoogduin, C. A. L., and Duivenvoorden, H. J. (1988). A decision model in the treatment of obsessive-compulsive neurosis. *British Journal of Psychiatry* 152:516–521.

Hoogduin, C. A. L., and Hoogduin, W. A. (1984). The outpatient treatment of patients with an obsessional-compulsive disorder. *Behaviour Research and Therapy* 22:455–459.

Insel, T. R., and Akiskal, H. (1986). Obsessive-compulsive disorder with psychotic features: a phenomenologic analysis. *American Journal of Psychiatry* 12:1527–1533.

Jenike, M. A., Buttolph, L., Baer, L., et al. (1989). Open trial of fluoxetine in obsessive-compulsive disorder. *American Journal of Psychiatry* 146:909–911.

Julien, R. A., Rivere, B., and Note, I. D. (1980). Traitement comportenmental et cognitif des obsessions et compulsions resultats et discussion. *Seance du Lundi* 27 *Octobre* 1123–1133.

Karno, M., Golding, J. M., Sorenson, S. B., and Burnam, A. (1988). The epidemiology of obsessive-compulsive disorder in five US communities. *Archives of General Psychiatry* 45:1094–1099.

Kasvikis, Y., and Marks, I. (1988). Clomipramine, self-exposure, and therapist-accompanied exposure in obsessive-compulsive ritualizers: two year follow-up. *Journal of Anxiety Disorders* 2:291–298.

Kenny, F. T., Mowbray, R. M., and Lalani, S. (1978). Faradic disruption of obsessive ideation in the treatment of obsessive neurosis: a controlled study. *Behavior Therapy* 9:209–221.

Kenny, F. T., Solyom, L., and Solyom, C. (1973). Faradic disruption of obsessive ideation in the treatment of obsessive neurosis. *Behavior Therapy* 4:448–457.

Kozak, M. J., and Foa, E. B. (1994). Obsessions, overvalued ideas, and delusions in obsessive-compulsive disorder. *Behaviour Research and Therapy* 3:343–353.

Lelliott, P. T., Noshirvani, H. F., Basoglu, M., et al. (1988). Obsessive-compulsive beliefs and treatment outcome. *Psychological Medicine* 18:697–702.

Marks, I. M., Hodgson, R., and Rachman, S. (1975). Treatment of chronic obsessive-compulsive neurosis by in vivo exposure. *British Journal of Psychiatry* 127:349–364.

Marks, I. M., Lelliott, P., Basoglu, M., et al. (1988). Clomipramine self-exposure, and therapist-aided exposure for obsessive-compulsive rituals. *British Journal of Psychiatry* 152:522–534.

Marks, I. M., Stern, R. S., Mawson, D., et al. (1980). Clomipramine and exposure for obsessive-compulsive rituals—I. *British Journal of Psychiatry* 136:1–25.

Mawson, D., Marks, I. M., and Ramm, L. (1982). Clomipramine and exposure for chronic obsessive-compulsive rituals, volume III. Two year follow-up and further findings. *British Journal of Psychiatry* 140:11–18.

Meyer, V. (1966). Modification of expectations in cases with obsessional rituals. *Behaviour Research and Therapy* 4:273–280.

Meyer, V., and Levy, R. (1973). Modification of behavior in obsessive-compulsive disorders. In *Issues and Trends in Behavior Therapy*, ed. H. E. Adams and P. Unikel, pp. 77–136. Springfield, IL: Charles C Thomas.

Meyer, V., Levy, R., and Schnurer, A. (1974). A behavioral treatment of obsessive-compulsive disorders. In *Obsessional States*, ed. H. R. Beech, pp. 233–258. London: Methuen.

Montgomery, S. A., McIntyre, H., Oaterheider, M., and Sarteschi, P. (1993). A double-blind, placebo-controlled study of fluoxetine in patients with *DSM-III-R* obsessive-compulsive disorder. *European Neuropsychopharmacology* 2:143–152.

Montgomery, S. A., and Manceaux, A. (1992). Fluvoxamine in the treatment of obsessive-compulsive disorder. *International Clinical Psychopharmacology* 7 (Suppl. 1):5–9.

Ost, L. (1992). *Behavior therapy for obsessive compulsive disorder: long-term follow-up.* Unpublished manuscript.

O'Sullivan, G., Noshirvani, H., Marks, I., et al. (1991). Six-year follow-up after exposure and clomipramine therapy for obsessive-compulsive disorder. *Journal of Clinical Psychiatry* 52:150–155.

Pato, M. T., Zohar-Kadouch, R., Zohar, J., and Murphy, D. L. (1988). Return of symptoms after desensitization of clomipramine and patients with obsessive-compulsive disorder. *American Journal of Psychiatry* 145:1521–1525.

Perse, T. (1988). Obsessive-compulsive disorder: a treatment review. *Journal of Clinical Psychiatry* 49:48–55.

Perse, T. L., Griest, J. H., Jefferson, J. W., et al. (1987). Fluvoxamine treatment of obsessive-compulsive disorder. *American Journal of Psychiatry* 144:1543–1548.

Price, L. H., Goodman, W. K., Charney, D. S., et al. (1987). Treatment of severe obsessive-compulsive disorder with fluvoxamine. *American Journal of Psychiatry* 144:1059–1061.

Rabavilas, A. D., Boulougouris, J. C., and Stefanis, C. (1976). Duration of flooding sessions in the treatment of obsessive-compulsive patients. *Behaviour Research and Therapy* 14:349–355.

Rachman, S., DeSilva, P., and Roper, G. (1976). The spontaneous decay of compulsive urges. *Behaviour Research and Therapy* 14: 445–453.

Rachman, S., and Hodgson, R. (1980). *Obsessions and Compulsions*. Englewood Cliffs, NJ: Prentice-Hall.

Rachman, S., Marks, I. M., and Hodgson, R. (1973). The treatment of obsessive-compulsive neurotics by modelling. *Behaviour Research and Therapy* 8:383–392.

Rasmussen, S. A., and Eisen, J. L. (1989). Clinical features and phenomenology of obsessive-compulsive disorder. *Psychiatric Annals* 19:67–73.

———— (1990). Epidemiology of obsessive-compulsive disorder. *Journal of Clinical Psychiatry* 51:10–14.

Rasmussen, S. A., and Tsuang, M. T. (1986). Clinical characteristics and family history in *DSM-III* obsessive-compulsive disorder. *American Journal of Psychiatry* 3:317–382.

Roper, G., Rachman, S., and Marks, I. (1975). Passive and participant modeling in exposure treatment of obsessive-compulsive neurotics. *Behaviour Research and Therapy* 13:271–179.

Steketee, G. S., and Cleere, L. (1990). Obsessional-compulsive disorders. In *International Handbook of Behavior Modification and Therapy*, ed. A. S. Bellack, M. Hersen, and A. E. Kazdin, pp. 307–332. New York: Plenum.

Steketee, G. S., Foa, E. B., and Grayson, J. B. (1982). Recent advances in the treatment of obsessive-compulsives. *Archives of General Psychiatry* 39:1365–1371.

Stern, R. S. (1978). Obsessive thoughts: the problem of therapy. *British Journal of Psychiatry* 132:200–205.

Stern, R. S., Lipsedge, M. S., and Marks, I. M. (1975). Obsessive ruminations: a controlled trial of thought-stopping technique. *Behaviour Research and Therapy* 11:650–662.

Thoren, P., Asberg, M., Chronholm, B., et al. (1980). Chlorimipramine treatment of obsessive-compulsives. *Archives of General Psychiatry* 37:1281–1285.

Zohar, J., and Insel, T. (1987). Obsessive-compulsive disorder: psychobiological approach to diagnoses treatment and pathophysiology. *Biological Psychiatry* 22:667–687.

CHAPTER SEVEN

Childhood Phobias

The understanding of anxiety in childhood and adolescence has undergone the same radical changes as those described in the introductory chapter with regard to adults, both in diagnosis and in treatment. There seems to be an easier acceptance of symptomatic treatment for childhood phobias than for those of adulthood. For example, a parent with a child who refuses to attend school will be likely to seek therapy that promises short-term symptom relief. For the parent's own phobia, however, there may be no effort to seek therapy, or a traditional exploratory psychotherapy may be attempted. The effectiveness of the treatment now available for anxiety in childhood might perhaps have a salutary effect on the mental health of the future adult, in that a rapid remission encourages a more normal and age-appropriate developmental progression. But, as Dr. Koplewicz points out, diagnostic accuracy in anxiety disorder in childhood is of special importance to avoid missing the diagnosis of a more insidious and serious pathological process.

Childhood Phobias

Harold Koplewicz

ANXIETY DISORDERS

Anxiety disorders of childhood and adolescence, according to the *DSM-IV*, are separation anxiety disorder and selective mutism. However, generalized anxiety disorder, simple phobia, social phobia, and obsessive compulsive disorder, which are all listed in the adult section of the *DSM-IV*, can and often first occur during childhood or adolescence. All of these disorders are pathologic states of normal anxiety conditions. Several hypotheses have been postulated for their etiology:

1. Normal developmental maturation does not occur in a group of anxious children.

2. The parents, usually the mother, condition these children to be anxious. This hypothesis is hard to prove, since most parents of anxious children are nonsymptomatic, and they are the ones requesting help for their child.

3. Certain children are predisposed to anxiety disorders in the same way certain children are predisposed to chronic ear infections, seizures, or any other physical illness.

Even though the etiology of the anxiety disorders is still unknown, effective treatment approaches, including psychotherapy and pharmacotherapy, have been developed. The possibility that more than one hypothesis is true often indicates an individualized treatment approach, utilizing psychotherapy, parent counseling, and medication. This chapter will review the current state of the art in the treatment of the anxiety disorders of childhood and adolescence.

Avoidant Disorder of Childhood and Adolescence

Anxiety normally occurs at certain developmental stages throughout childhood. Its absence may be a pathological sign. Alternatively, anxiety is termed a disorder when the anxiety reaction continues past the normal developmental stage and causes the child discomfort and dysfunction. Normal stranger anxiety occurs in infants between the ages of 7 and 11 months. For example, while being examined by a physician, the baby may look up at the doctor's face and begin to cry. One hypothesis for the baby's anxiety reaction is that his brain has developed to the stage that he can distinguish his mother and father from strangers, and he becomes "distressed" at the difference. The absence of stranger anxiety may be a symptom of certain pathological conditions. The differential diagnosis would include hearing or visual impairment or possibly neglect or abuse.

A nonpathological absence of stranger anxiety would result from the effects of multiple caretakers on normal children. A child from a large extended family being examined by his pediatrician would look up at the doctor and think, "This isn't my mother, this isn't my father, this isn't my Uncle Pete, this isn't Cousin Rose," and by the time he had compared the doctor to all the images in his mind of his relatives, he would be back in his mother's arms. Therefore, no anxiety or distress would be expressed. Similarly, children of working parents may also have multiple caretakers and may not experience stranger anxiety.

Stranger anxiety that persists past the age of 2½ years is a pathologic condition. For example, a child may have a warm, satisfying relationship with his parents and immediate family but become socially uncomfortable and isolated when a stranger or friend of the family enters the house. The child or adolescent experiences intensive and pathological self-consciousness. As the child enters adolescence, these symptoms cause greater dysfunction. This condition is known as social phobia. It is common, but frequently these children and adolescents suffer quietly and do not present for treatment.

CASE EXAMPLE

Elizabeth was a 16-year-old who presented to a children's anxiety clinic at her parents' request. She had always been a shy child. In elementary school, although she was a good student, she often refused to read out loud or answer questions in class. She had one close friend and spent most of her free time with her parents. During adolescence Elizabeth's social awkwardness became more obvious and problematic. Her socially anxious behavior interfered with the psychosocial development tasks of adolescence. Her behavior in social settings included only speaking when spoken to and refusing to eat in public. She was socially isolated and withdrawn from her classmates.

At the recommendation of her guidance counselor, Elizabeth's parents took her to a therapist. The doctor utilized an analytic approach, which resulted in nonsignificant gains. Essentially, Elizabeth spent the sessions in silence. After several months the parents took her to an anxiety clinic at a university-affiliated hospital. The differential diagnosis included social phobia and schizoid disorder. The prognosis for a child with social phobia is possibly a continuation of her symptoms into adulthood. The child with schizoid disorder presents with peculiar social skills but is not anxious about his social deficits. The prognosis for this child may include schizophrenia.

Most individuals have experienced social phobic reactions at a large cocktail reception. One has the sensation of being scrutinized. Eating in a restaurants and using public bathrooms may be problematic. It is easier to treat a child with social phobia than an adult with the disorder. The adult has a lifelong pattern, while the child's symptoms may be of only a few years duration.

In the adult population, patients who have social phobia have been treated with group therapy and with either Nardil or placebo (Liebowitz et al. 1986). Both groups received social skills training. The group that also received Nardil had a significaint decrease in symptoms over the placebo group. Nardil is effective in the treatment of atypical depression. Rejection sensitivity is commonly seen in atypical depression and is probably a key feature of social phobia, therefore providing a possible rationale for efficacy of an MAOI antidepressant in this anxiety disorder.

TREATMENT

The treatment of choice for social phobia is group therapy. A social skills training group is the most effective route (Cartledge and Milburn 1986), most often optimally composed of eight to ten patients, all of whom have social skills deficits. The group may include both sexes with an age range of approximately three years (e.g., 12–15 years, 15–18 years). The treatment is short term, consisting of 12–18 sessions. Each session is goal specific—teaching how to conduct phone conversations, speaking in front of a group, dealing with parents. The group therapy includes relaxation techniques. The patients are encouraged to have contact with their group members outside of sessions.

Consideration of pharmacotherapy is indicated in patients with severe anxiety or rejection sensitivity that limits the effectiveness of psychotherapy. In these cases, a short-term trial of a minor tranquilizer should be made an adjunct to the psychotherapy. In adolescent patients who will comply with the necessary dietary restrictions, a trial of an MAO inhibitor can be considered. Recently, SSRIs (selective serotonin reuptake inhibitors) have been used for adolescents with social phobia. Prozac and Zoloft have both been used.

Selective Mutism

A special presentation of social phobia in childhood and adolescence is selective mutism. The prominent symptom in this disorder is the persistent refusal to speak in specific social situations. The symptoms interfere with the child's social and educational functioning. Open clinical trials of Fluoxetina (Prozac) have been effective with this group of patients. Parents and teachers report that the children speak with greater ease and more frequency.

Separation Anxiety Disorder

The normal child between 18 months and 2½ years old experiences separation anxiety. We expect that a child will be anxious when his mother leaves the room. Sometimes, a child playing comfortably in his own room will suddenly need to see his mother. The first day of nursery school or even kindergarten, children may become very upset and clingy, and experience separation anxiety. After a few days, this anxiety decreases and eventually disappears. The child becomes comfortable in the school setting. This is a normal sequence. When separation anxiety behavior persists past the age of 4 and causes distress and dysfunction, it is separation anxiety disorder (SAD). In SAD, children experience: (1) illogical worry that something is going to happen to threaten the integrity of the family, (2) distress upon separation, and (3) homesickness (*DSM-III-R* 1987). The illogical worries can be present in nightmares in which separation themes are prominent. Fears about kidnappers coming into the home and taking the child or killing the parents are common. The threat to the integrity of the family is a key feature to these worries. Distress upon separation presents most acutely on Monday and other schoolday mornings. These children will state that "Sunday night and Mondays are the worst days of the week." Homesickness can present with school refusal or termination of sleep over dates. Sleepaway camps will represent a great difficulty. Homesickness may affect a child so that he is terribly uncomfortable and often experiences physical symptoms at school. Younger children experience more gastrointestinal complaints while the adolescents more frequently complain of cardiovascular symptomatology (Gittelman-Klein and Klein 1980).

CASE EXAMPLE

Adam, a first-grader at a new school, was an attractive 6-year-old with curly blond hair. He was homesick and weepy and complained daily of stomachaches at school. Physical examination disclosed no organic etiology. Adam admitted to the pediatrician that the stomachaches occurred only on weekdays. He also realized that they disappeared with his mother's presence.

TREATMENT

The treatment approach should include the parents and school as well as the child. The first goal is to get the child to attend school. The longer the child has been out of school, the more difficult the treatment (Gittelman-Klein 1975). If the child does not respond within a month to a vigorous behavioral child-therapy approach, medication should be added to the treatment regimen. In the adult population with panic disorder and agoraphobia, 50 percent had childhood SAD (Klein 1964). Tofranil (imipramine) is effective in the treatment of panic disorder and has efficacy in children and adolescents with SAD (Gittelman-Klein 1971).

The relationship between panic disorder with agoraphobia and SAD is very close, and they occur together frequently. In one study comparing adult patients with panic disorder with agoraphobia versus simple phobia, 47 percent of those with panic disorder with agoraphobia also had SAD, while only 22 percent of those with simple phobia reported a current diagnosis of SAD. In adults with a diagnosis of panic disorder with agoraphobia, 50 percent report a history of childhood separation anxiety versus the adult simple-phobic population, which reports a history of 27 percent (Klein et al. 1980). In another study, parents of children with SAD were compared to parents of children with attention-deficit disorder with hyperactivity (ADHD). The parents of the separation-anxiety-disordered children reported histories of separation anxiety in 19 percent of the group versus 2 percent in the ADHD group (Gittelman-Klein and Klein 1980). In a survey done in the general population, adults with a diagnosis of depression with agoraphobia reported that 24 percent of their children had separation anxiety versus no incidence in the children of adults with depression without an anxiety disorder (Weissman 1982). Xanax (alprazolam), which has proven efficacy in the treatment of anxiety disorders in the adult population, has been used in an open clinical trial with children and adolescents with SAD with positive results (Koplewicz and Gittelman-Klein 1986, Sheehan et al. 1984). Newer medications have been used in open clinical trials with children and adolescents with SAD. The SSRIs as well as BuSpar have been used in this population with positive results. The side effects are of a nuisance quality and are not as serious or problematic as the tricyclics.

Simple Phobia

A normal child will experience fear of many common things, such as the dark or dogs, at 3 to 5 years of age. When the fear causes dysfunction and severe distress, it is considered a simple phobia— an illogical fear of a harmless object. Some common objects of simple phobias are snakes, elevators, bugs, and planes. Many children, adolescents, and adults experience simple phobic symptoms but never require treatment, because they are able to avoid the feared object and, therefore, do not experience distress or dysfunction. With support and reassurance, a simple phobic reaction in childhood may remit.

CASE EXAMPLE

Sam, a 3-year-old, had developed a fear of pigs. The onset of this phobic reaction occurred while he was visiting relatives who lived on a farm. Sam repeatedly asked to see the pig. When he was taken to the pen, however, a piglet ran at him and nipped his ankle. Although he suffered no physical harm, the entire day Sam spoke of nothing else but his fear of the pig eating him. For several weeks Sam had nightmares about the pig and was fearful of visiting his relatives, going for a drive in the country, or visiting the zoo.

TREATMENT

Children may develop phobias of many different types of animals or objects (such as snakes, elevators, bugs). If the condition persists and the child's functioning is impaired, a treatment that includes desensitization should be started. No medication has efficacy in the treatment of simple phobias.

Generalized Anxiety Disorder

Children may experience anxiety before tests, recitals, or plays. This is known as performance anxiety. However, a child who experiences excessive worries about performance before, during, and after the test may have an overanxious disorder. Such children often have "pseudoprecarious worries." They are overly concerned about the future and what others think of them. The overanxious child frequently presents to the pediatrician with physical complaints that prove to have no organic etiology.

CASE EXAMPLE

Jennifer, a 7-year-old, is described by her parents as a "nervous wreck." She has headaches and stomachaches all the time. Jennifer admits to worrying about everything: "I worry about money, I worry about the future, I worry where I will go to school when I am older." Jennifer refused to go to the rooftop playground at her school. She was fearful that a gust of wind would blow down the fence and possibly she would fall or get hurt. Her teachers state that she "tries her hardest" all the time. She requires their constant reassurance that she is doing her school work correctly. Her dinner conversation centers around test and school performance.

TREATMENT

The treatment for a child with overanxious disorder requires the participation of the school, the parents, and the child. The parents often are overachievers and may be anxious about their performance and the child's, but usually not to the child's pathologic extent. Behavioral therapy approaches can be effective with these

children (Ollendick and Gruen 1972). The parents require counseling on how to focus on other issues beside the child's performance. The initiation of low doses of minor tranquilizers may
be necessary because of the increased anxiety these children experience when performance discussions and teacher checkups are
eliminated. To date, a systematic study of the efficacy of minor
tranquilizers in the childhood population has not been done.
Recently, an open clinical trial of Prozac has been shown to have
a positive effect.

Obsessive-Compulsive Disorder

In school-age children, rituals and superstitions are not uncommon.
Fear of "stepping on a crack, breaking your mother's back" is an
example. Obsessive-compulsive disorder (OCD) usually presents in
school age or early adolescence. Its range of severity is wide. Obsessions are illogical ideas or thoughts that one has to keep repeating in one's head. A compulsion is a purposeless behavior or ritual.
The most common obsessions and compulsions are related to germ
contamination (*DSM-III-R* 1987). A feeling of dread is common
and necessitates the compulsive behavior. Quite often, children with
OCD are secondarily depressed.

CASE EXAMPLE

David, a 16-year-old, presented with a 4-year history of OCD.
At age 12 he became intensely worried about his height. He
began measuring himself repeatedly and comparing his height
to that of everyone he met. His concentration and then his
school functioning decreased. He described the symptoms as
ego-dystonic. David was demoralized and at times said he
wished he could die so his symptoms would end.

TREATMENT

Treatment for children and adolescents with OCD should include cognitive-behavioral therapy. Clomipramine (Anafranil), a tricyclic antidepressant, has been studied in this population and has efficacy in the treatment of OCD (Flament et al. 1985).

Fluoxetine (Prozac) has been studied in adults with OCD with positive results (Turner 1985). Prozac, Sertraline (Zoloft), and Fluroxamine (Luvox) have all been used with children and adolescents.

CONCLUSION

The anxiety disorders of childhood and adolescence are common. The treatment approach often requires the active involvement of the parents and school as well as the child.

The treatment of avoidant disorder of childhood and adolescence is social skills training. This treatment consists of a short-term group therapy. Further research following adult models is needed to test the efficacy of SSRIs in this disorder, as well as in selective mutism.

The treatment of separation anxiety disorder (SAD) consists of psychotherapy and pharmacotherapy. The utilization of behaviorally oriented psychotherapy is effective in 40 percent of children with school phobia (Gittelman-Klein and Klein 1971).

The treatment of separation-anxiety disorder (SAD) consists of psychotherapy and pharmacotherapy. The utilization of behaviorally oriented psychotherapy is effective in 40 percent of children with school phobia (Gittelman-Klein and Klein 1971). Tofranil is the only medication that has been studied with a double-blind design. The side effect profile of this medication includes both nuisance and serious adverse effects. The nuisance side effects interfere with compliance with this medication. The serious side effects include potential cardiovascular changes that require careful monitoring. Open clinical trials of alprazolam (Xanax) with children and adolescents with SAD have been promising. SSRIs have been used with excellent results and need further study.

Simple phobia is the most common anxiety disorder of childhood. Treatment is required only when the child experiences distress and dysfunction as a result of the phobia. The treatment of choice is desensitization. At present no drug treatments are available.

Children and adolescents with generalized anxiety disorder infrequently present to a mental health professional. Worries about performance and the future are symptoms that can be useful for academic success. Frequently, a child will experience physical symptoms secondary to the overanxious disorder before a psychiatric consultation is eventually obtained. The most efficacious treatment involves the parents and school as well as the child. In some cases, a short-term trial of a minor tranquilizer can be instituted along with psychotherapy. To date, there are no double-blind placebo-control studies of medication for this disorder.

The treatment of children and adolescents with obsessive-compulsive disorder includes behavioral-cognitive therapy and pharmacotherapy. Clomipramine (Anafranil) has proven efficacy for children and adolescents with OCD. Fluoxedine (Prozac) is a promising alternative to clomipramine; however, further research is required in the child and adolescent population.

The treatment of anxiety disorders in children and adolescents is very promising. Treatment models utilized in adults, which include psychotherapy and pharmacotherapy, are proving effective in the child and adolescent population.

REFERENCES

Cartledge, G., and Milburn, J. F., eds. (1986). *Teaching Social Skills to Children: Innovation Approaches*, 2nd ed. New York: Pergamon.

Diagnostic and Statistical Manual of Mental Disorders (1987). 3rd ed., rev. Washington, DC: American Psychiatric Association.

Flament, M., Rapoport, J. L., and Berg, C. J. (1985). Clomipramine treatment of childhood obsessive compulsive disorder: A double blind control study. *Archives of General Psychiatry* 42:977–983.

Gittelman-Klein, R. (1975). Pharmacotherapy and management of pathological separation anxiety. *International Journal of Mental Health* 4: 255–271.

Gittelman-Klein, R., and Klein, D. F. (1971). Controlled imipramine treatment of school phobia. *Archives of General Psychiatry* 25:204–207.

——— (1980). Separation anxiety in school refusal and its treatment with drugs. In *Out of School*, ed. L. Hersov, pp. 321–341. London: Wiley.

Klein D. F. (1964). Delineation of two drug-responsive anxiety syndromes. *Psychopharmacologia* 5:397–408.

——— (1980). Diagnosis and drug treatment of childhood disorders. In *Diagnosis and Drug Treatment of Psychiatric Disorders: Adults and Children*, 2nd ed. Baltimore: William and Wilkins.

Koplewicz, H. S., and Gittelman-Klein R. (1986). *Short-term psychotherapies of children and adolescents.* Paper presented at the Meeting of American Academy of Child and Adolescent Psychiatry, Washington, DC.

Liebowitz, M., Fyer, A. J., Gorman, J., et al. (1986). Pheuelzine and social phobia. *Journal of Clinical Psychopharmacology* 6:93–98.

Ollendick, T. H., and Gruen, G. E. (1972). Treatment of a bodily injury phobia with implosive therapy. *Journal of Consulting and Clinical Psychology* 38:389–393.

Sheehan, D. V., Coleman, J. H., Greenblatt, D. J., et al. (1984). Some biochemical correlates of panic attacks with agoraphobia and their response to a new treatment. *Journal of Clinical Psychopharmacology* 4:66–75.

Turner, S. (1985). Fluoxetine treatment of obsessive-compulsive disorder. *Journal of Clinical Psychopharmacology* 5:207.

Weissman, M. M., Kidd, K. K., and Prusoff, B. A. (1982). Variability in rates of affective disorders in relatives of depressed and normal probands. *Archives of General Psychiatry* 39:1397–1403.

CHAPTER EIGHT

Post-Traumatic
Stress Disorder

⟹⊷⊱⟸

The addition of Post-Traumatic Stress Disorder to the Anxiety Disorders was one of the major revisions to the field with the publication of the *DSM-III* in 1980. The category was further changed with the *DSM-IV* in 1994, when Acute Stress Disorder was delineated.

The contribution of Patricia Resick and Karen Calhoun is new to this book and provides an expanded discussion of diagnostic and assessment issues and theoretical models for treatment of the stress disorders. The discussion of theoretical models for PTSD is especially interesting because it highlights the similarities to as well as the differences from the other anxiety disorders.

PTSD includes diverse groups such as veterans, Holocaust survivors, and flood, fire, or earthquake victims, among others. The treatment section in this chapter concerns victims of rape and is an excellent example of a treatment model that is primarily based on cognitive techniques.

⟹⊷⊱⟸

Post-Traumatic Stress Disorder

PATRICIA A. RESICK
KAREN S. CALHOUN

INTRODUCTION

Post-traumatic stress disorder (PTSD) was introduced in the third edition of the *Diagnostic and Statistical Manual of Mental Disorders (DSM-III)* (1980). Previous editions had referred to stress reactions with terms like *gross stress reaction* and *transient situational disturbance*, but without empirical support or specific criteria. Classified as a form of anxiety disorder (no longer a neurosis), the *DSM-III* description of PTSD was based on the existing empirical literature, most of it derived from studies of combat veterans. But it was recognized that exposure to other forms of trauma could lead to similar symptoms. This stimulated a convergence of disparate areas of research on different types of trauma, which is resulting in rapid developments in theory and treatment. It is now commonly accepted that the type of trauma experienced (although each has some unique features) is less important than trauma severity and individual reactions and vulnerabilities. In this chapter we focus on rape-related PTSD.

The criteria for PTSD in the fourth edition of the *Diagnostic and Statistical Manual of Mental Disorders (DSM-IV)* (1994), shown in

Table 8–1, represent refinements over *DSM-III* and the revised third edition criteria based on recent research advances. Major changes include use of the term *traumatic event* and the requirement that the event be threatening to the life or physical integrity of oneself or others, *and* that the response to the event involve intense fear, helplessness, or horror. The inclusion of an individual's reaction to the event resulted from research showing that fear of death or injury is a strong predictor of PTSD symptoms. The three major characteristics of the disorder (reexperiencing, avoidance and numbing, and increased arousal) remain intact, with minor changes. Internal as well as external cues are now recognized as having potential to trigger reexperiencing. Physiological reactivity has been moved from the list of indicators of increased arousal to the reexperiencing list.

The specification of delayed onset is retained in cases where onset of symptoms occurs more than 6 months after the trauma. The acute–chronic distinction, dropped in *DSM-III-R*, is reintroduced and refined, setting the differentiating duration point at 3 months rather than 6.

Newly introduced in *DSM-IV* is acute stress disorder, to be applied to short-term (less than four weeks) severe reactions to trauma. The criteria include two types of symptoms, dissociative reactions and PTSD symptoms. In order to be diagnosed, the trauma victim must experience at least three types of dissociative reactions during or after the event, he or she must have PTSD symptoms from each of the main symptom clusters (reexperiencing, avoidance, and arousal), and the symptoms must cause significant distress or impairment in important areas of functioning. The disturbance must last for at least 2 days and no more than 4 weeks after the traumatic event. Although there has been some research indicating that dissociation during the traumatic event is a predictor of later PTSD, there has been no research thus far examining this particular configuration of symptoms. It is unknown how many people develop acute stress disorder following traumatic events or whether this

Table 8–1. *DSM-IV* Diagnostic Criteria for Post-Traumatic Stress Disorder

A. The person has been exposed to a traumatic event in which both of the following have been present:

    (1) the person has experienced, witnessed, or been confronted with an event or events that involve actual or threatened death or serious injury, or a threat to the physical integrity of self or others

    (2) the person's response involved intense fear, helplessness, or horror (in children, disorganized or agitated behavior)

B. The traumatic event is persistently reexperienced in one or more of the following ways:

    (1) recurrent and intrusive distressing recollections of the event, including images, thoughts, or perceptions (in young children, repetitive play may occur in which themes or aspects of the trauma are expressed)

    (2) recurrent distressing dreams of the event (in children, there may be frightening dreams without recognizable content)

    (3) acting or feeling as if the traumatic event were recurring (includes a sense of reliving the experience, illusions, hallucinations, and dissociative flashback episodes, including those that occur upon awakening or when intoxicated) (in young children, trauma-specific reenactment may occur)

    (4) intense psychological distress at exposure to internal or external cues that symbolize or resemble an aspect of the traumatic event

    (5) physiological reactivity upon exposure to internal or external cues that symbolize or resemble an aspect of the traumatic event

C. Persistent avoidance of stimuli associated with the trauma and numbing of general responsiveness (not present before the trauma), as indicated by at least three of the following:

    (1) efforts to avoid thoughts or feelings associated with the trauma

    (2) efforts to avoid activities, places, or people that arouse recollections of the trauma

    (3) inability to recall an important aspect of the trauma

(4) markedly diminished interest or participation in significant activities
(5) feeling of detachment or estrangement from others
(6) restricted range of affect (e.g., unable to have loving feelings)
(7) sense of a foreshortened future (e.g., does not expect to have a career, marriage, children, or a normal life span)

D. Persistent symptoms of increased arousal (not present before the trauma), as indicated by at least two of the following:
(1) difficulty falling or staying asleep
(2) irritability or outbursts of anger
(3) difficulty concentrating
(4) hypervigilance
(5) exaggerated startle response

E. Duration of the disturbance (symptoms in B, C, and D) is more than one month.

F. The disturbance causes clinically significant distress or impairment in social, occupational, or important functioning.

Specify if:
Acute: if duration of symptoms is less than three months
Chronc: if duration of symptoms is three months or more

Specify if:
With Delayed Onset: onset of symptoms at least six months after the stressor

Diagnostic criteria for Acute Stress Disorder

A. The person has been exposed to a traumatic event in which both of the following were present:
(1) the person experienced, witnessed, or was confronted with an event or events that involved actual or threatened death or serious injury, or a threat to the physical integrity of self or others
(2) the person's response involved intense fear, helplessness, or horror

B. Either while experiencing or after experiencing the distressing event, the individual has three (or more) of the following dissociative symptoms:

(1) a subjective sense of numbing, detachment, or absence of emotional responsiveness

(2) a reduction in awareness of his or her surroundings (e.g., "being in a daze")

(3) derealization

(4) depersonalization

(5) dissociative amnesia (i.e., inability to recall an important aspect of the trauma)

C. The traumatic event is persistently reexperienced in at least one of the following ways: recurrent images, thoughts, dreams, illusions, flashback episodes, or a sense of reliving the experience; or distress on exposure to reminders of the traumatic event.

D. Marked avoidance of stimuli that arouse recollections of the trauma (e.g., thoughts, feelings, conversations, activities, places, people).

E. Marked symptoms of anxiety or increased arousal (e.g., difficulty sleeping, irritability, poor concentration, hypervigilance, exaggerated startle response, motor restlessness).

F. The disturbance causes clinically significant distress or impairment in social, occupational, or other important areas of functioning or impairs the individual's ability to pursue some necessary task, such as obtaining necessary assistance or mobilizing personal resources by telling family members about the traumatic experience.

G. The disturbance lasts for a minimum of 2 days and a maximum of 4 weeks and occurs within 4 weeks of the traumatic event.

H. The disturbance is not due to the direct physiological effects of a substance (e.g., a drug of abuse, a medication) or a general medical condition, is not better accounted for by Brief Psychotic Disorder, and is not merely an exacerbation of a preexisting Axis I or Axis II disorder.

---

grouping of symptoms, including these dissociative reactions, is more predictive of later PTSD than just knowing how severe the PTSD symptoms were in the immediate aftermath of the event.

Reexperiencing phenomena such as flashbacks and nightmares are considered the hallmark symptoms of PTSD. Nightmares are often exact replications of the traumatic experience, or of earlier traumas, memories of which are reactivated by a new event. Flashbacks are characterized by extreme emotional and physiological arousal during which the person may feel immobilized and unaware of immediate surroundings. They may be described as "waking nightmares." Almost any stimulus associated with the trauma can trigger flashbacks, even when its connection with the traumatic experience goes unrecognized. For example, a rape victim did not understand why she could not tolerate the odor of roses until she recalled a vase of roses in the room in which she was attacked. She remembered thinking at one point during the assault how inappropriate their presence seemed. When clients do not understand the origins of their symptoms, which often happens in cases of delayed onset, it increases their perception that the symptoms are both unpredictable and uncontrollable.

Avoidance symptoms, including emotional numbing, are usually viewed as attempts to control or protect against the negative affect and arousal associated with reexperiencing. Avoidance behavior can be extreme, as in the case of a rape victim who became agoraphobic and refused to leave her house for years. Emotional numbing is not well understood. Litz (1992) described emotional numbing as a "complex, multiply determined problem that is best characterized as a selective emotional-processing deficit. This emotional deficit is chiefly manifested during symptomatic states (and is thus episodic in nature) and entails a muting of positively valenced responses and a heightened reactivity to negative events" (p. 429). It may be combined, in some cases, with a fear of losing control, a fear reinforced by the outbursts of extreme anger (increased arousal symptoms) that many victims experience. Such outbursts are more readily seen in male combat veterans than in female sufferers of PTSD. However, they are not at all uncommon among women and are all the more frightening when inconsistent with their pretrauma behavior and self-concept. Emotional numbing presents one of the most difficult treatment challenges and may persist long after other symptoms disappear. Emotional numbing often includes failure to enjoy sex, not only for rape victims but for others as well. Resick (1987) found this effect, for example, among male robbery victims. Feldman-Summers and colleagues (1979) found that rape victims rated their level of sexual satisfaction significantly lower than did control subjects, even though they were equally orgasmic. Thus, some aspects of emotional numbing might be an irreversible effect of trauma.

Studies have shown that PTSD is a very common consequence of rape. Kilpatrick and colleagues (1987) found that 57% of women in a community sample who had been raped developed PTSD at some point in their lives. More recently, a nationwide survey by the National Victim Center (Kilpatrick et al. 1992) found that 31% of rape victims developed PTSD at some point, compared to 5% of nonvictims. At the time of the survey, 11% had diagnosable PTSD. The report estimated that based on their rape incidence results, 1.3 million American women currently have rape-related PTSD and approximately 211,000 will develop it each year. Prospective studies report even higher rates. Rothbaum and colleagues (1992) found that 94% of women entering a longitudinal study following rape met criteria for PTSD at approximately 2 weeks postrape and about 50% at 12 weeks.

Given the high incidence of sexual assault, it is probable that female victims make up the single largest group of those suffering from PTSD. For example, in the Kilpatrick and colleagues (1992) study, 13% of women reported having been victims of at least one completed forcible rape. Of these, 39% had been raped more than once. Men are also victimized by sexual assault (overwhelmingly by other men). However, little is known about the prevalence or consequences. Forman (1982) found that 5.7% of reported rapes involved male victims. This may well be an underestimate since men are assumed to be even more reluctant than women to report sexual assault. Kaufman and colleagues (1980) found that 10% of victims were male. These were adult samples. If sexual assault of children is included, the percentage of male victims is higher. Burnam and colleagues (1988) found that 18% of sexual assault victims in the Los Angeles area were male, combining child and adult victims. Men may be less likely than women to disclose a history of sexual assault when seeking treatment, so therapists should be alert to signs of it. Very little research has been done on male victims, but there are indications that they suffer as much as women. Goyer and Eddleman (1984) identified PTSD symptoms in thirteen male sexual assault victims who sought treatment at a naval psychiatric center. Kaszniak and colleagues (1988) reported a case of an adult male who had functional retrograde amnesia for all autobiographical information after being sexually assaulted at gunpoint by two men. Male victims have been found to be at higher risk for substance abuse than women (Burnam et al. 1988), although gender did not predict probability of any other disorder.

THEORETICAL MODELS OF PTSD

A large number of theoretical models have been proposed in attempts to organize observed patterns of reactions in PTSD and to explain the development of these patterns. The models vary considerably in their level of comprehensiveness and they tend to overlap a great deal. The major trends in development of theoretical models are outlined here.

  Prior to the recognition of PTSD as a syndrome, the majority of theoretical ideas concerning stress reactions were psychodynamic in origin. Freud (1937), in observing traumatized World War I veterans, noted two of the major characteristics now identified with PTSD. These were repetition (reexperiencing) and denial (avoidance). Horowitz (1976) incorporated these ideas into his information processing model of response to trauma. This model has been highly influential. It incorporates not only traditional psychodynamic ideas but also ideas from cognitive theories of emotion and information processing. According to this model, adjustment to a traumatic event requires incorporating it into existing cognitive schemas or developing new schemas. Until this process is complete, the trauma remains in active memory. In active memory the information concerning the traumatic event is out of conscious awareness and the mechanisms of denial and emotional numbing are employed to keep the individual from being overwhelmed by it. However, representations of the events stored in active memory tend to be repeated as part of the attempt to process and integrate them. This results in intrusive thoughts and images about the trauma that are accompanied by intense emotions. Horowitz refers to oscillation between periods of intrusive ideas and emotions and periods of denial and numbing. Reexperiencing phenomena such as nightmares and flashbacks are intrusions aimed at facilitating information processing. However, uncontrolled intrusions can lead to retraumatization and out-of-control emotions. Avoidance and numbing are seen as control processes aimed at regulating information processing so the individual is not overwhelmed. However, excessive controls may prevent complete cognitive processing of the event. Horowitz (1986) continued the development of this model and incorporated new ideas. For example, he notes the potential for strong, positive social support to help protect against the development of PTSD. In research on stress, one of the most consistent empirical findings has been the buffering effect of social support. Although Horowitz's model is among the most comprehensive, it fails to address one of the great puzzles in this area: Why do some individuals develop PTSD and others exposed to the same trauma do not? In addition, the clinical procedures suggested by this model are less explicit and testable than those generated by other theoretical models.

Biological models attempt to explain the development of PTSD on an entirely different level. Van der Kolk and colleagues (1984) developed a biological model based on the observation that PTSD shares many similarities with the animal model of inescapable shock. Both involve exposure to severe and uncontrollable stress. Van der Kolk and colleagues (1984) postulated that PTSD symptoms result from changes in neurotransmitter activity. The hyperamnesia symptoms, exaggerated startle responses, and aggressive outbursts are thought to be associated with noradrenergic overreactivity to trauma-relevant stimuli followed by depletion of these brain biochemicals. Decreases in central nervous system levels of noradrenalin are thought to account for symptoms such as anhedonia, social withdrawal, and affective numbing. Endogenous opiates released during reexposure result in stress-induced analgesia. Subsequent depletion of the endogenous opiates is experienced as aversive, setting up a cycle of behavior in which the victim may seek exposure to stress repeatedly in an attempt to regain the analgesic effects.

Kolb (1987) proposed another model for the pathophysiology of PTSD. Both Kolb (1987) and McGaugh (1990) emphasized the effects of exposure to stressors on the central nervous system. Excessive stimulation experienced in traumatic events may cause damage or alteration of neuronal pathways. Other recent research supports trauma-induced change in brain neurochemical systems as contributing to PTSD symptoms. For example, Charney and colleagues (Charney et al. 1990, Charney et al. 1991) found that changes in serotonin function may be associated with anhedonic symptoms.

Although such biological models are intriguing, it should be remembered that they are preliminary in nature and leave many of the puzzles of PTSD unexplained. For example, delayed onset of symptoms, impact of mediating variables, and individual differences in response to trauma have not been addressed by most of these models (Jones and Barlow 1990).

Two-factor learning theory models of PTSD symptom development were proposed by Keane and colleagues (1985). Kilpatrick and colleagues (1979) used similar explanations for rape-related PTSD symptoms. According to this model, any stimulus associated with the traumatic event can become, through the process of classical conditioning, capable of eliciting a conditioned response similar to that associated with the original trauma. Additional stimuli, associated indirectly with the trauma, create similar reactions through stimulus generalization and higher-order conditioning. Avoidance behaviors are learned in order to escape or prevent the conditioned response. Thus, repeated negative reinforcement of avoidance makes it very resistant to extinction. This explains the persistence of anxiety symptoms long after other symptoms decrease significantly. The principles of higher-order conditioning in stimulus generalization are used to explain why symptoms often worsen over time as more and more stimuli elicit traumatic memories and physiological arousal. Keane and colleagues (1985) suggested that delayed onset of PTSD may actually result from symptoms gradually worsening over time until they reach a critical point.

Behavioral models of PTSD development continue to evolve and have begun to incorporate additional variables such as individual characteristics, including social support as well as cognitions. Foy and colleagues (1992) proposed a behavioral model in which the maintenance of PTSD symptoms is influenced substantially by buffering factors such as social support and vulnerability factors such as family history of psychopathology.

Information processing models of PTSD are based on Lang's (1977, 1979, 1985) theory of emotion. Lang posited a semantic memory network of interconnected points of information including trauma-relevant stimuli, information about response events, and information about the meaning of both stimuli and responses. Foa and colleagues (1989) suggested that traumatic events create especially large and complex fear networks that are activated readily because of the large number of interconnections formed through conditioning and generalization. Associations that were once considered neutral or safe may now be connected with fear. This leads to a sense of unpredictability and uncontrollability that is important in the development and maintenance of PTSD. Chemtob and colleagues (1988) have developed a similar information processing model of PTSD. However, it appears to fit combat-related PTSD better than rape or other single-event traumas.

Theoretical models are becoming increasingly sophisticated and comprehensive as our knowledge mounts concerning the effects of trauma. For example, Creamer and colleagues (1992) proposed a cognitive processing model for reactions to trauma that includes a feedback loop among intrusions, avoidance, and symptom levels. Like other cognitive processing models, Creamer's model views the successful processing or integrating of the trauma as central to successful recovery. This model sees the cognitive processing mechanisms involved in recovery over time as occurring in five stages. Stage 1 is objective exposure. The major factor at this stage is the severity of the traumatic stressor. Stage 2 is network formation. This is determined primarily by subjective perceptions and meaning attached to the experience. Stage 3 is labeled intrusion. During this stage, the memory network is activated in an attempt to process and resolve the trauma-related memories. Stage 4, avoidance, is characterized by the use of escape and avoidance as coping strategies in response to intrusions. During Stage 5, which is labeled outcome, recovery is achieved through network resolution processing. Such factors as pretrauma functioning and biological processes are not incorporated into this model although the authors acknowledge their importance.

In a more comprehensive recent model, Jones and Barlow (1992) proposed that variables important in the etiology and maintenance of other anxiety disorders, along with anxious apprehension, explain the development of PTSD. The role of biological vulnerability is acknowledged in this model and family and twin studies are cited to support this role. Jones and Barlow (1992) postulate that what is inherited may be a predisposition to respond to stress with chronic autonomic overarousal or noradrenal lability. This is consistent with findings that combat veterans with PTSD exhibited higher resting heart rate than did controls (Blanchard et al. 1982, Blanchard et al. 1986). Central to this model is the observation of similarities between PTSD and other anxiety disorders, in particular panic disorder. If an individual with biological and psychological vulnerabilities is exposed to a trauma and develops anxious apprehension, the stage is set for PTSD. Anxious apprehension involves distorted processing of information along with extremely negative affect. The individual perceives the traumatic event and subsequent reexperiencing as unpredictable, uncontrollable aversive events and reacts with chronic overarousal, hypervigilance, and narrowing of attention. This sets up a feedback loop in which hyperarousal, hypervigilance, and narrowing of attentional focus increase intrusive thoughts and reexperiencing.

ASSESSMENT

The first essential step in assessment is to identify sexual assault or other major trauma in the client's history. Many rape victims fail to disclose their trauma history unless specifically asked. This is consistent with their general pattern of avoidance of trauma-related reminders. Even when seeking treatment, trauma victims often fail to recognize that their psychological problems are associated with their assault. Kilpatrick (1983) suggested several other reasons victims might not be forthcoming with this information. They may fear a negative reaction to disclosure, especially if previous disclosure has resulted in disbelief or blame. Additionally, many victims do not recognize or identify their experience as a rape, especially if the assailant was an acquaintance or a relative. In actuality, the majority of rapes are committed by someone known to the victim.

Resnick and colleagues (1991) suggest supportive, nonevaluative questioning of sexual assault history. Saunders and colleagues (1989) developed a ten-question screening interview to detect history of crime victimization including rape. Its use as part of a standard intake at a mental health center resulted in identification of sexual assault in 41.7% of female clients, compared to 13.3% using a standard intake. A self-report instrument that can be used for screening identification of rape and other forms of sexual assault is the Sexual Experiences Survey by Koss and Gidycz (1985). This is a ten-item self-report instrument that assesses types of coercion or force, as well as types of molestation or sexual assault. It was reported to have internal consistency of .74 and a test-retest reliability over a 1-week interval of .93.

There are two major aims in assessment: diagnosis and treatment planning. A third purpose is suggested by the high rates of comorbidity with PTSD. Depression, anxiety disorders, and substance abuse are especially common comorbid disorders. Whether the primary purpose of assessment is diagnosis or treatment planning, a multidimensional, multiaxial approach is necessary. Because a cross-sectional view taken at a single point in time may fail to capture the full range and pattern of symptoms, a longitudinal approach to assessment has been advocated by Denny and colleagues (1987) and Sutker and colleagues (1991). Certainly for purposes of treatment, ongoing assessment of symptom patterns and treatment effectiveness is essential. For a more comprehensive discussion of issues and procedures in assessment of rape-related PTSD, the reader is referred to Resnick and colleagues (1991).

Researchers in combat-related PTSD have led the field in development of assessment procedures (Keane et al. 1984, Keane et al. 1987, Keane et al. 1988). Several of these procedures have been adapted for use with civilian victims. Keane and colleagues (1987) report the development of a comprehensive structured assessment battery that is useful not only for diagnostic purposes but for the development of treatment goals and the evaluation of treatment outcome. Although developed for assessment of combat-related PTSD, the principles embodied in this battery are relevant to other forms of trauma as well. The battery includes both objective and subjective data collected through structured interview formats, as well as quantifiable psychological inventories. It assesses past and present functioning in a wide range of cognitive, affective, behavioral, and physiological areas (Wolfe and Keane 1990).

A note of caution regarding assessment is in order. Suicide risk should always be carefully assessed and monitored. The National Women's Study (Kilpatrick et al. 1992) found that 13 percent of rape victims had made a suicide attempt. This is compared to 1 percent of the nonvictims. Additionally, 33 percent of the rape victims compared to 8 percent of nonvictims stated that they had seriously considered suicide at some point.

COGNITIVE PROCESSING THERAPY FOR RAPE-RELATED PTSD AND DEPRESSION

Over the past five years we have been working to develop and test a therapy specifically tailored for the symptoms that are observed most frequently in treatment-seeking sexual assault victims. The result of this effort is cognitive processing therapy (CPT). CPT is based on information processing theory. However, unlike some of the information processing theories, which view PTSD symptoms as developing from a readily potentiated fear schema, we view the symptoms as developing from an inability to resolve conflicts between the traumatic event and prior beliefs about the self or others, as well as the consequent avoidance of a range of strong affects such as anger, shame, or guilt, not just fear. Given this approach to the problem, CPT focuses on the content of cognitions and includes components which help the client to 1) access her memory of the event, 2) identify and experience her emotions until they have extinguished, and 3) identify and challenge beliefs about the event itself and beliefs about herself and the world that have been altered because of the rape.

CPT is a twelve-session therapy which systematically builds the client's skills to deal first with the rape and then with the effects of the rape in other areas of her life. After an initial assessment conducted prior to therapy, the first session has three purposes: to describe the symptoms of PTSD (and depression if relevant) to the client; to give her an explanatory model of the symptoms; and to describe the course of treatment. At the end of the session the client is given the assignment to write an impact statement, an essay about what it means to her that she was raped. The purpose of this assignment is to begin to identify stuck points, conflicts and beliefs that have prevented the client from recovering and have changed her view of herself and the world. The therapist will look for overgeneralized beliefs about danger, trust, power and control, esteem, and intimacy, as well as self-blame statements or other statements that may indicate that the client has distorted the event (assimilation) rather than accepting it ("Maybe it wasn't rape since I had dated him before").

At the second session the client reads her impact statement and the client and therapist discuss the meanings the rape has for the client. The therapist has the client identify emotions and begin to recognize the difference between thoughts and emotions. The client is given A-B-C forms, which have columns for the client to record events, thoughts, and feelings. She is encouraged to begin noticing how different thoughts and interpretations may lead to different emotions. The client is given a number of the sheets to work on between sessions and is encouraged to complete at least one sheet on the rape. The rest of the events recorded on the forms can relate to daily situations.

Session three begins with a review of the A-B-C sheets. Corrections are made if the client confuses thoughts with feelings, and the therapist mildly challenges the validity of cognitive distortions that become evident. The next assignment is for the client to write her account of the rape, the exposure component of CPT. The account should not be a dry factual account but should include sensory details, thoughts, and feelings. The client is instructed to write her story as soon as possible and to read it every day. She is also told to pick a time and place to write and read her account that allows her to feel her emotions. She is advised to let herself feel her feelings, and that while it feels intense to begin with, it gets easier over time.

At session four the client reads her account to the therapist. If she is not expressing any emotions, or if she appears to be skipping over part(s) of the event, the therapist gently challenges the client's avoidance. The therapist also challenges the client's self-blame, or any questions regarding whether the event was a rape or whether the client could reasonably have done something different (knowing what she knew then, not what she knows now). The client is then given the assignment to rewrite her account, adding more details and including her current thoughts and feelings. She is again instructed to read her account every day. If the client has been subjected to more than one rape, she should also begin writing her account of the other event(s).

As with the previous session, at session five the client reads her new account aloud. The therapist looks for details that were omitted from the first account. Usually during the first writing assignment, the client experiences the same feelings she had at the time of the rape, feelings that may have been left unaltered because the client has successfully avoided thinking about it except for brief intrusive recollections or flashbacks. However, by the time she has been reviewing the event for two weeks, there is a difference in the type as well as intensity of feelings. For example, at the time of the rape she may have felt confused, terrified, or numb. While writing or reading the second account she may feel angry or sad. These new feelings should also be validated and allowed to proceed until extinguished. The therapist may have to help the client discriminate anger from aggression and allow her to own her justifiable anger while not aggressing against others verbally or physically.

At this point in therapy the focus shifts to skill development in challenging beliefs and cognitive patterns. The client is given a list of questions that can be used to challenge specific beliefs. The client is asked to pick one of her stuck points and to challenge it with twelve questions. The therapist helps the client the first time during the session and reviews all of the questions and possible answers on a stuck point. For the next session, the client is asked to challenge one or two stuck points.

At session six the client and therapist review the client's homework, discussing any difficulties the client may have had in challenging her stuck points. Throughout the therapy, the therapist has been using a Socratic style of cognitive therapy, and now teaches the client to apply it to herself. She is taught to question her assumptions and interpretations through questions, answers, and more questions. After analyzing single beliefs, the therapist introduces another worksheet to help the client determine if she has faulty thinking patterns that may cut across situations. She is asked to notice and record examples of patterns such as overgeneralizing, mindreading, or emotional reasoning (e.g., "I feel fear so I must be in danger").

After discussion of the faulty thinking patterns the client observed since the last session, the therapist introduces a worksheet that will be used throughout the rest of the therapy. The Challenging Beliefs Worksheet has six columns that build upon the earlier A-B-C sheets. In addition to identifying the precipitating event or belief, thoughts, and emotions, the client is asked to rate the extent of her emotions with a SUD rating and to rate the strength of her beliefs. She is then asked to answer the twelve Challenging questions, determine if any of the faulty belief patterns are present, and then generate an alternative interpretation. Finally, she is asked to rerate her emotions and to rate the strength of her new statement. After successfully challenging a distorted belief, the client is asked to reread the worksheet until she becomes comfortable with the new statements and the old belief is dismantled completely.

Following the introduction and illustration of this new worksheet, the therapist begins exploring the first of five themes: safety. The therapist and client discuss the client's prior beliefs regarding safety, including two loci: safety/dangerousness of others, and the client's beliefs regarding her abilities to protect herself. They discuss whether prior positive beliefs were shattered or whether negative beliefs were seemingly confirmed. The client is asked to complete at least one worksheet on the topic of safety to challenge her post-crime beliefs and to complete worksheets on other stuck points that remain regarding self-blame or other distorted rape beliefs. She is also given a module on safety to read and consider that discusses self and other safety, possible stuck points and reactions, and possible resolutions for these stuck points.

At the eighth session, the therapist and client review the worksheets the client completed and correct any problems she may have had. At this point the therapist may need to help the client challenge her beliefs or look for other stuck points that may underlie the one she is working on. As the therapy proceeds the therapist will intervene less and the client will take over the job of challenging and correcting her own beliefs. Next, the topic of trust is introduced. This topic is particularly salient for those clients who were raped by an acquaintance. The client may question whether others are to be trusted and whether she can trust her own judgment about people. If other people who should have been supportive react badly to the crime and the victim, she is even more likely to feel betrayed and generalize mistrust. The client is again assigned worksheets to complete on trust, safety, and other topics as needed and is given a module to read on trust.

At the ninth session, after going over the trust worksheets, the client and therapist discuss power and control. They discuss the client's feelings of helplessness or need to control situations and relationships. At the tenth session, the topic that is introduced is esteem: self-esteem and regard for others. At the eleventh session, the therapist and client explore stuck points regarding self-intimacy or intimacy in relationships. Self-intimacy refers to the ability to regulate affect without relying on external substances such as alcohol or food. Such abilities to self-soothe may have been disrupted by the rape or may have been a problem prior to the crime. Intimacy topics include friendships and family relationships as well as more intimate relationships. Along with the assignment of worksheets and the module, the client is also asked to rewrite her impact statement to see how she currently views her experience. At the final session the client and therapist go over the worksheets, compare the new impact statement with the first one, review the entire therapy process, and establish goals for the future.

It should be noted that this therapy has been developed within the context of ongoing research, so the number of therapy sessions has remained fixed. Clinicians implementing CPT are encouraged to tailor it to suit the particular needs of their clients. For example, a client may not have safety issues, but might have stuck points regarding trust and control. The therapist may opt to skip the safety module and spend extra sessions on the themes that are particularly relevant to the client. A client with multiple victimizations such as incest may need more time for exposure and more time for particular modules (e.g., trust). For our purposes we introduce all five topics to ensure we have covered the most prevalent issues.

The results of CPT are quite strong thus far, and the therapy appears to be effective for both group and individual formats (Resick 1993, Resick and Schnicke 1992, 1993). Although subjected to research, this approach to therapy still needs to undergo systematic clinical trials with random assignment to groups. It will also be important to determine if CPT can be modified to be used to treat PTSD from other precipitating events such as combat or disaster. The treatment manual has been published as a book which includes all of the handouts as well as case materials (Resick and Schnicke 1993).

REFERENCES

Blanchard, E. B., Kolb, L. C., Gerardi, R., et al. (1986). Cardiac response to relevant stimuli as an adjunctive tool for diagnosing post-traumatic stress disorder in combat veterans. *Behavior Therapy* 17:592–606.

Blanchard, E. B., Kolb, L. C., Pallmayer, T. P., and Gerardi, R. T. (1982). The development of a psychophysiological assessment procedure for PTSD in Vietnam veterans. *Psychiatric Quarterly* 54:220–228.

Burnam, M. A., Stein, J. A., Golding, J. M., et al. (1988). Sexual assault and mental disorders in a community population. *Journal of Consulting and Clinical Psychology* 56:843–850.

Charney, D. S., Delgado, P. L., Price, L. H., and Heninger, G. R. (1991). The receptor sensitivity hypothesis of antidepressant function. A review of antidepressant effects on serotonin function. In *The Role of Serotonin in Psychiatric Disorders*, ed. S. Brown and H. van Praag, pp. 27–57. New York: Brunner/Mazel.

Charney, D. S., Woods, S. W., Krystal, J. H., and Heninger, G. R. (1990). Neurobiological mechanisms of human anxiety. In *Bases of Psychiatric Treatment*, ed. R. Pohl and D. Gershon, pp. 242–283. New York: Karger.

Chemtob, C., Roitblat, H., Hamada, R., et al. (1988). A cognitive action theory of posttraumatic stress disorder. *Journal of Anxiety Disorders* 2:253–275.

Creamer, M., Burgess, P., and Pattison, P. (1992). Reaction to trauma: A cognitive processing model. *Journal of Abnormal Psychology* 101:453–459.

Denny, N., Robinowitz, R., and Penk, W. (1987). Conducting applied research on Vietnam combat-related post-traumatic stress disorder. *Journal of Clinical Psychology* 43:56–66.

Diagnostic and Statistical Manual of Mental Disorders (1980). 3rd ed., rev. Washington, DC: American Psychiatric Association.

——— (1987). 3rd ed., rev. Washington, DC: American Psychiatric Association.

——— (1994). 4th ed. Washington, DC: American Psychiatric Association.

Feldman-Summers, S., Gordon, P. E., and Meagher, J. R. (1979). The impact of rape on sexual satisfaction. *Journal of Abnormal Psychology* 88:101–105.

Foa, E. B., and Kozak, M. J. (1986). Emotional processing of fear: exposure to corrective information. *Psychological Bulletin* 99:20–35.

Foa, E. B., Steketee, G. S., and Rothbaum, B. O. (1989). Behavioral/cognitive conceptualizations of post-traumatic stress disorder. *Behavior Therapy* 20:155–176.

Forman, B. D. (1982). Reported male rape. *Victimology* 7:235–236.

Foy, D. W., Osato, S. S., Houskamp, B. M., and Neumann, D. A. (1992). Etiology of posttraumatic stress disorder. In *Posttraumatic Stress Disorder*, ed. P. A. Saigh, pp. 28–49. New York: Macmillan.

Freud, S. (1937). Moses and monotheism. *Standard Edition* 23.

Goyer, P., and Eddleman, H. (1984). Same-sex rape of nonincarcerated men. *American Journal of Psychiatry* 141:576–579.

Horowitz, M. (1976). *Stress Response Syndromes.* New York: Jason Aronson.

——— (1986). *Stress Response Syndromes,* 2nd ed. New York: Jason Aronson.

Jones, J. C., and Barlow, D. H. (1990). The etiology of posttraumatic stress disorder. *Clinical Psychology Review* 10:299–328.

———— (1992). A new model of posttraumatic stress disorder: Implications for the future. In *Posttraumatic Stress Disorder*, ed. P. A. Saigh, pp. 147–165. New York: Macmillan.

Kaszniak, A. W., Nussbaum, P. D., Berren, M. R., and Santiago, J. (1988). Amnesia as a consequence of male rape: a case report. *Journal of Abnormal Psychology* 97:100–104.

Kaufman, A., Divasto, P., Jackson, R., et al. (1980). Male rape victims: noninstitutionalized assault. *American Journal of Psychiatry* 137:221–223.

Keane, T. M., Caddell, J. M., and Taylor, K. L. (1988). The Mississippi Scale for combat-related PTSD: studies in reliability and validity. *Journal of Consulting and Clinical Psychology* 56:85–90.

Keane, T. M., Fairbank, J. A., Caddell, J. M., et al. (1985). A behavioral approach to treating posttraumatic stress disorder in Vietnam veterans. In *Trauma and its Wake*, vol. 1, ed. C. R. Figley, pp. 257–294. New York: Brunner/Mazel.

Keane, T. M., Malloy, P. F., and Fairbank, J. A. (1984). The empirical development of an MMPI-subscale for the assessment of combat-related post-traumatic stress disorders. *Journal of Consulting and Clinical Psychology* 52:888–891.

Keane, T. M., Scott, W. O., Chavoya, G. A., et al. (1985). Social support in Vietnam veterans: a comparative analysis. *Journal of Consulting and Clinical Psychology* 53:95–102.

Keane, T. M., Wolfe, J., and Taylor, K. L. (1987). Posttraumatic stress disorder: evidence for diagnostic validity and methods of psychological assessment. *Journal of Clinical Psychology* 43:32–43.

Keane, T. M., Zimering, R. T., and Caddell, J. M. (1985). A behavioral formulation of posttraumatic stress disorder in Vietnam veterans. *Behavior Therapist* 8:9–12.

Kilpatrick, D. G. (1983). Rape victims: detection, assessment and treatment. *Clinical Psychologist* 36:92–95.

Kilpatrick, D. G., Edmunds, C. N., and Seymour, A. K. (1992). *Rape in America: A Report to the Nation*. Arlington, VA: National Victim Center.

Kilpatrick, D. G., Veronen, L. J., and Resick, P. A. (1979). The aftermath of rape: recent empirical findings. *American Journal of Orthopsychiatry* 49(4):658–669.

Kilpatrick, D. G., Veronen, L. J., Saunders, et al. (1987). *The Psychological Impact of Crime: A Study of Randomly Surveyed Crime Victims* (Final report, Grant No. 84-IF-CX-0039). Washington, DC: National Institute of Justice.

Kolb, L. C. (1987). A neuropsychological hypothesis explaining post-traumatic stress disorder. *American Journal of Psychiatry* 144:989–995.

Koss, M. P., and Gidycz, C. A. (1985). Sexual Experiences Survey: reliability and validity. *Journal of Consulting and Clinical Psychology* 53:422–423.

Lang, P. J. (1968). Fear reduction and fear behavior: problems in treating a construct. *Research in Psychotherapy* 3:9–102.

——— (1977). Imagery in therapy: an information processing analysis of fear. *Behavior Therapy* 8:862–886.

——— (1979). A bio-informational theory of emotional imagery. *Psychophysiology* 16:495–512.

——— (1985). The cognitive psychophysiology of emotion: Fear and anxiety. In *Anxiety and the Anxiety Disorders*, ed. A. H. Tuma and J. D. Maser, pp. 131–170. Hillsdale, NJ: Erlbaum.

Litz, B. T. (1992). Emotional numbing in combat-related post-traumatic stress disorder: a critical review and reformulation. *Clinical Psychology Review*, 12:417–432.

McGaugh, J. L. (1990). Significance and remembrance: the role of neuromodulatory systems. *Psychological Science* 1:15–25.

Resick, P. A. (1987). *Reactions of Female and Male Victims of Rape and Robbery.* (Final report, NIJ Grant No. MH37296). Washington, DC: National Institute of Justice.

——— (1992). Cognitive treatment of crime-related post-traumatic stress disorder. In *Aggression and Violence throughout the Life Span*, ed. R. Peters, R. McMahon, and V. Quinsey, pp. 171–191. Newbury Park, CA: Sage.

Resick, P. A. (1993). *Group versus individual format of cognitive processing therapy for post-traumatic stress disorder in sexual assault victims.* Paper presented at the Lake George Research Conference on Post-Traumatic Stress Disorder, Bolton Landing, NY, January.

Resick, P. A., Jordan, C. G., Girelli, S. A., et al. (1988). A comparative outcome study of behavioral group therapy for sexual assault victims. *Behavior Therapy* 19:385–401.

Resick, P. A., and Markaway, B. E. G. (1991). Clinical treatment of adult female victims of sexual assault. In *Clinical Approaches to Sex Offenders and their Victims,* ed. C. R. Hollin and K. Howells, pp. 261–284. New York: Wiley.

Resick, P. A., and Schnicke, M. K. (1990). Treating symptoms in adult victims of sexual assault. *Journal of Interpersonal Violence* 5:488–506.

——— (1992). Cognitive processing therapy for sexual assault victims. *Journal of Consulting and Clinical Psychology* 60:748–756.

——— (1993). *Cognitive Processing Therapy for Rape Victim: A Treatment Manual.* Newbury Park, CA: Sage.

Resnick, H. S., Kilpatrick, D. G., and Lipovsky, J. A. (1991). Assessment of rape-related posttraumatic stress disorder: stressor and symptom dimensions. *Psychological Assessment* 3:561–572.

Rothbaum, B. O., Foa, E. B., Riggs, D. S., et al. (1992). A prospective examination of post-traumatic stress disorder in rape victims. *Journal of Traumatic Stress* 5:455–475.

Saunders, B. E., Kilpatrick, D. G., Resnick, H. S., and Tidwell, R. P. (1989). Brief screening for lifetime history of criminal victimization at mental health intake. *Journal of Interpersonal Violence* 4:267–277.

Sutker, P. B., Uddo-Crane, M., and Allain, A. N. (1991). Clinical and research assessment of posttraumatic stress disorder: a conceptual overview. *Psychological Assessment* 3:520–530.

Van der Kolk, B., Boyd, H., Krystal, J., and Greenberg, M. (1984). Post-traumatic stress disorder as a biologically based disorder: implications of the animal model of inescapable shock. In *Post-traumatic Stress*

Disorder: Psychological and Biological Sequelae, pp. 124–134. Washington, DC: American Psychiatric Press.

Veronen, L. J., and Kilpatrick, D. G. (1983). Stress management for rape victims. In *Stress Reduction and Prevention*, ed. D. Meichenbaum and M. E. Jaremko pp. 341–374. New York: Plenum Press.

Wolfe, J., and Keane, T. M. (1990). The diagnostic validity of post-traumatic stress disorder. In *Post-traumatic Stress Disorder: Etiology, Phenomenology, and Treatment*, ed. M. Wolf and A. Mosnaim. Washington, DC: American Psychiatric Press.

PART II

Specific Treatment
Techniques

CHAPTER NINE

Cognitive-Behavioral Treatment of Panic Attacks

Dr. Barlow and his colleagues at the State University of New York at Albany have made their notable contributions through years of experimental research on a variety of issues that have direct applicability to the clinical treatment of anxiety disorders. Since panic disorder and the treatment of panic attacks have become central to this field, the effective cognitive-behavioral techniques briefly elucidated in this chapter are essential skills for the practioner to acquire.

Cognitive behavioral therapy (CBT) consists of several treatment modules: psychoeducation, progressive muscle relaxation, cognitive therapy, exposure to external anxiety cues, and exposure to internal anxiety cues. This chapter places emphasis on Dr. Barlow's leading concept that the desensitizing of panic attacks must occur not only in the phobic situations, but also to the fear of bodily sensations (such as rapid heart beat or dizziness) that are associated with mounting anxiety and panic.

For a more detailed view of this treatment program, please write to Dr. David H. Barlow, Boston Center for Anxiety and Related Disorders, Boston University, 1 Kenmore Square, Boston, MA 02215.

Cognitive-Behavioral Treatment
of Panic Attacks

Janet S. Klosko
David H. Barlow

At the Phobia and Anxiety Disorders Clinic, our treatment of panic attacks grew from experience with treatment of the phobic aspects of agoraphobia. In our clinic and elsewhere, studies showed consistently that treatment that focused upon exposure to feared situations significantly decreased avoidance behavior in most agoraphobic patients (Barlow 1985). Moreover, when we measured panic attacks directly, we found that exposure treatment, still focused upon avoidance of feared situations, also decreased panic attacks. For example, a clinical replication series of sixteen agoraphobic patients at our clinic showed that almost half the patients who reported panic attacks pre-treatment were panic-free post-treatment (Klosko and Barlow 1986).

Concurrent with our research on treatment of agoraphobia we began a treatment project on treatment of panic disorder. At that time, like *DSM-III*, we viewed panic disorder in the same class as generalized anxiety disorder—both being disorders of anxiety states—rather than in the same class as agoraphobia. We began treatment of panic attacks with the application of self-control procedures, such as biofeedback and relaxation, and cognitive therapy. In a controlled-outcome study, we demonstrated some success (Barlow et al. 1984).

As our work continued, gradually our treatments of phobia and panic grew closer together. This occurred partly because it was so rare to find patients with panic attacks who did not exhibit phobic avoidance. Most often we found that even in patients diagnosed with panic disorder rather than agoraphobia, most exhibited avoidance responding, though their avoidance might be subtle. For example, it was not unusual to find patients with panic disorder avoiding exercise, or heat, or the drinking of alcohol—or any other activity that might elicit panic-like sensations. They feared and avoided symptoms of panic attacks. We came to see similarities in agoraphobic avoidance of external anxiety cues a.... avoidance of internal anxiety cues. Our view emerged that internal events can serve as phobic stimuli and that individuals, through a process of interoceptive conditioning, starting usually from the first panic attack, can develop phobic avoidance of internal events. Consequently for us the distinction blurred between agoraphobia and panic disorder. We began to view patients with these diagnoses on a continuum, with fear of panic as the key feature.

We thus began to experiment with exposure treatments of anxiety states. Particularly, we designed treatments in which, in addition to learning self-control and cognitive strategies, patients underwent exposure to panic symptoms and cues. Our evidence suggests this is an effective treatment of panic attacks (Klosko and Barlow, 1986).

ASSESSMENT

Initial Assessment

All patients who present to the Anxiety Disorders Clinic undergo initial assessment by administration of the Anxiety Disorders Interview Schedule (ADIS) (DiNardo et al. 1985). The ADIS is a structured interview designed to provide *DSM-III* and *DSM-III-R* diagnoses of anxiety and affective disorders and to rule out psychosis, substance abuse, and somatoform disorders. It provides detailed symptom ratings and includes the Hamilton Anxiety Scale (Hamilton 1959) and the Hamilton Depression Scale (Hamilton 1960). In addition, the ADIS assesses psychiatric and psychological history, situational and cognitive factors that influence anxiety, and comorbidity of anxiety disorders with one another and with other mental disorders. Reliability tests of the ADIS for 125 subjects, using Kappa coefficients, indicate good reliability for all anxiety disorders (Barlow 1985). Patients who participate in panic disorder treatment projects at the clinic have been given a primary diagnosis of panic disorder, with a clinician's severity rating of at least 4 on a 0-to-8 scale.

Patients generally respond positively to the ADIS. It presents them with aspects of their experience structured in a way they find educational. Often patients feel understood. After administration of the ADIS, the interviewer meets with the patient, explains the diagnosis, and describes treatment. Most patients who are offered treatment at the clinic agree to participate.

Pre- and Post-treatment Assessment Measures

In addition to the ADIS, psychophysiological and self-report assessment measures are administered to all patients pre- and post-treatment.

PSYCHOPHYSIOLOGICAL MEASURES

Psychophysiological assessment lasts about an hour. A polygraph measures physiological responses of patients (forehead muscle tension, heart rate, skin resistance, and finger temperature) to relaxation and stressor tasks. This procedure has been described in detail by Andrasik and co-authors (1982).

SELF-REPORT MEASURES

Self-report measures include both standardized questionnaires and self-monitoring. Questionnaires measure such factors as panic and generalized anxiety symptoms, fear and avoidance, somatic symptoms associated with anxiety, interference with functioning, depression, personality, and life events.

Patients engage in daily self-monitoring for two weeks pre- and post-treatment, and throughout treatment. Self-monitoring is a crucial part of treatment. Patients use a diary called the Weekly Record that provides information about levels of anxiety and related variables. This record was constructed by staff at the clinic over the course of several years. We have also developed a set of procedures to maximize compliance with recording, including instruction, review, and feedback. Patients record in the diary current levels of anxiety, depression, and pleasant feelings on 0-to-8 scales, four times each day. Such data serve as measures of background levels of these variables. In addition, patients record the following information about each discrete episode of anxiety they experience that they rate 4 or higher on the 0-to-8 scale: date and time of onset and offset of the anxiety episode; maximum level of anxiety during the episode; whether or not the patient considers this episode of anxiety a panic attack (according to *DSM-III* criteria); whether the patient considers the context of the episode stressful or nonstressful; and the symptoms the patient experiences. Data serve as measures of anxiety episodes and panic attacks, both spontaneous and situational. In addition, there is space in the diary for patients to describe the situation in which the episode occurred, relevant behavior and cognitions, and any comments they may have.

Recently, the clinic has begun to experiment with psychological induction of panic symptoms as an assessment measure.

Treatment

Generally patients receive fifteen sessions of cognitive-behavioral treatment in weekly meetings. Treatment is administered individually, although recently we have treated small groups of panic disorder patients. Treatment begins with presentation of the rationale. Patients are told they will learn skills to control panic disorder symptoms in three response systems: physiological, cognitive, and behavioral. They are given education about the disorder. Individual symptoms are explained, with emphasis on the notion that the symptoms are not dangerous. Active treatment phases are composed of one or more of the following components: progressive muscle-relaxation training; cognitive therapy; exposure to external anxiety cues; and exposure to internal anxiety cues and panic symptoms.

PROGRESSIVE MUSCLE RELAXATION TRAINING

This treatment component is based upon the model for training described by Bernstein and Borkovec (1973). It begins with a tension-relaxation phase, in which patients are taught to tense and relax muscle groups and to discriminate muscle tension levels. Exercises are gradually reduced from sixteen to four muscle groups. Then patients are taught relaxation by recall, in which they recall sensations of muscle release in muscle groups. Finally, patients are taught cue-controlled relaxation, in which they learn to associate the subvocalized word "relax" with muscle relaxation. Patients are instructed to practice relaxation at home twice a day and to maintain records of such practice. They are encouraged to use cognitive and relaxation skills learned in treatment in their daily lives and to carry out homework assignments for practice of use of the skill.

COGNITIVE THERAPY

This treatment component was based upon the model for therapy described by Beck and Emery (1979). It includes presentation of didactic material, self-monitoring of automatic thoughts and self-statements, hypothesis testing, and behavioral experiments in the form of graduated homework assignments, from low to high anxiety.

EXPOSURE TO EXTERNAL ARXIETY CUES

This treatment component consists of graduated in vivo exposure to phobic or otherwise stressful situations. Patients and therapists together construct hierarchies of feared situations, from low- to high-anxiety items. Patients expose themselves systematically to the situations through structured homework assignments.

EXPOSURE TO INTERNAL ANXIETY CUES AND PANIC SYMPTOMS

This treatment component was developed by clinic staff through experience in treatment of panic disorders. It consists of exposure to internal cognitive and physiological cues of anxiety and panic using procedures such as imagery training of both stimulus and response propositions of images (Lang et al. 1983); induction of symptoms through imagery of anxiety-provoking situations and sensations; voluntary hyperventilation (Clark et al. 1985); physical exertion (such as running in place, spinning one's head); or other idiosyncratic methods for eliciting frightening physical symptoms, accompanied by deliberate catastrophic interpretations. Exposures proceed up a hierarchy of feared cognitions and somatic sensations, both in sessions with the therapist and in homework assignments the client carries out between sessions.

Patients are followed up at 3 months, 6 months, 1 year, and 2 years. Our research indicates that patients maintain positive treatment changes (Barlow et al. 1984). Many continue to improve after treatment ends. Treatment is designed to work against establishment of dependency relationships between patient and therapist. The emphasis on self-control strategies, graduated mastery experiences, generalization practices, and homework assignments between sessions increases the likelihood of maintenance of treatment gains.

CASE EXAMPLE

When she presented for treatment, M. was a 26-year-old married woman with a 4-month-old infant. She could barely discuss her first panic attack, which had occurred in the hospital after the birth of her baby, under the influence of Demerol. She thought she had been given too much Demerol and was dying. Two weeks later, at home, following an argument with her husband, she had an attack out of the blue. Her husband rushed her to the emergency room. Doctors there told her there was nothing wrong and sent her home. A week later she was back in the emergency room with another attack, and doctors there gave her Xanax. Despite her continuation on Xanax, the attacks persisted. Before she started treatment at the anxiety clinic, she withdrew from Xanax, a requirement of the particular research project in which she participated.

Interview and self-monitoring revealed that M.'s most severe panic symptoms were tachycardia, difficulty breathing, and shaking. She avoided hospitals; all drugs, including alcohol, and situations in which others took drugs (e.g., bars); arguments; and exercise. She avoided thinking and talking about anxiety and panic. For reasons she did not understand, late every afternoon she experienced panic symptoms. The most disturbing seemed to be feelings of unreality, which she connected with going crazy. She reported intense fear of panic, and preoccupation with death and dying. The last she related to a "bad trip" she had experienced on LSD as a teenager, during which she had the sense that she had died. (Interestingly, questioning revealed M. actually had had her first panic attack during this "bad trip." She attributed the experience to the drug, however, and did not consider it a panic attack.)

The early course of M.'s treatment illustrated a pattern that seems common to many cases of panic disorder. In the first few weeks she stopped panicking completely. At that time she felt elated; she felt she would never panic again. She was told that in all likelihood she would panic again and that, moreover, treatment would not be effective without her continued experiences of anxiety. By the fifth week of treatment she reported panic attacks again. In the early weeks she was taught relaxation and rebreathing skills to control the physiological components of anxiety. Through use of her self-monitoring records, she identified carefully the thoughts she associated with anxiety. In her case, such thoughts tended to be interpretations of physical sensations as dangerous, either because they signaled a panic attack or because she thought they meant something was physically wrong. She was told as she learned to control anxiety symptoms, she would fear her sensations less.

For the exposure component of treatment, we developed a hierarchy of fear situations, activities, and sensations, from low to high anxiety. Her hierarchy was as shown in Table 9–1.

M. was encouraged to adopt a stance of approach to, rather than avoidance of, anxiety symptoms, in order to practice controlling them. We started with low-anxiety hierarchy items. Between sessions, in homework assignments, she was instructed to enter feared situations, or engage in feared activities, until she reached a criterion of anxiety she felt able to control. Gradually we increased the criterion. For example, one of her

Table 9–1. Patient M's Anxiety Hierarchy

Anxiety	Rating	Feared Situation / Activity / Sensation
2	(low)	Swimming until her heart rate increased
2		Arguing with her husband when she disagreed with him
3		Numbness in her hands and legs
4		A sense of pressure in her head
4		Feeling unsure of herself at a staff meeting
4		Getting a floating feeling out of the blue
5		Getting shaky out of the blue
7		In a room with friends who were smoking marijuana, feeling the sensations of the drug
7		Visiting the hospital maternity ward where she had her baby
8	(high)	Taking Demerol at the hospital

first assignments was to swim until her anxiety reached a 3, to stop and control the anxiety until it was a 1, then to repeat the exercise several times. Toward the end of treatment she visited the hospital unit in which she had suffered her first attack, and she relived in imagination her Demerol experience.

In sessions, M. used such techniques as visualization, voluntary hyperventilation, and physical exercise to induce symptoms and practice controlling them. For example, early in treatment she induced lightheadedness, a low-anxiety item, by holding her breath and breathing shallowly. At other times she induced chest pain by tensing her chest muscles, and she induced trembling by tensing her arms and legs. Through visualization she reexperienced episodes of anxiety and panic she had experienced in the past week, and she rehearsed episodes she anticipated in the week to come. Toward the end of treatment, M. became willing in sessions and at home to visualize her first panic attack. At the end of treatment she still had panic attacks, but they were less frequent, less intense, and less severe; she feared and avoided panic symptoms significantly less; and she was no longer judged to have a clinical disorder. At 3-month follow-up, she had continued to improve.

FUTURE DIRECTIONS

We plan to pursue the development of treatment of panic attacks in a number of directions. Clinical experience continues to suggest ways to improve treatment, which we may study experimentally at a later time. Presently, with a group-comparison design, we are conducting a component-analysis study of our panic treatment. We are also conducting a placebo-controlled study that compares psychological treatment of panic to medication treatment with alprazolam. A next step would be to look at the combination of psychological and medication treatments. We do not expect the effect of combining psychological and medical treatments of panic to be simply additive. Clinical experience indicates medication at times interferes with psychological treatment. Patients tend to attribute decreases in symptoms to medication, and therefore they tend not to develop an adequate sense of mastery and self-control. Further, effective exposure treatment requires the patient to experience anxiety symptoms, and masking of symptoms by medication may make this difficult. We also are conducting single-case and group studies that evaluate the effectiveness of adding the component of exposure to interoceptive cues to treatments of agoraphobia.

REFERENCES

Andrasik, F., Blanchard, E. B., Arena, J., et al. (1982). Psychophysiology of recurrent headache: methodological issues and new empirical findings. *Behavior Therapy* 3:407–429.

Barlow, D. H. (1985). The dimensions of anxiety disorders. In *Anxiety and the Anxiety Disorders*, ed. A. H. Tuma and J. D. Maser, Hillsdale, NJ: Lawrence Erlbaum.

Barlow, D. H., Cohen, A. S., and Waddell, M. T. (1984). Panic and generalized anxiety disorders: nature and treatment. *Behavior Therapy* 15:431–449.

Barlow, D. H., O'Brien, G. T., and Last, C. G. (1984). Couples treatment of agoraphobia. *Behavior Therapy* 15:41–58.

Beck, A. T., and Emery, G. (1979). *Cognitive Therapy for Anxiety and Phobic Disorders*. Philadelphia: Center for Cognitive Therapy.

Bernstein, D. A., and Borkovec, T. D. (1973). *Progressive Relaxation Training*. Champaign, IL: Research Press.

Clark, D. M., Salkovskis, P. M., and Chalkley, A. J. (1985). Respiratory control as a treatment for panic attacks. *Journal of Behaviour Therapy ·d Experimental Psychiatry* 16:22–30.

DiNardo, P. A., Barlow, D. H., Cerny, J., et al. (1985). *The Anxiety Disorders Interview Schedule—Revised*. Albany, NY: Center for Stress and Anxiety Disorders.

DiNardo, P. A., O'Brien, G. T., Barlow, D. H., et al. (1983). Reliability of *DSM-III* anxiety disorder categories using a new structured interview. *Archives of General Psychiatry* 40:1070–1078.

Hamilton, M. (1959). The assessment of anxiety states by rating. *British Journal of Medical Psychology* 32:50–55.

——— (1960). A rating scale for depression. *Journal of Neurology, Neurosurgery, and Psychiatry* 23:56–62.

Klosko, S. S., and Barlow, D. H. (1986). Cognitive-behavioral treatment of panic attacks. Poster presented at Association for the Advancement of Behavior Therapy, Chicago, IL.

Lang, P. J., Levin, D. N., Miller, G. A., and Kozak, M. J. (1983). Fear behavior, fear imagery, and the psychophysiology of emotion: the problem of affective response integration. *Journal of Abnormal Psychology* 92:276–306.

CHAPTER TEN

Cognitive Therapy
for Evaluation Anxieties

Dr. Aaron Beck is well known for the extraordinary impact his work on cognitive therapy has had on the current reconceptualization of psychotherapy. His central thesis is that cognition, or how we understand and process information, is a central function in our adaptation to our environment. A disturbance in cognition will lead to a disturbance in feeling and behavior. Correcting the disturbance in cognition will correct the disturbance in feeling and behavior. This emphasis on information processing is an obvious shift from the historical interest in affect, impulse, and conflict on the one hand and behavior on the other.

In this chapter Dr. Beck discusses a variety of social phobias, including performance anxiety, test anxiety, and anxiety in social situations. The treatment implications flow naturally from his conceptualization of these disorders. The term *evaluation anxieties* refers to a primary fear of being observed and evaluated and a primary cognitive distortion in which a critical evaluation is a catastrophe in terms of total failure, loss of love, loss of self-esteem, and so on. The anxiety may lead to an inhibition of functioning in social situations, which then itself becomes the problem.

Cognitive Therapy
for Evaluation Anxieties

AARON T. BECK
GARY EMERY
RUTH L. GREENBERG

THE ESSENCE OF EVALUATION ANXIETIES

Before the Fall

A person entering a socially threatening situation is like someone walking a tightrope. He feels *vulnerable* to a serious mishap if his performance is not *adequate*. For *safety*'s sake, he must conform to a rigid set of *rules* regarding appropriate actions and movements. The greater his *confidence* in his skill, the less likely he is to make a potentially fatal *misstep*. If he has a *failure* of nerve his *performance* may be sabotaged by primitive reflex reactions—freezing, motor *inhibition*. Thus, this exercise is a test of his *ability* and *maturity*. Smooth performance reaffirms his *image* of himself and maintains his *status*. Failure would shatter this image. Finally, every action *is observed* by a crowd of *evaluators* and appraised as clumsy or skillful, and he is *judged* according to his confidence and competence. The italicized words here represent crucial aspects of the psychology of evaluative anxiety that will be described in this chapter.

The potential fall of the performer is paralleled by the "fall from grace" anticipated by an anxious person in the myriad of evaluative situations of everyday life. As in the case of the tightrope walker, *errors, missteps, inappropriate actions represent only a fraction of his overt behavior, but the damage is to the entire person*—or so he fears.

COMMON FEATURES
OF EVALUATIVE THREATS

There are certain commonalities among the various situations in which an individual may experience "evaluation anxiety." The situations may be grouped as follows: (1) social situations—initiating or maintaining a person-to-person relationship; participating in a social gathering (for example, a party); (2) school or vocational situations—performance evaluation by teacher, supervisor, or peer group; taking a test or examination; confrontation with a superior over a conflict of interest; athletic competition, (3) transactions in the "outside world" while shopping or traveling, with salespersons, waiters or waitresses, taxi drivers, strangers.

A complex web of factors in these situations may aggravate or mitigate fears. These factors involve the question of evaluation and vulnerability and include the following: (1) the relative status of the individual and the evaluator in the area of power or social desirability; (2) the individual's skill in presenting an attractive or effective "front"; (3) his confidence in his ability to perform adequately in a given threat situation; (4) his appraisal of the degree of threat, the severity of potential damage, and the probability of its occurring; (5) the threshold of certain automatic "defenses" (verbal inhibition, blockage of recall, suppression of spontaneity) that can undermine individual performance; (6) the rigidity and attainability of the "rules" relevant to acceptable performance, behavior, and appearance; (7) the anticipated punitiveness of the evaluator for nonadherence to rules or substandard performance, and so on.

Vulnerability

The individual who is anxious when entering into an evaluative situation has a network of implicit questions.

1. "To what degree is this a *test* of my competence or acceptability? How much do I have to prove myself to me or others?"

2. "What is my status relative to that of my evaluators?" If the individual feels parity with or superior to the evaluator, then the rules are less narrow and more flexible and the prospective "punishment" for failure is less important.

3. "How important is it to establish a position of strength about relative power status (as in dealing with service personnel) or a position of acceptability in dealing with social evaluators (as in blind dates or speaking before an audience)?"

4. "What is the attitude of the evaluator? Is he accepting and empathetic or rejecting and aloof? Are his judgments likely to be objective or harsh and punitive?"

5. "To what degree can I count on my skills (such as verbal fluency) to carry me through the difficult evaluation?"

6. "What is the likelihood of my being undermined by distracting anxiety and inhibitions?"

Status and Ranking Order

A good part of the pressure to perform well is related to relative position on a vertical scale of power or social desirability. In a situation of confrontation with authority (teacher, supervisor, service personnel), the individual's perception of relative power determines his self-confidence and performance. If a person presents an appearance of self-confidence and competence, he reduces his "inferiority" on the power scale. If he perceives that he is lower, he is more likely to be less confident and less competent and thus will be vulnerable to being reduced in power even more. The dominance–submission dimension is generally also involved. The more dominant the individual perceives an evaluator to be, the more his own submissive tendencies are likely to be mobilized. Service personnel (physicians, cab drivers, receptionists, cashiers) are invested with authority and dominance by virtue of their position, which they can use to intimidate the individual.

In the case of a social confrontation in which a person wants to make a good impression, he is under pressure to maximize his social assets—attractiveness, dress, fluency, maturity, poise, grace. A high "score" on these assets may (depending on the values of the evaluator) make the person more desirable and thus ensure success in other encounters. A low "score" sets him up to be rejected.

A person may want to shun this type of confrontation because failure is painful. Moreover, avoidance leaves open the question of whether he is inferior, whereas a failure confirms his inferiority. Thus, social fearfulness is expressed in part by the experience of painful anxiety and the desire to reduce or avert the anxiety by avoiding or withdrawing from the aversive situation.

Self-Confidence

Confidence in one's ability to perform adequately in the confrontation is related to the perceived magnitude of one's expectations, their difficulty, and the anticipated punishment for inadequate performance.

A disparity in the individual's sense of his power or desirability in relation to that of the evaluator increases the magnitude of the task, because the criteria for acceptable performance are higher, and therefore the demands on him are greater. When he perceives himself in a "one-down" position, a person is less certain that he can fulfill these demands; thus his global confidence in his competence is reduced. Moreover, if he anticipates a drastic punishment for inadequate performance (loss of job, suspension from school, termination of a relationship), his self-confidence may be further undermined. Other factors being constant, there is a reciprocal relationship between self-confidence and sense of vulnerability. As one goes up, the other goes down.

Rules and Formulas

In an obviously evaluative situation (for example, test taking, public speaking, making a date), there is a pressure to conform to arbitrary, rigid rules in order to avoid "punishment." The individual fears that he may not be sufficiently facile, fluent, and unflappable and thus experiences anxiety and other symptoms that militate against his attaining his goal. Deviations from these rules during performance raise negative evaluations and self-doubts, such as "I look timid, frightened," "What I say sounds stupid," "I'm so awkward," or "Will I foul it up?"

In public speaking, he believes he must adhere to stringent rules regarding the volume and tone of his voice, his articulateness and speed of speaking, his fluency and control of speech. The individual, thus, may fear that any departure from the rules may make him susceptible to disapproval and devaluation. In a social situation, deviation from the established canons may bring rejection.

In other types of interpersonal transaction (asking for information, requesting a raise), a breach of the rules may evoke hostility and overt devaluation. In such encounters, the individual is faced with such rules as "You shouldn't impose on people." Thus, if he makes a legitimate request or asserts his rights in a reasonable way, he may fear that "This seems like an imposition."

Automatic Protective Reactions

AUTOMATIC INHIBITION

Reflex reactions in a dangerous situation have been discussed previously. Many people are susceptible to automatic inhibitory reactions that impede flow of speech, thinking, and recall. The function of these reactions under more primitive circumstances may have been to protect the individual from taking action that would provoke attack. Today this function is anachronistic and actually leads to dysfunction. Consequently, it is likely to evoke just the kind of attack that the individual would like to avoid. There does not appear to be any volitional component in this freezing reaction. It is mobilized completely contrary to a person's intentions and wishes.

ANXIETY

Anxiety seems to be the product of a different system than is reflex inhibition. The function of anxiety seems to be to spur the person to take some action to reduce the danger. Then, he may be motivated to avoid going into a threatening situation or, if in the situation, to escape or minimize the danger by being inconspicuous (for example, not speaking up in class). It is obvious that, far from providing safety, the safety or protective patterns (inhibition blocking and anxiety–avoidance–escape) have a negative effect on performance. In fact, the anticipation of these reactions is in itself often sufficient to arouse anxiety and then to impair performance.

FAINTNESS

People in evaluative situations not infrequently feel faint and often fear that they will lose consciousness. This type of response is obviously highly inappropriate in an evaluative situation and may be a throwback to a primitive fear of being physically injured—as is the blood-injury phobia.

SOCIAL PHOBIAS AND SOCIAL ANXIETIES

Social phobias and social anxieties are concerned with one's exaggerated fear of being the focus of attention and devaluation by another person or persons. According to the third edition of the *Diagnostic and Statistical Manual of Mental Disorders (DSM-III)*,* the essential feature of social phobia is "a persistent irrational fear of, and compelling desire to avoid, a situation in which the individual is exposed to possible scrutiny by others" (1980, p. 228). This definition is probably too broad, in that it would encompass a huge proportion of the population as well as a significant number of patients now appropriately diagnosed as having a generalized anxiety disorder. In contrast to the definition of social phobia, the official definition of agoraphobia does specify that "normal activities are increasingly constricted as the fears or avoidance behavior dominate the individual's life" (p. 226). This restrictive criterion applied to the definition of social phobia would be more in keeping with the general concept of phobia. Moreover, *DSM-III* includes as examples of social phobias "fears of speaking or performing in public, using public lavatories, eating in public, and writing in the presence of others" (p. 227). Certainly the fear of speaking in public should not be included, since a very high proportion of the general population has this fear. If the more restrictive definition is used, a relatively small percentage of people with social anxiety would be considered social phobics.

PARADOXES OF SOCIAL ANXIETY

Unlike the phobias described in the previous chapters, a major feature of the social anxieties is that the actual fear (anticipation of being nervous and inhibited), prior to entering a situation, appears

---

Editor's note: The *DSM-IV* revisions of the criteria for social phobia are in keeping with the ideas expressed here by the author.

plausible and indeed seems to have a reasonable probability of being realized. Although a person with a phobia of heights, bridges, or elevators runs a minimal risk of falling or suffocating, an individual who is afraid that he will become tongue-tied when trying to carry on a conversation with a blind date, or that his mind will go blank during an examination or interview, can reasonably expect these events to occur. The most interesting feature is that actually having the fear seems to bring on the undesirable consequence. A vicious cycle is created, whereby the anticipation of an absolute, extreme, irreversible outcome tends to make a person more fearful, defensive, and inhibited when entering the situation. On the other hand, the person who does not experience the fear of inept performance in a particular situation is substantially less likely to respond ineptly.

An important aspect of social anxiety, in which the fears are grossly inaccurate, is the individual's expectation that his inept performance in a social situation will be a fatal blow to his social aspirations. The expectation that one's life will be ruined by a specific rejection or failure is rarely borne out by experience. The content and the probability of such dire consequences are grossly exaggerated. Even when the extreme outcome does not occur after a particular unsettling experience, the individual, nonetheless, expects the bad thing to happen next time.

The Fear of Being Evaluated

The central fear in the so-called social anxieties is that of negative evaluation by another person or persons—a fear that separates the social and the performance anxieties from agoraphobia. In the latter syndrome, a person may be afraid of wide-open spaces, fields, or beaches, where there are no people, as well as closed-in groups or crowds of people. In agoraphobia, the fear of social disapproval appears to be secondary to the fear of losing control, fainting, going crazy, and so on. In contrast, in the social anxieties the central fear is of being the center of attention, of having one's "weaknesses" exposed, and consequently of being judged adversely by one or more people.

There is a symbolic confrontation in the social anxieties, whether the individual is calling a stranger on the telephone, trying to initiate a conversation in a social setting, or performing before a group. When the socially anxious person is engaged in a one-to-one encounter with another person or group of people, he believes that he is being scrutinized, tested, and judged. Under observation are his performance, fluency of speech, self-assurance, and freedom from anxiety.

Unlike the agoraphobic, who is hypersensitive to internal signals suggestive of impending mental or physical collapse, the social phobic is hypersensitive to signals from other people regarding his acceptability. If he is receiving positive responses, he interprets them as a sign that he is making a good impression, and he feels less vulnerable and more self-confident. On the other hand, if he receives and integrates negative responses, he feels more vulnerable and less confident.

The physiological responses of the socially anxious individual may be similar to those of the agoraphobic person but are not as pronounced. As we shall discuss, he may feel the same type of sympathetic symptoms (rapid pulse rate, sweating) or parasympathetic symptoms (faintness, drop in blood pressure) as the agoraphobic; however, these evoke the fear that he will not perform adequately (which may be accurate), whereas the agoraphobic has the fear of an internal disaster (practically never accurate). It should be noted that some patients with public-speaking anxiety do, indeed, fear panic attacks, and some actually have a panic attack, but they are in the minority.

The Primal Defenses

The single factor that seems to be the most crippling to the socially anxious person is not the subjective experience of anxiety per se, although this indeed proves a handicap, but the various inhibitions, specifically those that interfere with his performance. Thus, the various types of inhibition—such as interference with verbal fluency, thinking, recall, and remote memory—are the most disabling factors in this disorder and, once they are involved in the vicious cycle, perpetuate the fear of going into the phobic situation.

These paradoxical responses to a threat, rather than priming the individual for more effective performance, actually impair his performance. The explanation seems to be, as we have said, that a primitive defensive system is mobilized as the individual goes into the social situation. This system, reminiscent of "freezing" and "atonic immobility" (Gallup 1974), prepares the individual to cope with a *physical* assault but does not, of course, prepare him to perform effectively and maturely. Furthermore, the nature of this primitive innate response pattern is *designed* to produce immobility and muteness. Thus, paradoxically, the defense against a challenge to speak up and actively participate in a particular situation triggers just the opposite of the demands.

DIFFERENTIATING SOCIAL PHOBIA FROM AGORAPHOBIA

In a landmark article, P. L. Amies and colleagues (1983) brought out in a systematic way a number of features that differentiate these two syndromes and consequently help to clarify the understanding of each. Eighty-seven people with symptoms of social phobia were compared with fifty-seven people with the symptoms of agoraphobia to determine whether the symptoms were part of distinct syndromes [the authors used the nonrestrictive diagnosis of social phobia according to *DSM-III* (1980)—*Ed.*]. The pattern of phobic situations was different in these two groups, as was the pattern of autonomic symptoms. Symptoms that could be observed by others were more frequent among the social phobics, whereas fainting was more frequent among the agoraphobics.

Situations that Provoke the Phobic Symptoms

The social phobics reported more severe anxiety in being introduced, in meeting people in authority, in using the telephone, whereas the agoraphobics reported more severe anxiety in being alone or in unfamiliar places, in crossing streets, and in public transport. The list of phobic situations is presented in Table 10–1.

In reviewing the situations that differentiate these two types of phobia, it becomes clear that the social phobic is concerned specifically about interpersonal situations, and that the center of the concern is being scrutinized by other people. The agoraphobic, in contrast, is concerned about being alone in unfamiliar or challenging places that present many kinds of stimulation and represent varying degrees of distancing or blocking from his home base (security). The social phobic, then, seems to encompass the notion of a *child being subjected to evaluation* by adults, whereas the agoraphobic seems to resemble the *child who has been placed in a strange place* for the first time. In the case of the social phobic, the other person or persons are involved in *paying attention* to the "child"; in the case of the agoraphobic, the other people *ignore* him even to the point of not caring whether something disastrous happens to him.

In the Amies, Gelder, and Shaw (1983) study, the notion of being attacked is supported by the finding that the agoraphobic group is much more likely than the social phobic group to experience fears of small animals (mice, rats, bats), snakes, deep water,

Table 10–1. Comparison of Major Fears in Agoraphobia and Social Phobias

More severe when main complaint is social phobia	*More severe when main complaint is agoraphobia*
Being introduced	Being alone
Meeting people in authority	Unfamiliar places
Using the telephone	Crossing streets
Visitors to home	Public transport
Being watched doing something	Department stores
Being teased	Crowds
Eating at home with acquaintances	Open spaces
Eating at home with family	Small shops
Writing in front of others	Mice, rats, bats
Speaking in public	Snakes
	Flying Insects
	Deep water
	Airplanes
	Blood, wounds

Source: Adapted from P. L. Amies, M. G. Gelder, and P. M. Shaw, "Social Phobia: A Comparative Clinical Study," *British Journal of Psychiatry* 142 (1983): 176. Used with permission.

airplanes, injections, and so on. The typical agoraphobic's clustering of these fears suggests that this group is basically afraid of some kind of physical damage or attack.

Somatic Symptoms

Certain somatic symptoms tend to be far more pronounced in the agoraphobic than in the social phobic. As noted in Table 10–2, the agoraphobic is more likely to have typical "collapse" symptoms: weakness in the limbs, difficulty breathing, dizziness/faintness, and actual fainting episodes. This differentiation suggests that

Table 10–2. Comparison of Major Symptoms in Social Phobia and Agoraphobia

Item	Social phobia (%)	Agoraphobia (%)	p Less than
Blushing	51	21	0.001
Twitching of muscles	37	21	(0.07)
Weakness in limbs	41	77	0.001
Difficulty in breathing	30	60	0.001
Dizziness/faintness	39	68	0.01
Actual fainting episode	10	25	0.05
Buzzing/ringing in ears	13	30	0.05
Palpitations	79	77	NS*
Tense muscles	64	67	NS
Dry throat/mouth	61	65	NS
Sinking feeling in stomach	63	54	NS
Feeling sick	40	40	NS
Trembling	75	75	NS

Source: Adapted from P. L. Amies, M. G. Gelder, and P. M. Shaw, "Social Phobia: A Comparative Clinical Study," *British Journal of Psychiatry* 142 (1983): 176. Used with permission.
*NS = Nonsignificant.

in the agoraphobic, a different primal defensive response has been mobilized. This system—the parasympathetic—is generally associated with blood phobias but evidently also plays a role in agoraphobia.

THE PHENOMENA OF SOCIAL ANXIETY

In a clinical study, Nichols (1974) discusses the features of social anxiety in thirty-five cases observed over a 3-year period. The following clinical observations were drawn from different phases of therapy work, and each item was observed in at least 50 percent of cases:

1. The *perception* of disapproving or critical regard by others.

2. The *expectation* of disapproving or critical regard by others.

3. A strong tendency to perceive and respond to criticism from others that is nonexistent.

4. A feeling of being less capable and less powerful than others—low self-esteem.

5. Having rigid ideas of appropriate social behavior, and not being able to vary behavior in order to deal with difficulties.

6. Negative fantasy/imagination that produces aniticipatory anxiety.

7. Heightened awareness and fear of being evaluated and judged by others.

8. A sense of being watched.

9. A discrimination and fear of situations from which sudden withdrawal would be unexpected and likely to attract attention.

10. A sense of being trapped/confined in such situations (that is, being socially closed).

11. An exaggerated interpretation of the sensory feedback related to tension or embarrassment.

12. Detection of bodily sensations within social situations.

13. A fear of being seen to be "ill" or losing control (that is, the physical signs of panic).

14. The experience of a progressive buildup of the discomfort.

15. The unpredictability of the anxiety response; the time available for prior fantasy and mood of the day seemed to be important determinants.

Nichols suggests that the incidence of social anxiety is related to some specific phase in development. He offers the late teens as a possible starting point. Finally, he adds that, in the development of social anxiety, the role of personality traits and their associated cognitive aspects becomes important.

Shame and Social Image

The experience of shame is important in discussions of social anxiety because the socially anxious person is fearful of being shamed in many situations. Shame is an affect related to a person's conception of his public image at the time that he is being observed or believes he is being observed. His notion of his social image may be accurate or inaccurate; but if he *believes* that his image has been tainted, and he cares about the observer's opinion of him, then he is likely to feel shame. It should be noted that the possibility of being thought of as weak, inferior, or inept may be just as threatening as actually being talked about in these terms. In other words, what others think of him is the crucial ingredient of shame induction—irrespective of whether they communicate this opinion.

The key factor in the activation of shame is *exposure* to observation by one or more persons. This affect is triggered when a person realizes that he has been observed violating specific social norms, expectations, or demands, especially in relationship to appropriate appearance and behavior. His "deviant" appearance or behavior are judged (he assumes) to be reflections of his weakness, inferiority, ineptness, character flaws, or immaturity. The public sanctions for lack of conformity, by and large, take the form of making the individual feel inferior, depreciated, and immature. The actual social consequences may consist of covert depreciation or open expressions of disapproval, ranging from mild mimicking to overt ridicule. It should be noted that if a person manages to conceal his "substandard" behavior or engages in a shameful activity in private, then he does not feel shame.

A person who feels shame sees himself as relatively helpless in attempting to counteract his depreciated public image. He believes he is subject to painful group reprisals, such as public humiliation and ridicule, and is *powerless* to ward off these attacks. The social opinion is absolute, finalistic, irrevocable. It is futile for him to try to modify or appeal the group verdict, and he must accede to the right of the members of the group to amuse themselves at his expense. Any protestations only increase their enjoyment of his embarrassment. The individual acknowledges his "inept" behavior by statements such as "I made a public display of myself" and hangs his head or attempts to hide to avoid their gaze.

In his mind, the antidote for shame is to vanish from the shameful situation. A person will say, for example, "I would like to fade away," or "I felt like merging into the woodwork." In contrast, anxiety is generally accompanied by the inclination to flee or by passive immobility.

Public relations deal in the currency of public appraisal, such as admiration or devaluation. A specific social group emphasizes surface values (peculiar to that group)—acceptable appearance, smooth performance, appropriate manners and dress, maturity—and gives public rewards (admiration, respect, special privileges). A person who deviates from the group norm may receive punishment through disdain, ridicule, isolation. We should emphasize that if the opinion of members of the group is irrelevant or immaterial to him he does not feel shame.

When we talk about the public image at a particular time, we do not imply that the "unacceptable" behavior is necessarily observed by a group. The interaction may be with another person with whom there is no personal relationship but who is a representative of the social group—that is, a stranger on the street or a telephone operator. Along the same lines, it appears that strangers can enforce shame more readily than can one's intimates. Thus, it may be practically impossible for parents to shame a child for his infractions of their domestic rules. Yet the child can be exquisitely sensitive to shame induced by strangers or by his own peer group for minimal deviation from group norms.

Shame is a form of *social influence*. Other people attempt to produce shame in us so as to control our behavior now and in the future. Typically, a person is exposed to a situation that produces shame. Although this may be the first experience in which he links this type of situation with this unpleasant affect, the memory is stored, and it influences the ways he approaches similar situations in the future. In a sense, a particular rule is set up by the individual: "If I behave in such a way, then I will be ridiculed and feel shame." It is the affect of shame that puts teeth into the rule. The individual thus is inclined to follow the rule and avoid the shame that would result from its violation.

Anxiety and shame differ in many ways. For one thing, anxiety generally occurs before one enters a stressful or threatening situation and may continue during the situation. But it is relieved when the situation is over. The feeling of shame starts during the exposure to the shameful experience and may continue for a time after the experience has ended.

Fear of Loss of Love or Abandonment

In intimate relationships, the demands are more personal than in public relationships and have to do with satisfying the specific needs and expectations of a particular person rather than with preserving an image. The expectations generally center on intangible qualities such as consideration, understanding, and caring. If a person does not meet those expectations of the significant other person, the sanctions take the form of withdrawal of affection or rejection. The affect derived from this sort of sanction is sadness. The qualities valued in intimate relations (kindness, empathy, warmth) are more often associated with character traits, whereas those admired by the group are related to appearance and performance. In intimate relationships, a person is less likely to be concerned about group norms and, to a certain extent, can drop his façade. The concern in the intimate relationship is usually with unconditional and total acceptance without having to preserve appearances.

Fears of loss of love or abandonment may at times become entangled with the same concerns about performance as do the other evaluation anxieties. In these cases, the individual fears that he will not live up to the expectations or demands of a loved one. He may then slide into the same rut as the socially anxious person: (1) a sense of vulnerability because the other person has the power to terminate the relationship. He may come to fear that nothing he can do is good enough; (2) a sense of being continually judged and possibly disapproved of; (3) a defensive inhibition, so that his actual behavior becomes stilted and artificial; (4) "catastrophizing" about the consequences of rejection. For example, a woman was in a continuous state of high anxiety over the possibility of being rejected by her lover. She believed that he was judging everything about her—how she dressed, spoke, prepared meals, arranged their social life. She worried that a single misstep would induce him to break the relationship. She sought continual reassurance that he was not displeased with her. Ultimately, he did leave her—not because of any deficiencies in her performance but because he could nor tolerate her incessant requests for reassurance.

Public Speaking Anxiety

The various disabilities and symptoms involved in severe public speaking anxiety encapsulate the various facets of evaluation anxiety: vulnerability to being the center of scrutiny or to being judged harshly, negative predictions, reduced self-confidence, sense of incompetence, being handicapped by involuntary inhibition, impaired control of thoughts and speech, adherence to stringent rules, expectation of punishment for breaking the rules.

ON BEING ABLE TO FUNCTION

The first hope of a person who attempts to speak in public is to be able to function. The speaker must be able to maintain an upright position, keep his balance, open his mouth, and speak intelligibly. If he cannot do this, it means that he has no control over the functioning of his mind and body—a devastating blow to his self-confidence. Since control over mind and body is ultimately essential for survival, the undermining of his functioning by the primal mechanisms represents a symbolic threat. Specific symptoms such as swaying, a quavering voice, faint feelings, loss of fluency, rigid postural control, all mean to him, "I can't control myself—I can't perform adequately—anything can happen to me." The sense of being victimized by internal processes is similar to the experience of the agoraphobic, except that it does not imply the presence of a life-threatening or disintegrating disorder.

This demonstration of lack of control is perceived (or so the speaker believes) by the audience. The person then experiences not only the fear of being unable to function but also the greater fear that his lack of functioning will be judged by the audience as an indication of his sickness, nervousness, immaturity, neurosis, or inadequacy.

ROLE OF ANXIETY

Although the subjective aspects of anxiety are difficult to describe, they seem to be universally experienced in response to a sense of threat in the evaluative situation. The physiological symptoms are initially of the sympathetic type: increase in blood pressure, pulse, and perspiration. These symptoms, however are not infrequently followed by a faint, dizzy, or wobbly feeling (parasympathetic). The faint feeling is sometimes a result of the drop in blood pressure and may be related to the pooling of blood in the lower extremities. Similarly, dry mouth and/or sweating are autonomic reactions.

Anxiety itself serves as a stimulus to further negative conceptualization. First, the unpleasant experience itself serves to distract the person from the task at hand just as would a sudden sharp pain. Second, he interprets anxiety as a dramatic sign that he is not functioning well (and *will not* function well). The anxiety itself, rather than any focused systematic assessment of his capability, is taken as the index of dysfunction. He has a concept such as "This is a sign that I'm not making it." Next, his global self-confidence is eroded. As the individual's attention is diverted to his anxiety, and as his cognitive-motor apparatus is diverted to danger, there is likely to be an increase in his overt nervousness as well as increased difficulty in performance.

PERFORMANCE FEEDBACK

The typical individual with public speaking anxiety uses feedback from the audience to tell him whether he is effective. If the response is negative, then his functioning is likely to suffer. If he decides that the audience considers him inadequate, this judgment may activate his notions of inadequacy and trigger nonadaptive "protective" responses. He may become disabled, impaired, possibly even mute. In actuality, he could function if he *believed* that he was capable of functioning in these circumstances. The negative response from the audience makes him believe that he cannot function at a good level and thus starts the vicious cycle.

The dysfunctional attitudes interact, are often accentuated by a negative response from the audience, and lead to a barrage of negative thoughts. ("They can tell I'm nervous. They believe I'm weak. They're downgrading me.") As a result, the individual subjectively experiences a decrease in his sense of being able to influence the audience, and he feels his power draining out of him. As he becomes increasingly "weak and powerless," he senses great danger and feels vulnerable to attack or disapproval from the audience. The net effect is a catastrophic drop in his confidence in his functional capacities to see him through this crisis.

COGNITIVE SET DURING SPEECH

A person's cognitive set prior to presenting a speech includes a wide variety of negative attitudes and evokes unpleasant cognitions. The overall set is one of perceiving the audience itself as threatening, ready to pounce on any misstep. His view of their expectations is that he must speak clearly and articulately, that his content must be appropriate and interesting, that his manner must be free and confident, but not too casual or informal. He believes that any deviation from these rules will evoke a critical response. His self-perception is that he will be naked, exposed, and inadequate and that, furthermore, he will suffer crippling inhibitions and painful anxiety that will impair his performance and open him to criticism or ridicule. This set is manifested in automatic thoughts such as "I won't be able to do it," "They will be disappointed in me," or "I will make a fool of myself."

At the onset of the speech, the cognitive set consists of self-monitoring and evaluation of the audience response. This set is represented by negative evaluations and dire predictions: "I look silly"; "I'm not expressing myself well"; "I'll forget what I want to say"; "I sound childish"; "I won't be able to go on"; "I'll be forced to stop"; "I'll be disgraced." The interpretation of the audience response is based on selective focus and is expressed in such thoughts as "They're bored"; "They think I look pathetic"; "They wish this was over."

The cognitive set thus primes the person to meet a danger. The public speaker is prepared to deal with an adversary whom he perceives as more powerful than himself and who is poised to attack or to abandon him. The speaker feels vulnerable and exposed and does not perceive that he has effective weapons to ward off the anticipated attack. Hence a primitive defensive response is evoked— rigidity, inhibition of articulation. The problem is that the audience is not an enemy out to attack him, and that, consequently, the defensive protection does not protect him at all. In fact, it cripples his functioning and sets him up for what he wishes desperately to avoid: reduced control over his cognitive and physical functioning and his appearing to the audience to be weak and incompetent.

Test Anxiety

Test anxiety can illustrate the processes involved in the anticipation of a specific confrontation with an evaluative situation—apprehension regarding available resources for dealing with the "danger"— and in the mobilization of primitive defenses against the threat. Let us take the case of a good student who is anxiety-prone. Several months before the exam, he is confident that he will do well and is probably reasonably realistic in appraising his ability to be adequately prepared. He may even overestimate his chances for success ("self-serving bias").

At some point, as the date of the exam approaches, the possibility of not doing well enters into his thinking. As the exam assumes the character of a serious threat, his orientation to the test starts to point toward the consequences of failure—a blow to his self-esteem, an obstacle to future plans, a personal defeat, a disgrace in the eyes of his friends, a disappointment to his family.

Focusing on the prospect of his performance's being evaluated, in addition to the possibility of failure and its consequences, affects his self-confidence. As the notion of threat takes hold, there is an automatic shift in his cognitive organization to a *vulnerability set*. The student's attention is drawn to his various possible weaknesses— omissions in his coverage of the material, deficiencies in comprehension, difficulties in collating and expressing what he has learned. These flaws are given progressively greater salience and tend to overshadow his positive achievements and abilities. In fact, he may seriously question what he has learned and his ability to cover the additional material necessary for the test. Raising such questions casts doubt on how successfully he will perform on the test.

As the threat of doing poorly (by his standards) increases, his anxiety increases and may propel him to greater efforts to cover the material. As he studies, each difficulty, delay, or obstacle becomes a threat in itself and elicits a warning such as "You'll never.be prepared in time."

Now let us suppose that the day of the exam has arrived. The vulnerability set is dominant. The student is concerned about his own weaknesses and the probability of examination questions or demands that may attack unknown gaps in his knowledge or comprehension. As the student looks at the exam, his cognitive set influences him to see the demands as enormous and his own resources as minimal. If the questions are realistically difficult, then the discrepancy between the demands and his own resources may be great. This discrepancy is translated into a threat: "I may not be able to handle this. I may blow it."

At this point one of the most disabling—and intriguing— phenomena associated with test anxiety may occur. His mind goes blank, he has difficulty regaining access to material with which he is thoroughly familiar, and his reasoning ability seems to be paralyzed. The blocking is a component of test anxiety (as well as of other evaluation anxieties) that is difficult to explain. One possible explanation is that the individual perceives the task as overwhelming his available resources. For example, the questions may seem far beyond his comprehension or knowledge or ability. The perception (or misperception) that the test is overwhelming may have the same effect on him as when a task is indeed overwhelming. It can be postulated that when confronted with a demand that overtaxes its capacity, the cognitive apparatus shuts down part of its capacity, just as an electric company under analogous circumstances automatically shuts down part of its capacity. Another possible explanation of the massive inhibition of recall, reasoning, and verbal expression may be that the primitive inhibitory reflexes are activated in this confrontation to serve the anachronistic function of diverting all attention to the danger.

The cognitive component is obvious in cases of progressive test anxiety. While the student continues to grapple with the questions or instructions, he tends to exaggerate flaws in his knowledge and understanding and in his responses. Each flaw takes on the form of a danger and increases the prospect of a failure.

Most students, of course, seem able to mobilize their resources when confronted with an actual test, and once they begin writing, their thoughts begin to flow and the vulnerability set is damped down. The seriously test-anxious subject, however, is unable to turn down or turn off the vulnerability set. He continues to operate at two levels: one deals with actual questions on the exam; the other with continual warnings, predictions, and self evaluations. Notions such as "You're stupid," "You'll never finish in time," "You can't understand," place a great tax on his cognitive capacity and thus reduce efficiency and performance (Sarason and Stoops 1978). Some students pass from the defensive phase (body rigid, fists clenched) to the helpless phase (feeling faint, limp, and so on)—a response that suggests a parasympathetic reaction. Others may respond with a panic attack—overwhelming anxiety and uncontrollable desire to escape—and, indeed, may abruptly leave and not return.

A SYNTHESIS

To the sensitive subject, being evaluated (for example, taking an examination, speaking in public, or going out on a date) is akin to being subjected to a painful probing. It may be likened to a dentist's probing teeth for an area of decay or a cavity. The evaluative situation is viewed as a confrontation or challenge that puts the subject on the defensive. He assumes that it is incumbent on him to prove himself to the evaluators and to *conceal* his presumed defects, ineptness, ignorance; whereas it is their role to *reveal* his ignorance, stupidity, and ineptness. Because he views the other persons (audience, graders of the test, dates) as looking for weaknesses, he assumes that they will pounce on every slip, flaw, or sign of nervousness and downgrade him for it. Thus, he stiffens after each misstep and imagines the immediate negative reaction of the evaluators and the long-range negative effects.

Since he regards himself as vulnerable, his reaction is self-protective: he automatically retracts into his shell so as to conceal any soft parts. In actuality, this retraction is expressed in the form of inhibition. Unfortunately for him, the inhibition not only conceals weaknesses (since it prevents him from saying or writing anything "stupid") but also interferes with effective presentation of the self. Consequently, the subject is undone by the very primal (reflex) mechanism designed to protect him.

The premonitory fears lead to stiffness *before* an encounter. The subject braces himself to absorb the impact of the aggressive scrutiny of the evaluators. This type of inhibition, however, interferes with spontaneous self-expression. Thus, at the onset of an encounter, his mind goes blank, he stutters, and he cannot focus on what he has to say or write. Moreover, he perceives the examination questions as being more difficult than they are, the audience as more unfriendly, and the date as more disdainful. He also underestimates his coping capacity. "Breaking the ice" consists of lifting the inhibition through action, by discovering that he does not need to retract and can allow free play of his personality or skill without reprisal.

REFERENCES

Amies, P. L., Gelder, M. G., and Shaw, P. M. (1983). Social phobia: a comparative clinical study. *British Journal of Psychiatry* 142:174–179.

Diagnostic and Statistical Manual of Mental Disorders (1980). 3rd ed. Washington, D.C.: American Psychiatric Association.

Gallup, G. T., Jr. (1974). Animal hypnosis: factual status of a fictional concept. *Psychological Bulletin* 81:836–853.

Nichols, K. A. (1974). Severe social anxiety. *British Journal of Medical Psychology* 47:301–306.

Sarason, I. G., and Stoops, R. (1978). Test anxiety and the passage of time. *Journal of Consulting and Clinical Psychology* 46:102–109.

CHAPTER ELEVEN

Imaginal Desensitization
and Relaxation Training

———————

Reid Wilson's chapter lends a valuable new slant to the picture of imaginal desensitization. Imaginal desensitization was initially developed by John Wolpe and was one of the first techniques used in the treatment of phobia. It pairs verbally presented imagery of a phobic situation with a relaxation response. This technique has been replaced by in vivo desensitization, that is, exposure to the phobic situation in reality rather than in imagination, since the latter has been shown to be the more effective technique. However, imaginal desensitization continues to have its place in the treatment of phobias, especially in an office practice, as a rehearsal to lessen anticipatory anxiety before exposure to a phobic situation that the patient is preparing to perform between sessions. In this chapter the addition of Ericksonian techniques provides some provocative and new material, addressing the issue of the resistant patient and the patient who has difficulty with visualization in imaginal techniques.

———————

Imaginal Desensitization
and Relaxation Training

R. REID WILSON

A guiding principle in psychotherapy is to identify and address the client's resistance to change before exploring the avenues of potential change. In individuals experiencing a panic or phobic disorder, such resistance can be readily identifiable.

For those whose problem developed from a spontaneous panic attack or a traumatic event, any consideration of facing the phobic situation can stimulate that dramatic memory. This recall reminds them of their perceived inability to cope with any such event in the future, since during their last attempts their loss of control (over their physiology or their circumstances) was of overwhelming proportions. They project this same failed strategy into their future, so that their view of coping with a similar situation tomorrow ends in failure as well.

Since these panic-prone individuals cannot perceive themselves successfully implementing coping strategies, when they do plan for challenging events they mentally prepare for the worst possible scenarios. Since the mind responds to imagery in a way similar to reality, these imagined scenes stimulate increased anxiety. Thus phobic clients are in the proverbial "catch-22": until they experience themselves successfully facing the panic-provoking situation, they remain fearfully immobile, yet they avoid facing the feared situation until they are certain they will succeed. They skirt confrontation until they can be guaranteed that they will experience zero anxiety. Thus avoidance becomes their primary pseudosolution.

This avoidance, however, is costly. When adopted as their response to anxiety, it leads to a more and more restricted lifestyle. And as these individuals limit their activities in response to irrational fear, this coping style reinforces low self-esteem, harsh self-criticism, and depression.

As they enter treatment, these clients will often present rigid attitudes about their capabilities, their worth, their projected image in public, and their treatment options. Dogmatic themes reflecting the need for containment will surface: "I *must* hide my anxiety from others." "I *can't* let myself feel any anxiety." "If I don't control these feelings they *will* run wild." Underneath this position is often a loss of self-worth and a sense of hopelessness. Although not always stated openly in the treatment session, probing can reveal messages such as, "There is something inherently flawed about me," or "I don't have what it takes to cope with the world's pressures." Their hopelessness is reflected in their poor attitude toward the potential of treatment options and in their unwillingness to attempt new coping strategies: "I've had it too long"; "I've tried everything—it's too ingrained"; "This will never help—I can't improve."

Thus, the therapist seeking to treat clients with phobias, panic disorder, or agoraphobia must account for any powerful, traumatic memories of the clients' past, the image and sensation of impending failure in their future, their psychic preparation for catastrophe, their strong investment in avoidance as the only safe and realistic option, and their restricting, self-defeating attitude regarding their change potential. For clients who enter treatment with such a rigid frame of reference, cognitive-behavioral assignments alone can meet with resistance in the form of "forgetfulness," unwillingness to comply, brief or feeble attempts at the therapeutic strategies, canceled appointments, and treatment dropouts.

The use in treatment of imaginal exposure through visualizations offers many benefits in this difficult therapeutic relationship. The chief benefit is the ability of these techniques to circumvent clients' resistance enough to allow them to entertain the possibility of change. This is accomplished through a special structuring of the therapist's language that encourages clients to become more receptive to presented ideas. Clients are gently guided through experiences that allow them to increase their control over physical and psychological responses before entering the actual fearful situation. This enables clients to build coping skills in less traumatic settings. If clients perceive that they can practice skills without suffering the "trauma" of anxiety, they become more willing to comply with the therapeutic request. Simultaneously, as they entertain the possibility of change through actively participating in a positive visualization, they begin the process of shaping: the gradual building up of a behavior by successive approximations toward the goal.

Consider the example of a client who wishes to overcome his fear of flying in an airplane. Perhaps he has flown successfully in the past but five years ago experienced a difficult flight and subsequently became frightened by the idea of flying again. A comprehensive initial assessment is important to identify the specific experiences, fears, and hesitations of each client, and a number of cognitive and behavioral interventions may be needed.

After an initial evaluation, suppose you assess that positive visualization would be a useful adjunctive tool. If imagery is to be beneficial within such a treatment, its function will be threefold: to develop clients' self-efficacy (their belief that they are capable of performing the task successfully) (Bandura 1977), to reduce clients' anticipatory anxiety, and to reinforce coping techniques that can be used during moments of anxiety.

The first therapeutic consideration should be how to reduce the chance that clients will resist your suggestions. Since pressure to perform will stimulate their fears, they are likely to respond to directives with resistance. For instance, a more traditional approach to imagery for fearful flying might contain the following directives:

> Close your eyes now and begin to relax. Relax the muscles of your face, jaw, shoulders, and back. Just let go of tensions more and more. Now, I want you to see an image of yourself floating comfortably on a raft in a swimming pool. Just enjoy the warmth of the sun on your body. You're feeling so very comfortable now. Maintaining that sense of comfort, imagine yourself sitting on a plane, relaxed, enjoying a flight to your favorite vacation spot.

To receptive clients this approach is straightforward and supportive: you help clients access feelings of comfort and encourage clients to maintain those feelings as they place themselves into the fearful situation. However, if you ask a fearful flier to participate in this particular imagery, you will probably meet with resistance. Instead of comfort, the client will probably begin to experience anxiety, with images of himself feeling trapped as the plane door closes or feeling anxious as the plane passes into a stormy region.

PROBLEMS WITH TRADITIONAL IMAGERY

What is it about this approach that stimulates resistance? First is the theme of relaxation. For many panic-prone individuals merely the idea of relaxing is frightening, since one of their primary fears is of losing control. "Control" means remaining consciously tense, braced, and vigilant. "Relaxing" means surrendering that conscious control over their body. This they will not purposely do until they experience an alternative method of maintaining control. In fact, as you suggest relaxation, they usually will respond to that "threat" with greater tension.

Second is the theme of being trapped. This traditional approach to imagery instructs clients in an authoritarian fashion to follow a specific path: close your eyes, relax your body, see an image, enjoy your flight. Such requests can stimulate a sense of being confined and restricted in thoughts, feelings, and actions. Once again, for some phobic clients the mere idea of having to perform in a specific manner will instantly stimulate anxiety and tension.

The third difficulty with this approach is the increased likelihood that you will lose rapport with clients. If you make a request that clients cannot perform, and if you continue to push for compliance, you will lose a basic therapeutic alliance. If you require that clients "relax" in order to proceed with the imagery, what happens if they don't feel relaxed at that moment? When you ask them to imagine themselves floating comfortably on a raft, what if they are afraid of water? If you state, "You are feeling so very comfortable now," when clients are actually tense and uncomfortable, what will happen to your rapport? While you are encouraging a pleasurable experience, these clients are probably experiencing failure and are subvocalizing this failure: "This isn't working; I can't do it; there is no way I can feel relaxed." In this paradigm, by the time you now tell clients to visualize themselves "sitting on a plane, relaxed, enjoying a flight to your favorite vacation spot," you have long lost therapeutic rapport.

These therapeutic mistakes are some of the primary reasons that clients will quickly abandon the use of visualization or will associate it with relaxation training, saying, "I've already tried that and it didn't work." However, if you define visualization as focusing of concentrated attention inward, everyone is capable of that skill. In fact, panic-prone individuals unwittingly use a negative form of visualization. They focus their concentrated attention inward to retrieve a memory image of failing at their task in the past. As the mind associates to an experience, it will respond physically, so clients now begin to notice sensations that they felt during that past event: their stomach gets tense and their heart begins to race. They next turn their concentrated inward attention to an imagined future time when they might attempt to face the same problem situation. Since they are now feeling tense and anxious and since they are calling up an image of an event in the future that is similar to the past traumatic event, they project their past behavior into this future situation, telling themselves, "I knew I couldn't do it."

IMAGERY THAT OFFERS CHOICE

A dilemma arises when attempting to balance clients' needs to remain consciously in control at all times and the therapeutic need for clients to loosen conscious control in order to entertain novel solutions to old problems. Panic-prone individuals tend to create "rules" for interpreting and responding to anxiety-provoking situations: "Here is a restaurant. I have experienced panic in restaurants before; therefore, I might experience one today in this restaurant. I cannot cope with a panic attack; therefore, it is in my best interest not to enter this building." The deeper the clients' belief in this logic, the more difficulty therapists will encounter as they attempt to modify it. If clients remain controlled by this information-processing style, every event will be rigidly classified as either fearful or not fearful, and their response to fearful events will follow that same predictable pattern of anxiety and avoidance.

By building a new and different imaginal exposure paradigm that accounts for clients' needs to remain in control, to experience choices and options instead of feeling trapped, and to experience success and mastery instead of repeated failure, you can create imagery experiences that move clients closer to their therapeutic goals while simultaneously sidestepping resistance. This change in your therapeutic approach can assist clients in breaking through their rigid beliefs into creative problem solving that allows them to freely and openly entertain novel ideas, in the same way that all scientists, mathematicians, musicians, and artists produce creative new themes to expand their technique. As these individuals suspend their need for linear logic, they gain access to their ability to notice resemblances and correspondences in seemingly unrelated objects or events. In this way they form a gestalt with new complex images to solve old problems.

One of the best methods for clients to accomplish this is to allow special kinds of *imagery*, not words, to do their creative thinking. These images can contain more information than cognitive statements (thus the expression, "a picture is worth a thousand words") and can hold more emotional impact, which makes concepts more concrete to the mind. Once a novel solution for an old problem is produced through imagery, *then* clients can enlist the help of their cognitions to incorporate that change into their conscious daily living through specific rules or guidelines. This is a two-step process. In step one, complex imagery is used to generate options for change; in step two, clients choose among those options and select how to implement that solution.

PARADIGM FOR VISUALIZATION

To move from theory to practice, here is one way we might use visualization within a therapeutic session to assist clients in bypassing resistance and entertaining the possibility of change.

1. Select a therapeutic task that is the client's next appropriate step toward the treatment goal.

2. Identify the client's internal resources needed to accomplish this task.

3. Orient the client toward the task by indirectly discussing those needed resources.

4. Present one or more therapeutic images that are within the client's skill level, using option-oriented language. Suggest specific changes in the client's physiology, emotions, or images, while continuing to use option-oriented language.

5. Imply the client's ability to produce those changes in the future.

Returning to the example of the fearful flyer early in treatment, consider an initial therapeutic task (step 1) to be self-efficacy: the sense that he can actually accomplish this goal through his own efforts. The image of success would certainly compete with his typical picture of considering taking a flight and becoming too upset or panicky to follow through. And it would be an invaluable resource, since one's ability to image positive change will have a direct impact on one's willingness to exert effort toward change.

The important internal resources (step 2) would be the client's willingness and ability to use imagery and to imagine a positive future. By discussing these resources in an indirect fashion and through asking rhetorical questions, you begin to stimulate the client's selective memories and images for these resources (step 3). This process plants the seeds for the next important step by enlisting the fundamental skills needed to produce a more complex therapeutic image.

SUCCESS IMAGERY

When selecting a therapeutic image for such clients (step 4), the therapist will need to design a task that stimulates the least resistance. If we ask the client to imagine flying in comfort before the client believes he can accomplish this feat, we will run into resis-

tance. So, instead, ask the client first to see himself *already having suc-*
ceeded at his goal of flying, without yet considering how he will succeed.
This circumvents the client's resistance ("I can't . . . ") while setting the stage for more specific images supporting a self-efficacy
belief ("What would it be like if I could . . .").

Let me illustrate the actual presentation of these steps to this
hypothetical client. The illustration here begins with step 3: orient
the client toward the task by indirectly discussing the needed internal resources. Keep in mind that the objective at this step is to
begin to stimulate the client's ability to retrieve or develop complex imagery as it relates to the spoken phrases.

> *Therapist:* As you have been talking, I've been developing a grow-
> ing sense of just how much you would like to be rid of this
> whole problem, to not even think about how easy it is to
> get on a plane, and fly anywhere you want. [*pause*] Do you
> have any idea how you will feel when you have succeeded
> at this task?
>
> *Client:* Well, I'd feel great . . . I'd feel a sense of freedom.
>
> *Therapist:* You'll feel great, yes. And can you just sense how
> good you'll feel inside you as you step off a plane after a
> comfortable flight? . . . Because you have experienced that
> comfort before, haven't you? You used to fly with ease. Do
> you remember?
>
> *Client:* Yes, I remember, but it seems so long ago.
>
> *Therapist:* Yes, so long ago. And what I am really curious about
> is whether you can remember what it feels like to be com-
> fortable, long before you ever had this hesitation? Looking
> back, what do you think it is like in your body when you
> are feeling comfortable, at ease?
>
> *Client:* Well, I think my shoulders would be relaxed, I'd be
> breathing easily, my heart rate would be slow. And my mind
> wouldn't be racing.

Therapist: I can't tell whether you're feeling any of that right now. I wonder, is it possible for you to notice your shoulders relaxing? . . . And just let your breathing be nice and gentle as you listen to my words? [*pause*] And it must be a good feeling to have your mind quiet down, since there's nothing you have to be working at right now. As if you're letting your body and mind have a break as I talk. [*pause*] And wouldn't it be nice to be able to look ahead with these same feelings? . . . and having these feelings with you more often in the future? [*pause*] Just imagine how things might seem different if you somehow could call up these feelings whenever you wanted to.

Here are my objectives for the client in the exchange above. Develop a feeling sense of what it would be like if this problem were behind you (first paragraph). See a glimpse of yourself getting off a plane with physical and emotional comfort by retrieving a memory of accomplishing that feat in the past (second and third paragraphs). Produce those sensations of comfort right now in this room, then imagine the results of having these feelings again in the future (fourth paragraph).

Even though I had concrete and specific goals, there was no pressure on the client to perform; it was as if we were simply having a casual conversation. Nonetheless, the content of my statements and questions makes certain presuppositions. For instance, the first question ("Do you have any idea how you will feel when you have succeeded at this task?") presupposes that the client *will* accomplish his stated goal. In order for the client to answer, he must conjure up an image of succeeding. At the same time, the indirectness of the question lowers the risk of conscious resistance, relative to a more direct request ("Imagine yourself now flying successfully"); therefore, the client more easily creates the picture in his mind. Next, I ask him to remember that this success is an experience he actually has in his repertoire of past successes. Rather than focusing on his comment that "it seems so long ago," I casually suggest he find out whether he can recall the memory of *physical* comfort, then experience that comfort now ("Is it possible for you to notice your shoulders relaxing?"). Finally, I present the rhetorical questions and comments regarding these comfortable feelings continuing into the future.

The client is now psychologically and physically ready to begin step 4, which will be the first direct request for imagery.

> *Therapist:* While you're enjoying this physical comfort right now, I thought you might enjoy a brief little experience. As you continue to let those shoulders stay relaxed, and breathing easily, I wonder if you'd let your eyes close and try a little experiment? [*Client's eyes close*]
>
> Take a moment to pretend that you can drift through time into the future. And let yourself drift, as far into the future as you need to to imagine yourself in a time and place where you have long overcome this problem . . . where this difficulty is in the distant past . . . as many months or years or decades as you need to, and then just get to know what it is like to have succeeded. Here, now, in the future, you have the ability that you were seeking, the ability that you knew was inside you. All those problems between you and your goal have faded away because you have already reached your goal for some time. And you can now enjoy all the changes that come with attaining that goal. [*pause*]
>
> Let yourself fully experience how you feel now that you have made it. . . . And look around; how does your world appear to you now? . . . And who is around you: someone you know or someone new?
>
> And what is the feeling of success like? . . . Does that feeling of confidence and pride influence the way you walk

down a street? . . . or hold your head on your shoulders? And if someone were looking at your face, would that person be able to see your sense of accomplishment? Would your smile, your eyes, reveal your good feelings?

So tell me, in a few words, while you continue feeling comfortable, what it's like to feel successful.

Client: Yes, I like it. I'm in Australia with my wife and, we're having fun on our own, without the kids!

If the client progresses as smoothly as this hypothetical one has, a second image can be suggested within step 4 that will take advantage of this current state of mind and move him one step closer to the current therapeutic goal of self-efficacy.

Would it be acceptable with you if we tried another image? [*Client nods his head*] Fine. Just let that image fade away as you focus on the comfort or your body here, and your nice easy breathing. . . . I would like you to see yourself having *just completed* your first flight, and the flights went *perfectly*, almost magically . . . beyond your dreams of success: no bumps, no difficulties, no tensions, just smooth as glass. And you are now stepping off that plane. [*pause*] Let yourself begin to know what it feels like inside you to have accomplished this task. . . . As you are walking away from the plane, notice how this success is expressed in the movement of your feet. . . . And if some people are greeting you, I wonder if they will see the pride and relief and joy on your face. . . . And notice how they respond to your response. Really get to know how your body expresses your confidence, and absorb those feelings like a sponge.

This visualization capitalizes on the client's ability to experience success and moves that psychophysiological response closer in time to the feared task. However, three suggestions diminish resistance. First, the image is still of a time *after* the feared task, not during it. Second, the client is asked to imagine having completed a "magically perfect" flight. Third, the suggestions offered after the initial request for an image presuppose that the client is experiencing "success." In other words, in order for the client to comply to the indirect requests ("Really get to know how your body expresses your confidence"), he must accept the premise that he has just succeeded in the flight. Instead of struggling to imagine flying comfortably, he must busy himself in the discovery of how his sense of success might influence how he walks or how other people might react when they see him smiling.

If, upon questioning, the client continues to express success in generating these images and physical responses, a third and final visualization can be presented.

> In a moment I would like you to imagine the entire process of taking a commercial plane flight, from calling the airlines for a reservation to landing in some vacation location and enjoying your pleasures. I would like you to see yourself packing your clothes, driving to the airport, boarding the plane, taking the flight, and so forth. And I'd like you to experience that whole process—easily, comfortably, pleasantly—from start to finish, in 30 seconds. Go ahead and start now.

With about 10 seconds remaining in this imagery I would suggest to the client that he should soon see himself on the ground, enjoying his vacation. After the 30 seconds I would ask him to open his eyes and describe his experience.

This final visualization now takes the client through an imaginal experience of a successful flight sometime in the future. Two variables increase the likelihood that he will not have difficulty with this image. First, he has just had two visualizations giving him the feelings and the state of mind that support success: he has experienced himself long in the future with this success in his past, and he has seen himself take pride immediately after his first flight. Second, he is placed in a time bind: he has a great number of tasks to accomplish in his mind within 30 seconds of lapsed time. With all likelihood he will be so consumed by these elements that he won't have enough time or consciousness to become anxious. And he is reminded to end the imagery with the pleasant experience of his vacation.

Please note that the "30-second" guideline is not an absolute. A shorter exposure, such as the image of riding on an elevator or driving over a bridge, will require a visualization as brief as 10 seconds in order to maintain the therapeutic objectives.

This particular paradigm can be called *success imagery*, since the emphasis is on the positive experience either during or after an accomplishment and not on confrontations or struggles within the task. Other variations of success imagery can be adapted for a variety of fears associated with panic or phobias, such as driving a car, grocery shopping, eating at a restaurant, riding an elevator or escalator, standing in line, or entering a crowd.

A few guidelines will assist you in their use. First, regardless of the task, the outcome picture should be something the client desires, for it will be this goal that motivates the client. When developing an outcome picture, help the client adjust the future images until they reflect a pleasing goal. Second, by using silent pauses give the client time after each suggestion to develop an internal response—physically, emotionally, and with imagery. The more you and the client take time to enhance each presented image—using colors, textures, sounds, physical sensations, and emotions—the stronger will be the influence of the image. And, third, embellish your suggestions using option-oriented language to reduce resistance.

These visualizations given below are presented as though they were verbatim instructions to the client, but they are only illustrating the general flow of the imagery. In the next section you will learn how to enrich these directions in ways that enhance client responsiveness.

Illustrative Imagery—Option One

Imagine yourself in some comfortable, safe place. Let yourself remain there for a few minutes, enjoying the pleasant experience. Continue in that scene until you can feel your body reflecting your comfort and sense of safety. Take a mental scan through your body; notice how that comfort feels.

Now, while you maintain that feeling, call up the image of your task. This transaction is an important one. Only see the *picture* of the task in your mind; turn off the sound and turn off the feelings associated with the picture. You should take on the role of a detached observer of the scene, as though you are the director reviewing the film clip. Keep your sense of bodily comfort from the previous scene.

While you are feeling physically relaxed, watch yourself, on that screen, simply float through the task. Don't bother making your actions realistic. Literally see yourself gliding through the entire experience, like you are comfortably floating on a pocket of air. Do it with ease. Face no threatening moment. Have no difficulties. End your scene by reaching your goal and *enjoying* it when you get there. Spend as much of your imagery time enjoying your goal as you took to reach your goal.

As you complete that task in your mind, return to your first scene of that comfortable, safe place. Spend a few minutes experiencing that comfort in your body and mind again.

Option Two

Follow the same process as in Option One, and add these instructions.

If, at any time, while you are viewing your task, you feel sensations of discomfort, take a mental eraser and wipe away that scene completely. Return your comfortable, safe scene to the screen. Stay in that scene as long as you need to in order to regain your sense of

ease. Then, maintaining those comfortable feelings, return to floating through your task from the beginning.

You can stop that task image as many times as you like, taking
as long as you need to regain your sense of comfort. You don't even
need to get through the task in your mind the first few times that
you try it here. Consider that you are playing with these ideas and
images. It doesn't really matter how far you get in any particular
session.

It is important, however, that you take time to end each imagery
session feeling at ease. When you are ready to stop, return to imagining your comfortable safe scene until you feel that comfort reflected in your body.

Option Three

Feel free to reduce the number of steps or change any particular step
to create a process specifically designed for the client's task. It is
unnecessary to go through all steps every time.

This session will require that clients first write down their
answers to the questions below. Have them keep the sheet of paper
in their lap.

1. What is my task?

2. When will I do this?

3. How long will I take?

4. What worried thoughts do I have about this task?

5. What self-critical thoughts do I have about accomplishing this task?

6. What hopeless thoughts do I have about this task?

7. What can I say (in place of those negative thoughts) to
support myself during this task?

8. How can I increase my sense of safety while working on
this task?

A. Call up your success image. Give yourself a clear, positive goal. Take a nice calm breath as your body responds to that image.

B. Now, let that image fade away as you visualize yourself briefly somewhere in the middle of your task. See yourself totally in control of the situation, smoothly handling the scene even if you can hold onto that sense for only a few moments. Take another nice calm breath as you let that image fade away.

C. Glance down at your answers to question 4, "What worried thoughts do I have about this task?" Take your answers one at a time. Look at your first answer, then close your eyes and repeat that one statement or question in your mind. If you can, visualize a few or the key words of that worried thought at the same time. Now, take a calming breath as you let that thought, and those words, fade from your mind. Don't bother responding to the thought, or replacing it with a positive thought. Simply let it fade out, and let any of your associated tensions fade away. Return to that sense of calmness to your body. Completely dissolve that negative thought without responding to it.

Once you have returned to that state of calmness and ease, glance down at your next answer.

Proceed in the same fashion as above. After completing this process for each of the client's answers to question 4, use this same method with each answer to questions 5 and 6.

D. Spend as much time as you need to again develop your quiet mind and body. Consider this a rest period: no work, no effort, just drifting comfortably, letting your body soothe itself.

E. Now turn your attention to question 7, "What can I say to support myself during this task?" Reflect on your statements one at a time. Close your eyes and recite the first one to yourself. Think only about the statement, not about your task. Let the statement sink in. Let your body respond as though you believe the statement. Get to know how your body feels as it is supported. After you are satisfied with your response to that first statement, recite that second statement, let it sink in, and notice your body's response as you let yourself believe the statement to be true, if only for a few

moments. Continue using this process with each of your supportive statements.

You may find that as you reflect on these statements a new and
different supportive stance rises up in your mind. Reflect on that
sentence and learn from it. If you like how your body feels as you
attend to it, jot down the new sentence for a later use.

F. Begin to mentally rehearse your task. Start with any active
preparatory steps you might want to take to increase your sense of
safety. Then, see yourself moving through each stage of the task in
the way that you have planned. Envision yourself at the beginning
of the task, in the middle, and as you are finishing it. Finally, see
yourself enjoying the completion of that task, smiling to yourself
at the accomplishment.

G. Take a few minutes to become quiet and calm, without having to work on any task. Use this time to focus on a pleasant image,
to experience comfortable body sensations, or to meditate on a
calming word.

Suggest to the client that "you can continue to practice your
success imagery a little bit each day, as many times as you need to,
in order to have confidence in your ability to begin practicing the
task itself."

OPTION-ORIENTED LANGUAGE

One of the therapist's most important goals in treating panic and
phobic disorders is to assist clients in breaking through rigid,
avoidance-oriented patterns of problem-solving in order to experience conscious competence in responding to stressful events. Imagery, especially success imagery, provides a safe therapeutic step
toward producing new, competing, internal responses to the old fear-
producing cues.

To maintain rapport with an individual who fears becoming
trapped or losing control, the therapist must word these visualizations in such a way as to support the client's freedom and choice.

(Fortunately, such option-oriented language structure also promotes the creative problem-solving style that I spoke of earlier.) In the general field of clinical hypnosis, technique has been slowly shifting away from a direct, dominant style of suggestion to an indirect permissive style. Erickson's (1954, 1964, Erickson and Rossi 1976, 1980) innovative techniques in the field of clinical hypnosis can be implemented in the treatment of anxiety disorders with simple linguistic changes that can significantly diminish the likelihood of client resistance to visualization.

Questions and Rhetorical Questions

The simplest way to avoid resistance is to avoid requesting change. Good technique involves suggesting change without requiring it. Questions and rhetorical questtons serve this function of directly stimulating clients' curiosity while indirectly orienting them toward the possibility of changing. In order to respond to most questions, the mind must first consider the question. It is in the *consideration* that you gain the therapeutic advantage. For example, the direct request, "Relax your body now," might become:

> Do you think that there are times when your body is less tense than others? And during those times when *your body becomes less tense*, might you notice it? Have you ever just flopped down in a chair, *letting your body feel like a rag doll?* Do you think, during those times, that your *shoulders loosen and drop* a little? Is it like telling your legs they're on a break, that they can *go ahead and become loose and relaxed*, while you *focus on something pleasant*, like how nice it is just to *sit and unwind?*
>
> And, I wonder, what would it be like right now if 100 percent of your attention was on *letting yourself be physically comfortable?* Would you shift your body at all? Would your *breathing become nice and easy?*

Whether the client responds orally to each question or simply contemplates it, the therapist must pause long enough after each in order to allow a mental response. In this way, a direct or rhetorical question turns into an indirect suggestion. Notice how in the first paragraph of the example the client is asked about past experiences with relaxation. As he associates to the questions in a positive manner, he is more likely to begin ideomotor responses: physical responses to the ideas suggested within the questions. By the second paragraph the client is oriented toward the suggestions and becomes more susceptible to a mention of current relaxation.

Review now the phrases in italics in those two paragraphs. Here, embedded within the questions, are the direct suggestions to produce physical and mental relaxation. While the conscious mind is somewhat distracted by the questions, these suggestions influence with less resistance. To increase the impact of these phrases, they can be spoken a little more slowly and quietly than the rest.

Qualifiers

Any time we give an explicit instruction or direction to a client, we invite resistance as well as compliance. *Qualifiers* are words or phrases that limit or modify the meaning of another word or phrase. In this context we want to modify the message, "Do/think/feel this." Any direct suggestion can become an indirect suggestion by adding qualifiers such as: *might, maybe, may, can, a little, somewhat, probably, can wonder,* or *don't know if.* Introductory phrases will offer the same benefit: *I wonder if . . . ? Do you suppose . . . ? Is it possible . . . ? You might be surprised if . . . ? I'm curious what it would be like if . . . ? I don't know if. . . .*

Here is an example of qualifiers with a client who is fearful of entering stores and restaurants. The embedded suggestions (indicated by italics) are designed for the client to feel physically relaxed while imaging sitting in a car outside a restaurant.

> I wonder if you can imagine what it might be like if you were able to *sit outside that restaurant in your car.* I don't know if you could *reassure yourself that you are safe.* Do you suppose, if you only had to sit

there and not even get out, that you could *feel physically comfortable?* Maybe, if you *feel safe,* you could see yourself *breathing easily, gently.* Perhaps *your hands are relaxed in your lap.* If you want to right now, you can *let your shoulders relax,* too. And the *muscles of your forehead may loosen* a bit.

Negative Adjectives or Adverbs

Adding a negative to a statement can increase an internal search through the cortex for information by adding some brief confusion. It also can overtly support a resistance to change while covertly encouraging a mental association to the idea. In some cases it even challenges clients to produce the suggested change by suggesting that they are not yet ready or able to change. Negatives would be any words with the prefix of *un-, a-, im-, miss-* or *ex-* and adverbs such as *not, won't, never, can't,* or *couldn't.* Examples are:

It's unnecessary to be *totally* relaxed.

You don't have to *picture yourself having accomplished it perfectly, feeling as in control* as you would like to.

It might be impossible for you to *imagine your hands loosening their grip on the steeling wheel,* yet. You can't quite say what the *control* will feel like.

I'm not sure whether or not you can remember *experiencing that success in a completely satisfying way* before.

All Possible Alternatives

With these suggestions the therapist gives the client a variety of options within a narrow field of endeavor, whether it is regarding images, emotions, physical sensations, or behavior. While the client experiences a sense of choice, almost all the choices are of a therapeutic nature. For instance, if we want the client to access a memory or a feeling of power in order to maintain that subjective state as he enters a fearful scene, we might say:

> Everyone has his own sense of *what personal strength feels like.* You may remember a time when you were *feeling powerful.* It could have been a few days ago in some conversation, or a few months ago as you experienced some change in your life. Or perhaps it was years ago, when you were a teenager, or a child, *feeling that energy of accomplishment or pride.*
>
> I don't know *what it feels like inside of you when you are strong.* Does it feel as though it comes from one physical place, like your heart, or your chest? Or perhaps you feel it throughout your body, *like a warmth or an energy field.* Or you may only *notice* the results of *your power,* by the way you hold your head, or stand, or your facial expressions, your tone of voice. You might not even *know what your strength is like as you feel a sense of power.*

Implications

Implications encourage clients to consider the possibility of change without challenging their rigid conscious beliefs. They do this by including phrases that presuppose change. For instance, the question, "As you begin to improve, I wonder how many new behaviors you will become comfortable with?" presupposes, first, the client *will* improve and, second, that he will learn new behaviors as he improves.

One structure for implications stems from "if . . . then" thinking, such as

> Now, if you *create a voice inside you that supports your efforts,* then you will *notice* just *how good you can feel,*

or

> If your *breathing becomes slow and gentle* here, then your *thoughts* might *quiet,* too.

Neither statement directs the client to respond, but both will stir the client's associations and mental process regarding the suggested behaviors. To create such statements, choose two behaviors, one that the client is already experiencing or could easily experience, and another, more relevant therapeutic goal. Use an introductory phrase such as, "Before . . . ," "As soon as . . . ," "While . . . ," or "After. . . ." Use a phrase to link the two behaviors, such as ". . . then you can . . . ," ". . . it will remind you of . . . ," ". . . you might experience/notice . . . ," ". . . the problem will . . . ," or ". . . your feelings will. . . ." ("As soon as you begin to get comfortable in your seat, then you can think about what you would like to have when you leave this session today.")

A second method of generating implications is to speak in more abstract terms regarding change. Instead of directly addressing how the client should modify his own behavior, speak of other people:

> One thing many clients have found useful is to *remember back to experiences years ago, before the problem ever existed* . . . to *remember breezing through a grocery store without a moment's hesitation.*

or

> Each person can *overcome obstacles* at his own safe pace.

Questions can also be posed that imply resources or behavioral options available for the client. For instance,

> As you *imagine yourself approaching the restaurant door,* which of your many skills might you use to *respond to your tension?*

or

> As you *see yourself walking up to that restaurant,* will you *take a nice, slow, calming breath,* or will you *tell yourself that you can manage this task and feel the relief* that comes with that knowledge, or will you just *forget all about your worries* and *enjoy your friends?* Maybe you will do something entirely different that will help you feel *safe and confident.*

VISUAL REHEARSAL WITH
OPTION-ORIENTED LANGUAGE

Consider another example of the five-step design, described previously, for incorporating a visualization experience into a treatment session. Suppose the therapeutic task (step 1) is for the client to begin using a special breathing technique to assist him in remaining calm as he enters an anxiety-provoking situation, such as a restaurant. The internal resources he will need (step 2) are to sit comfortably and visualize a scene, to perform that breathing process, and to respond physically to that process.

Assume that we have indirectly discussed these internal resources with the client (step 3). Here is a hypothetical transcript of steps 4 and 5 of such a brief visualization, using all the styles of option-oriented language: questions and rhetorical questions, qualifiers, negative adverbs and adjectives, all possible alternatives, and implications. It will begin by assisting the client in becoming physically comfortable and oriented toward the visualization experience. The client will then associate a special breathing pattern with a sense of emotional and physical comfort. Finally, the client will visually rehearse successfully using that breathing technique in two different scenes. Again, italics will indicate the embedded suggestions.

> We have talked quite a bit about your desire to remain calm in a variety of situations. Truly, all of us deserve to *feel a sense of being settled*, to be able to call "time out" and just *rest*. I guess resting could mean different things to different people. It could mean *not having to think very much*, simply *letting your mind be quiet*. No work. No effort. Or it might be *letting your legs get heavy and relaxed*, like they do after a good workout. Perhaps resting means to *rest your eyelids, your jaw, your shoulders, your chest*. Take a moment here to see what parts of *you can begin to rest*.
>
> And as you continue to notice what it is that changes in your body while you *let go of muscle tensions*, you may be able to discover

that your *breathing has slowed to a gentle rate*. And do you ever wonder just how *your breathing helps relax you?*

If you want to feel a few more of *those muscles loosen*, you can try something. In a moment I am going to ask you to take a nice long gentle inhale and then let it out ever so slowly through pursed lips. So slowly you could count from one to eight as you exhale. And as you let the air flow out easily, perhaps you will notice *your body becoming heavier and heavier, more and more relaxed*. And after you finish exhaling, just let yourself breathe gently, easily, from your abdomen.

Now on your next exhalation, take that long deep breath, filling your lower lungs, then your upper lungs. Fine. Now ever so slowly begin that gentle, long exhale. And you don't even need to notice how *your body begins to melt, to loosen, to feel so much at ease as you let go more and more.*

You'll probably find that you don't even need to pay attention to your breath now. Your body is totally capable of performing that simple task, just as it does for you every night as you sleep quietly. But you might notice with each *gentle exhalation* now you're *feeling more and more comfortable, more and more safe*. And physically you might notice a number of things: how *relaxed your stomach can feel*, a sense of *heaviness in your arms and legs*, or perhaps a *pleasant kind of tingling* somewhere in your body. I don't really know.

And after your next exhalation, take another one of those nice long deep breaths . . . then very slowly exhale. And as you are exhaling, you can find out if your body wants to *feel* any *more comfortable* or whether it *feels just fine* with this degree of *comfort*. When you are ready, tell me in few words what you are aware of now. [*If client responds positively, then continue.*]

Fine, and let's refer to that breathing pattern as a Calming Breath. As you continue, do you suppose you could think of any times in your day when this kind of feeling of *comfort and safety* would come in handy? And if you do think of a *nice time to retrieve this feeling*, just nod your head gently. . . . Fine. Go ahead and see yourself during that time . . . and when you are ready, let yourself have that nice Calming Breath . . . and notice what happens.

If *you feel physically at ease,* find out just how things look to you. And any time you notice even a twinge of tension, [*as client is exhaling*] let yourself have another *nice deep inhale* . . . and a *gentle, slow exhale,* as your body responds naturally to your desire for *physical comfort and ease.* Find out whether you notice. [*Use client's description of physiological changes after Calming Breath from above.*)

It might even seem as though the scene stops and waits for you to *feel comfortable* again before it proceeds. Otherwise, continue to move in that scene, noticing whatever or whoever interests you, while you explore whether or not you *enjoy feeling safe, trusting your body.* And tell me in a few words what you are noticing right now. [*Listen and respond to client's experience.*]

Fine. Now, if you are interested, you might want to consider one other image here. Would you like to? [*Wait for client agreement.*] Pretend for a minute that this simple breathing can bring you a sense of *physical ease and comfort,* just as you describe. I'd like you to pretend that as you take that deep inhalation, and let it out slowly, you will remember just how you feel today. Would that be all right with you?

In a moment, I'm going to ask you to see yourself entering a restaurant that would have, in the past, felt uncomfortable. But this time, consider allowing your body to take charge of itself. Simply see yourself in a moment, walking into that restaurant and taking that nice long inhale and that easy, gentle, slow exhale that is a Calming Breath to your body. And then find out how you like it when your body responds to that Calming Breath by [*again use client's description of physiological changes after Calming Breath*].

So go ahead and begin to unfold that scene now. [*As you see client take that deep inhalation, continue.*] And just allow your body to respond, without work, without effort, and maybe even to your surprise. As you continue to *feel safe,* continue to drift through that scene with a knowledge that that Calming Breath is there when you need it. Otherwise, just *enjoy your comfort,* and the taste of that food or the good company around you. And any twinge of anxiety can be a cue for you to let your body take care of itself with that Calming Breath.

Take all the time you want to *enjoy* your meal, then pay your bill and walk comfortably out to the parking lot. And give me a nod when you are there.

[*After head nod*] Speaking of enjoyable experiences, wouldn't it be nice if sometime soon you discovered that without even thinking about it you found yourself taking a Calming Breath, or noticing those *comfortable feelings in your body*, or, without even thinking, doing something that you once were avoiding? All because, in some way, a person can *begin to trust the body*. And the more you *trust the body*, the more you will be surprised at your *comfort* and your *control* in the coming weeks.

Now I doubt that you'll come in next week and say that you have been *having no symptoms* all week. That would even surprise me! But I wouldn't be surprised if you tell me next week about one time or another that you suddenly notice *how comfortable you can feel*.

But for now you can just notice what it's like to let a little light in your eyes as you begin to adjust to this room again.

CONCLUSION

The advantages of this special form of imaginal exposure have been outlined throughout the chapter. The common denominator of most of these benefits is that such visualizations enable clients to be more receptive to presented ideas. The therapeutic relationship can then be used to explore with greater frequency experiences that are outside of clients' usual frame of reference. In turn, as clients become capable of envisioning positive change in their lives, this encourages them to take responsibility for their own actions in the future.

In addition, at certain moments during imagery sessions there can be blending of conscious understandings and expectations with unconscious participation. New unconscious insights and learning can be immediately gratifying to clients' conscious needs. As described in Bandura's (1977) self-efficacy theory, the client can acquire a sense of confidence that he or she will have adequate resources to cope with the phobic situation. Even this benefit alone makes imaginal exposure a significant technique in the treatment of anticipatory anxiety and phobic avoidance.

REFERENCES

Bandura, A. (1977). Self-efficacy: toward a unifying theory of behavior change. *Psychological Review* 84:191–215.

Erickson, M. (1954). Pseudo-orientation in time as a hypnotherapeutic procedure. *Journal of Clinical and Experimental Hypnosis* 2:261–283.

—— (1964). An hypnotic technique for resistant patients: the patient, the technique and its rationale and field experiments. *American Journal of Clinical Hypnosis* 7:8–32.

Erickson, M., and Rossi, E. (1976). Two-level communication and the microdynamics of trance and suggestion. *American Journal of Clinical Hypnosis* 18:153–171.

—— (1980). The indirect forms of suggestion. In *The Collected Papers of Milton H. Erickson*, vol 1, ed. E. Rossi, pp. 452–477. New York: Irvington.

SUGGESTED READING

Wilson, R. (1985). Interspersal of hypnotic phenomena within ongoing treatment. In *Ericksonian Psychotherapy*, vol. 2, *Clinical Applications*, ed. J. Zieg, pp . 179–184. New York: Brunner/Mazel.

—— (1987). *Don't Panic: Taking Control of Anxiety Attacks*, 2nd ed. New York: HarperCollins /Perennial Library.

—— (1987). *Breaking the Panic Cycle: Self-Help for People With Phobias.* Rockville, MD: Phobia Society of America.

CHAPTER TWELVE

In Vivo Desensitization: Anxiety Coping Techniques

Jerilyn Ross is a pioneer in the treatment of anxiety disorders. She has been particularly effective as an advocate for public awareness of the seriousness of disability accompanying anxiety disorders and the need for dissemination of information concerning effective treatments. As president of the Anxiety Disorder Association of America, she has provided the energy and direction for significant growth and communication within the field.

The chapter on in vivo desensitization included in this volume is excerpted from her training manual for paraprofessionals who work with the phobic person "in the field." It addresses pragmatic issues of how to structure the experience for the patient most effectively and provides details of the in vivo approach that are rarely available without hard-won first-hand experience. The treatment manual style of this contribution gives a hands-on view of how this material is presented to the phobic person. Some topics not covered elsewhere in the book include keeping a therapy progress daily log book, motivating the patient to enter the phobic situation, methods for positive changes in attitude during the experience, and a variety of anxiety coping techniques.

In Vivo Desensitization: Anxiety Coping Techniques

Jerilyn Ross

When treating someone for a phobia, I believe that a major part of the work must take place directly in the anxiety-provoking situation. This is known as *in vivo* or *contextual* therapy. It involves gradually introducing the phobic person into the feared situation and teaching fear-reducing techniques while the phobic anxiety is being experienced. These techniques enable the person to deal with the symptoms, while developing confidence that the feared consequences of a panic attack will not occur. At the same time, the person learns how to change maladaptive thought and behavior patterns into adaptive ones. The patient is taught to define the thoughts and symptoms as they occur, to observe what is happening internally as these thoughts and symptoms appear and disappear, and to deal with anxious feelings in a positive way.

GOAL SETTING AND THE DAILY TASK SHEET

Goal Setting

A critical part of contextual therapy is helping the patient learn to set and to work toward specific goals. Goals give the patient an opportunity to measure progress and to feel a sense of accomplishment, both of which are important for growth.

While in treatment, the patient should be encouraged to set long-term (8- and 16-week goals) and short-term (weekly, daily, and sometimes even minute-by-minute) goals. The goals should always be specific: drive to Suzy's house, meet Tom for lunch at Restaurant X, go to a job interview. They should reflect what the patient really wants to do, since motivation is a key factor in accomplishing any goal. The goals serve as guidelines and milestones.

In setting goals, discourage the patient from saying, "After 16 weeks I would like to drive without anxiety." Explain that true growth comes when you are able to enter into and stay in the situation *in spite of* anxiety.

I encourage patients to set goals that may seem overly ambitious rather than ones that are very comfortable. I explain that they can always back off if they want to. As one patient said to me at a final group session, "Sixteen weeks ago when I reluctantly set my 16-week goal as driving on the highway to my cousin's house, I thought I was crazy and so were you for encouraging me to set that as my goal. Now I do it without even thinking about it!"

The Daily Task Sheet

Overcoming a phobia is not always immediately rewarding. The opposite of feeling phobic is not necessarily feeling good. Also, panic attacks are often unpredictable so that one can do something five times without feeling phobic and the sixth time have a panic attack. Because of these uncertainties, it is particularly important to attempt to make the process of overcoming the phobia as concrete as possible.

Often, progress not only seems slow but is unrecognized. One woman who had been in treatment for 16 weeks was upset during her last session because she was still unable to drive to her office alone. However, in looking back at a daily log, she was astonished to realize that 16 weeks earlier she had not only been unable to drive there at all, but was barely able to leave her house, let alone hold down a full-time job. It was important for her to see this written in her own hand, since it was so difficult for her to acknowledge her own progress and how disabled she had been. Her experience reflected a pattern that is common for phobic people and is a barrier to recovery.

The daily log or "task sheet" is designed to be used every day until the patient is no longer avoiding the phobic place, object, or situation. I constantly reinforce the idea that patience and perseverance are essential for recovery.

To maximize the effectiveness of using a "task sheet," I have the patient begin each week by setting a specific goal for that week and then breaking it down into daily tasks, noting the *day of the week* and the *specific task*. Specific tasks, for example, might be:

11. Drive to the grocery store alone.

12. Make a purchase in a specific department store.

13. Have lunch with a friend.

14. Get a haircut at the beauty parlor.

15. Ask one question at a business meeting.

16. Use an elevator to visit a friend on the fifteenth floor.

17. Attend a religious service.

18. Visit a museum.

19. Give a dinner party.

10. Use public transportation to visit a friend.

The primary purpose of the task sheet is to make note of the following:

With Whom

Will you do this task alone or with a support person? If the latter, note who that person will be.

Highest Projected Level

Think about and write down the anxiety level you think you will reach when you confront the phobic situation. Zero (0) level means no phobic anxiety. Ten (10) is absolute panic. The number given to the anxiety is a subjective rating.

Highest Actual Level

After you have completed your task, write down the highest phobic level you actually reached. Note how it compares to your Highest Projected Level. Usually the level that you actually reach is much lower than the one you thought you would reach. It is important to recognize this for three reasons: 1) the next time you think about entering a phobic situation and are afraid you will experience a high level of anxiety, you can recall that the last time was not as bad as you anticipated; 2) you can begin to develop trust that the anticipatory anxiety is almost always worse than the anxiety experienced while actually in the phobic situation; 3) even if your level is high, you will notice how quickly it comes down.

How Long

What is the duration of time spent in the practice session? This does not mean how long you felt uncomfortable, but rather the length of the practice situation itself.

PHYSICAL SYMPTOMS

Rapid heartbeat, sweaty palms, feelings of disassociation, "noodle legs," difficulty breathing, and so on. Notice how these vary from session to session.

THOUGHTS

Write down any thoughts, positive or negative, which either contributed to the phobic feelings or lessened them. Notice whether your thoughts involved magical or exaggerated thinking and, if so, what that did to your anxiety level.

WHAT YOU ACTUALLY DID

The more specific you are the better. For example: "Took the #2 bus to Joan's house."

HELPFUL TECHNIQUES

List anything that helped you stay in the phobic situation, such as "counted backwards from 100 by 3s," "talked to the bus driver," "counted the red cars on the highway."

SATISFACTION LEVEL

Although the temptation will be for you to rate yourself with a high grade only if you accomplish your task without feeling high levels of anxiety, it is important that you do just the opposite, that is, consider the practice session a success if you accomplish your task *in spite of* the high levels of anxiety. Remember, the fact that you completed the task even though it was not comfortable means you had a successful session, and that should be acknowledged and celebrated.

IN VIVO PRACTICE

Motivation for Practicing

It is important to structure the practice situation in a way that is both practical and motivational. The more you can set up real-life practice situations with real rewards, the more energy you will have toward pursuing your goal. Some examples of "practical" practice situations:

1. An agoraphobic woman who was afraid to drive alone accepted an interesting part-time job that was a distance from her home. Although difficult at first, her motivation to get to the office overcame her fear of what could happen to her if she had a panic attack en route. Thus, she was forced to practice every day and eventually became comfortable with the trip.

2. A public speaking phobic accepted the role of president of his synagogue and therefore had to confront the various committees and members on a regular basis. It was anxiety-provoking at first, but after a while his only complaint was that he had waited so long to accept the challenge.

Beginning the In Vivo Practice

The first step is difficult, and often the patient will procrastinate to avoid getting started. I help the person get started by suggesting the following:

Begin with something easy and manageable. *No step is too small.* Each step leads to the next, no matter how insignificant it may seem at the time.

If your goal is to go into the store and buy ten grocery items, begin by just walking into the store, picking up one item, and feeling good about it. If that is too difficult, just walk in and out of the store and feel good about that. If that is too difficult, just walk up to the door of the store and try to stand there for several minutes. If you feel you cannot do that, just get out of your car and walk within ten feet of the store. If that is too difficult, just drive into the parking lot near the store. Keep breaking down your steps until you find one that you can take. As you reach each step, wait a few seconds, take a deep breath, and take one more step. If necessary, take one step back, rest a few seconds, and then go forward again. If you feel foolish about only going as far as the entrance to the store, or only as far as the parking lot, think of the alternative: not to do anything at all. Take a deep breath and *go!*

To deal with the anxiety experienced in the phobic situation, I tell the patient to keep in mind that the more uncomfortable they feel during the practice sessions, the more they are truly practicing and progressing. As they continue breaking down the steps and move forward, they *should* experience some anxiety. The longer and more often they can practice at this level, the more progress they will make.

Staying in the Situation

Repetitive exposure to the phobic situation is a critical part of treatment. I explain to the patient the necessity for practice every day in the phobic situation in the following manner:

> In the past, you have found that when you leave the phobic situation your anxiety level goes down. You are therefore tempted to leave as soon as you begin to feel uncomfortable, assuming that this is the only way to be relieved of your phobic feelings. If you *remain* in the phobic situation, you will find that your anxiety level will also go down. Each time you stay long enough to see your anxiety level come down without having to leave, you reinforce the idea

that nothing will happen to you. This is difficult at first, but it becomes progressively easier with constant practice.

If you feel you absolutely *must* leave, try to wait out the panic and *then* leave. Let the feelings pass. The worst will only be a few seconds. Your aim is to delay your leaving long enough for the panic to diminish. Then you may leave, rest a while, and go back. It is very important for you to go back to a place where you felt uncomfortable as soon as you can. Go back, step by step, but be sure to *go back*.

Coping With Anticipatory Anxiety

For phobic/panic patients, the anticipatory anxiety is often worse than the panic attack itself. To help the patient cope with this, I distribute the following list of helpful hints:

1. When you find yourself thinking of what might happen (future thinking), use the technique of *staying in the present*. You are not presently in the phobic situation, so keep your thoughts focused on where you are at the moment, what is going on around you, who you are with, and so on.

2. When you begin to think of all the "what ifs," tell yourself, "So what!" Allow yourself to face the absolute worst. Say, "The worst that will happen to me is that I will go crazy, have a heart attack, or make a fool of myself." None of these things will happen to you because of your phobia. The more you face and accept your fears, the less intense they will become.

3. Think about a time you thought you could not do something and were then surprised at being able to do it. Think back to how much more difficult it seemed before you actually did it, how it really wasn't that bad (you *did* survive), and how pleased you felt with yourself afterwards.

4. Become aware of the discrepancy between your anticipated anxiety level and the level you reach while actually in the pho-

bic situation. Each time you are about to enter a phobic situation, ask yourself, "What level do I think I will reach?" Then notice what really happens. After several experiences, you will begin to see that the level of anxiety you actually reach is rarely as high as your projected level.

5. There is a tendency to rehearse the potential bad feelings again and again, because of a belief that this better prepares you for when the panic hits. Just the opposite is true. The less attention you give to your feelings and symptoms, the less vivid they become and, thus, the less frightening. When you find yourself rehearsing, change that *primary thought. Stay in the present.* Remember, you want to let go of those phobic thoughts so that they will eventually die of neglect.

6. To help disrupt the chain of anticipatory anxiety, you might try *thought stopping.* When you begin to anticipate a panic attack, give yourself the command, "*Stop!*" Say it to yourself or scream it out loud, but make sure you are firm about it. Say it as soon as you have anxious thoughts about entering a phobic situation. Also, put a rubber band on your wrist and snap it every time your phobic thought re-occurs.

Hints to Stop Fears of Loss of Control

I help patients cope with frightening thoughts and impulses by presenting the following:

Many people with anxiety disorders have experienced that sudden, overwhelmingly frightening, feeling that they are going to lose control of themselves and do something harmful or humiliating to themselves or to someone else. One might suddenly feel a compulsion to jump while standing on a high balcony, a sudden urge to head into oncoming traffic while driving, an overwhelming urge to scream in a theater or at a business meeting. This is a *common* experience. While these impulses seem very real and frightening when they occur, they are only *thoughts* and are in no way dangerous. You are responsible for your actions, but not for your thoughts and feelings. You have no control over which thoughts and feelings will enter your mind, but you do have complete control over what you do with them. As overwhelming as these frightening thoughts and impulses may seem, remember that you do *not* really want to hurt yourself or someone else, or make a fool of yourself, and so you *won't*. These thoughts are similar to dreams, and we all know how creative and bizarre dreams can be. Remind yourself that you have never acted on these or similar thoughts.

The more you *try* to lose your frightening thoughts and impulses the more difficulty you will have in getting rid of them. The more willing you are to accept them as frightening, but not dangerous, the more they will begin to diminish. Tell yourself, "I've experienced this before and nothing happened. The scary thoughts have passed before and I know they will pass again." Allow yourself to face the worst.

The worst will not happen; you know that intellectually. To really believe it, you must allow yourself to experience the worst, no matter how scared you are. For example, try sitting in the middle of the theater and imagine yourself screaming. Stand on a balcony and imagine yourself jumping. Accept the thought. The less you fight your thoughts, the less vivid they will become. Once you truly accept these thoughts and impulses, they will lose their nightmarish power and begin to become less important to you. Eventually they will disappear.

CONCLUSION

Treating a phobic patient with in vivo therapy can be as exciting and rewarding for the therapist as for the patient. Dramatic progress often occurs after just a few sessions. For the best results, allow for setbacks and display the same kind of understanding patience one would have while leading a child toward his first steps. To the patient, confronting a phobic situation is often that monumental!

CHAPTER THIRTEEN

In Vivo Desensitization: Contextual Analysis

⸺⸻⸺

Dr. Manuel Zane began one of the first phobia clinics in the United States at White Plains Hospital in 1972. He pioneered the idea, now so widely accepted, that the anxiety is gradually diminished in the context of the phobic situation itself. His approach, for which he coined the term *contextual therapy*, is now more commonly called *in vivo desensitization*. He advocates using contextual therapy as a research tool to observe directly the rapid changes that take place in the phobic person while in the phobic situation.

This chapter presents the "Six Points of Contextual Analysis and Treatment" he developed with Doreen Powell. These six points incorporate the core ideas in desensitization, and they can serve either as a guideline for the therapist in the field or as a self-help reminder for the patient.

⸺⸻⸺

In Vivo Desensitization: Contextual Analysis

Manuel D. Zane

EXPECT AND ACCEPT YOUR PHOBIA

When you enter, or try to enter, the phobic situation, expect that you are going to become frightened and have physical reactions, whatever they may be in your case—rapid heartbeat, difficulty in breathing, butterflies in the stomach, weak legs, sweating hands, blurry eyes, dizziness, lightheadedness, and so on. It is your past phobic experiences that automatically trigger your physical feelings. It is your phobic thoughts about what you imagine is going to happen that make your physical and mental reactions get worse and accelerate. Try to recognize these negative, phobic thoughts when they start to come and then change them. Substitute more realistic thoughts for the negative ones. This is difficult to do and takes some work, but with practice it can be done.

It is helpful if you can accept the fact that you have a phobia. Try not to get angry or upset at not being able to do what other people can do. Anger, envy, and embarrassment simply add other negative feelings to those with which you already must cope.

WHEN FEAR APPEARS, WAIT

This is very hard to do, but it can be accomplished with practice. When you find your fear level rising, stop, wait, and try not to run out or rush back to your place of comfort. Expose yourself to the fear little by little and stay with it. Remember that phobic people have a fear of the fear itself.

FOCUS ON THINGS IN THE PRESENT

Anticipatory thoughts of the phobic situation are usually negative and destructive. Try to stay with the present and not project ahead to what might be; generally, anticipatory thoughts are much worse than what actually occurs. Catch yourself running ahead when you start to say, *"What if this should happen?"*

LABEL YOUR FEAR LEVEL 1–10, AND WATCH IT GO UP AND DOWN

Number 10 is a fear level so bad that you almost cannot tolerate it; number 1 is the absence of fear. Many people, after being in a phobic situation, will tell you that they were up at 10 the whole time. When you state your level of fear in the situation, you will find the level goes up and down and doesn't usually stay at 10. When you are thinking about your level of fear, this is the first step in changing your thoughts. The reason is that when you concentrate on what your fear level is, it is harder for the negative thoughts to get through. Thus you change your thinking.

DO THINGS THAT LOWER AND KEEP MANAGEABLE THE LEVEL OF FEAR

Each individual has to find his own ways to handle his fear in particular situations. Here are some examples of what some people have done to keep the fear level manageable: one person sings when he is driving his car—the sound of his voice is a comfort to him. Another person tells himself, "I will just let it be, I won't fight it. Let the feelings come, they are only feelings, I'm not going to faint. I haven't done so yet, and even if I do, so what?" Another person keeps a picture of his family on the dashboard of his car. When he finds the feelings coming on, he quickly glances at the picture and asks himself, "What is so different from sitting here in my car than sitting at home in the living room?" He also touches the material of the seat of the car to bring his thoughts back to the present—to keep connected to the familiar environment. To touch familiar objects, to see and recognize familiar things, helps bring the fear level down.

TRY TO FUNCTION WITH FEAR

If you try to eliminate the fear altogether, you are fighting it and not letting it be. If you can accept it and let it be, it will decrease. Learning that you can do things to bring your fear level down is the first step to being able to cope in the phobic situation. Be proud of your achievements, however small, while expecting that your fear may reappear.

CHAPTER FOURTEEN

Psychoeducation

————————

This chapter is part of the psychoeducational material distributed to those attending Dr. Barlow's clinic. Most experts recommend the use of some body of educational material in the beginning stages of treatment, and this convention has considerable research support. This chapter addresses the questions frequently asked and provides an excellent manner of conveying this body of information.

Those who approach this book from a psychodynamic background may find the idea of "teaching" the patient objectionable. Notice, however, that all the authors in this section of the book emphasize the need to provide educational information. The reason is found in the nature of the panic attack, which is so overwhelming that it is experienced as a profoundly disturbing loss of psychological control. The anxiety-stricken patients often present with fears that they are going crazy or having a "nervous breakdown." Information about panic disorder relieves the patient's fear of loss of sanity. Further, because intense anxiety is so disorganizing in its effects on rational and purposeful thought, the information performs an additional service in the beginning stage of treatment as an understandable and supportive communication.

This chapter is an excerpt from the manual *Mastery of Your Anxiety and Panic* describing the treatment program for panic attacks and panic disorder developed at the center for Stress and Anxiety Disorders of the State University of New York at Albany. Information on obtaining this manual is available from Graywind Publications, The Psychological Corporation, c/o Customer Service, P.O. Box 839954, San Antonio, TX 78283-3954.

————————

Psychoeducation

RONALD M. RAPEE
MICHELLE CRASKE
DAVID H. BARLOW

PHYSIOLOGY OF ANXIETY

Anxiety is probably the most basic of all emotions. Not only is it experienced by all humans, but anxiety responses have been found in all species of animals right down to the sea slug. Anxiety experiences vary in severity from mild uneasiness to terror and panic. They can also vary in their length, from a brief flash to a constant ordeal. While anxiety, by its nature and definition, is an unpleasant sensation, it is not dangerous. This last point is the theme of this chapter. These pages describe the components (physical and mental) of anxiety in order that (1) you realize that many of the feelings you now experience are the result of anxiety and (2) you learn that these feelings are not harmful or dangerous.

Anxiety Defined

While a definition of anxiety that covers all aspects is very difficult to provide (indeed, whole books have been written on the subject), everyone knows the feeling that we call anxiety. There is no one who has not experienced some degree of anxiety, whether, for example, it is the feeling upon entering a school room just before an exam, or the feeling when one wakes in the middle of the night, certain of having heard a strange sound outside. What is less known, however, is that sensations such as extreme dizziness, spots and blurring of the eyes, numbness and tingling, stiff, almost paralyzed muscles, and feelings of breathlessness extending to choking or smothering can also be a part of anxiety. When these sensations occur and people do not understand why, then anxiety can increase to levels of panic, since people imagine that they must have some disease.

Fight/Flight Response

Anxiety is a response to danger or threat. Scientifically, immediate or short-term anxiety is termed the *fight/flight response*. It is so named because all of its effects are aimed toward either fighting or fleeing the danger. Thus, the number-one purpose of anxiety is to protect the organism. Back in the days when we were cave people, it was vital that when some danger faced us, an automatic response would take over, causing us to take immediate action (attack or run). Even in today's hectic world this response is necessary. Just imagine yourself crossing a street when suddenly a car speeds toward you blasting its horn. If you experienced absolutely no anxiety, you would be killed. Probably, however, your fight/flight response would take over and you would run out of the way to be safe. The moral of this story is simple: *the purpose of anxiety is to protect the organism, not to harm it.*

Systems of Anxiety

Anxiety manifests itself through three separate systems, any one of which can be primary in a particular person. The *mental system* includes the actual feelings of nervousness, anxiety, and panic and also thoughts, such as "There is something wrong." The *physical system* includes all the physical symptoms, such as dizziness, sweating, palpitations, chest pain, and breathlessness. The *behavioral system* includes the actual activities such as pacing, foot tapping, and avoidance. In panic attacks the physical system becomes the most important, since it is the physical symptoms that are most easily mistaken as indicating some serious disease.

The best way to think of all of the systems of the fight/flight response (anxiety) is to remember that they are all aimed at getting the organism prepared for immediate action and that their purpose is to protect the organism.

Physical System

NERVOUS AND CHEMICAL EFFECTS

When some sort of danger is perceived or anticipated, the brain sends messages to a section of your nerves called the *autonomic nervous system*. The autonomic nervous system has two subsections or branches: the *sympathetic nervous system* and the *parasympathetic nervous system*. These two branches of the nervous system are directly involved in controlling the body's energy levels and preparation for action. Very simply put, the sympathetic nervous system is the fight/flight system that releases energy and gets the body "primed" for action, while the parasympathetic nervous system is the restoring system that returns the body to a normal state.

The sympathetic nervous system tends to be largely an all-or-none system. When it is activated, all of its parts respond. In other words, either all symptoms are experienced or no symptoms are experienced; it is rare for changes to occur in only one part of the body. This may explain why most panic attacks involve many symptoms and not just one or two.

A major effect of the sympathetic nervous system is that it releases *two* chemicals, adrenaline and noradrenaline, from the adrenal glands on the kidneys. These chemicals are used as messengers by the sympathetic nervous system to continue activity, so that once activity in the sympathetic nervous system begins, it often continues and increases for some time. This activity, however, is stopped in two ways. First, the chemical messengers adrenaline and noradrenaline are eventually destroyed by other chemicals in the body. Second, the parasympathetic nervous system (which generally has opposing effects to the sympathetic nervous system) becomes activated and restores a relaxed feeling.

It is very important to realize that eventually the body will "have enough" of the fight/flight response and will activate the parasympathetic nervous system to restore a relaxed feeling. In other words, anxiety cannot continue forever, nor spiral to ever-increasing and possibly damaging levels. The parasympathetic nervous system is an inbuilt protector, which stops the sympathetic nervous system from getting carried away.

Another important point is that the chemical messengers, adrenaline and noradrenaline, take some time to be destroyed. Thus, even after the danger has passed and your sympathetic nervous system has stopped responding, you are likely to feel keyed up or apprehensive for some time, because the chemicals are still floating around in your system. You must remind yourself that this is perfectly natural and harmless. In fact this is an adaptive function. In the wilds, danger often has a habit of returning, and it is useful for the organism to be prepared to activate the fight/flight response.

CARDIOVASCULAR EFFECTS

Activity in the sympathetic nervous system produces an increase in heart rate and in the strength of the heartbeat. This is vital to preparation for activity, since it helps speed up the blood flow, thus improving delivery of oxygen to the tissues and removal of waste products from the tissues. There is also a change in the blood flow. Basically, blood is redirected away from places where it is not needed (by a tightening of the blood vessels) and toward places where it is needed more (by an expansion of the blood vessels). For example, blood is taken away from the skin, fingers, and toes. This is useful because if the organism is attacked and cut in some way, it is less likely to bleed to death. Hence, during anxiety the skin looks pale and feels cold, and fingers and toes become cold and sometimes experience numbness and tingling. In addition, the blood is moved to the large muscles, such as the thighs and biceps, which helps the body prepare for action.

RESPIRATORY EFFECTS

The fight/flight response is associated with an increase in the speed and depth of breathing. This has obvious importance for the defense of the organism, since the tissues need to get more oxygen in order to prepare for action. The feelings produced by this increase in breathing, however, can include breathlessness, a sense of choking or smothering, and even pains or tightness in the chest. Importantly, a side effect of increased breathing, especially if no actual activity occurs, is that blood supply to the head is actually decreased. While this reduction is small and is not at all dangerous, it produces a collection of unpleasant (but harmless) symptoms, including dizziness, blurred vision, confusion, a sense of unreality, and hot flushes.

SWEAT-GLAND EFFECTS

Activation of the fight/flight response produces an increase in sweating. This has important adaptive functions, such as making the skin more slippery so that it is harder for a predator to grab, and cooling the body to stop it from overheating.

OTHER PHYSICAL EFFECTS

A number of other effects are produced by activation of the sympathetic nervous system, none of which is in any way harmful. For example, the pupils widen to let in more light, which may result in blurred vision, spots in front of the eyes, and so on. There is a decrease in salivation, resulting in a dry mouth. There is decreased activity in the digestive system, which often produces nausea, a heavy feeling in the stomach, and even constipation. Finally, many of the muscle groups tense up in preparation for fight or flight, and this results in subjective feelings of tension, sometimes extending to actual aches and pains as well as trembling and shaking.

Overall, the fight/flight response results in a general activation of the whole bodily metabolism. Thus, one often feels hot and flushed. Afterwards, because this process takes a lot of energy, the person generally feels tired, drained, and washed out.

Behavioral System

As mentioned before, the fight/flight response prepares the body for action—either to attack or to run. Thus, it is no surprise that the overwhelming urges associated with this response are those of aggression and a desire to escape from wherever you are. When this is not possible (owing to social constraints), the urges will often be shown through such behaviors as foot tapping, pacing, or snapping at people. Overall, the feelings produced are those of being trapped and needing to escape.

Mental System

The number-one effect of the fight/flight response is to alert the organism to the possible existence of danger. Thus, a major effect is an immediate and automatic shift in attention to search the surroundings for potential threat. In other words, it is very difficult to concentrate on daily tasks when one is anxious. Therefore, people who are anxious often complain that they are easily distracted from daily chores, that they cannot concentrate, and that they have trouble with their memory. This is a normal and important part of the fight/ flight response, since its purpose is to stop you from attending to your ongoing chores and to permit you to scan your surroundings for possible danger. Sometimes an obvious threat cannot be found. Many humans, however, cannot accept having no explanation for something, and so they turn their search upon themselves. In other words, "If nothing out there is making me feel anxious, there must be something wrong with me." The brain now invents an explanation, such as, "I must be dying, losing control, or going crazy." As we have seen, nothing could be further from the truth, since the purpose of the fight/flight response is to protect the organism, not harm it. Nevertheless, these are understandable thoughts.

Panic Attacks

Up until now, we have looked at the features and components of general anxiety, or the fight/flight response. How does all this apply to panic attacks? After all, why should the fight/flight response be activated during panic attacks, since there is apparently nothing to be frightened of?

Following extensive research, it appears that what people with panic attacks are frightened of (i.e., what causes the panic) is the actual physical experience of the fight/flight response. Thus, panic attacks can be seen as a set of unexpected physical symptoms and *then* a response of panic or fear of the symptoms such as illustrated below:

$$\begin{bmatrix} \text{pounding heart,} \\ \text{dizziness, etc.} \end{bmatrix} \longrightarrow \begin{bmatrix} \text{fear,} \\ \text{panic} \end{bmatrix} \quad \begin{bmatrix} \text{pounding heart} \\ \text{dizziness, etc.} \end{bmatrix}$$

The second part of this model is easy to understand. As discussed earlier, the fight/flight response (of which the physical symptoms are a part) causes the brain to search for danger. When the brain cannot find any obvious danger, it turns its search inward and invents a danger, such as, "I am dying, losing control, and so on." This is illustrated below:

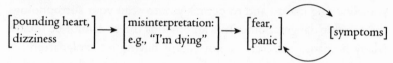

The first part of the model is harder to understand. Why do you experience the physical symptoms of the fight/flight response if you are not frightened to begin with? There are many ways these symptoms can be produced, not just through fear. For example, perhaps you have become generally stressed for some reason in your life, and this stress results in an increase in production of adrenaline and other chemicals, which from time to time produce symptoms. This increased adrenaline might be maintained chemically in the body even after the stressor has long gone. Another possibility is that you tend to breathe a little too fast (subtle hyperventilation), owing to a learned habit, and this also can produce symptoms. Because the overbreathing is very slight, you easily become used to it and do not notice that you are hyperventilating. A third possibility is that you are experiencing normal changes in your body (which everyone experiences but most don't notice), and, because you are constantly monitoring and keeping a check on your body, you notice these sensations far more strongly than most people.

Even if we are not exactly certain why you experience the initial symptoms, we can assure you that they are a part of the fight/flight response and therefore are *harmless*.

Thus, our final model of panic attacks (simplified) looks like this:

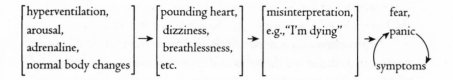

Obviously, then, once you truly believe (100 percent) that the physical sensations are not dangerous, then the fear and panic will no longer occur, and you will eventually no longer experience panic attacks. Of course, once you have had a number of panic attacks and have misinterpreted the symptoms many times, this misinterpretation becomes quite automatic, and it becomes very difficult to consciously convince yourself during a panic attack that the symptoms are harmless.

Anxiety Summarized

Anxiety is scientifically known as the fight/flight response, since its primary purpose is to activate the organism and protect it from harm. Associated with this response are a number of physical, behavioral, and mental changes. Importantly, once the danger has gone, many of these changes (especially the physical ones) can continue, almost with a mind of their own, owing to learning and other longer-term bodily changes. When the physical symptoms occur in the absence of an obvious explanation, people often misinterpret the normal fight/flight symptoms as indicating a serious physical or mental problem. In this case, the sensations themselves often can become threatening and can restart the whole fight/flight response.

MYTHS AND MISINTERPRETATIONS

Going Crazy

Many people, when they experience the physical symptoms of the fight/flight response, believe they are going crazy. They are most likely referring to a severe mental disorder known as schizophrenia. Let us look at schizophrenia to see how likely this is.

Schizophrenia is a major disorder characterized by such severe symptoms as disjointed thoughts and speech, sometimes extending to babbling, delusions, or strange beliefs (for example, that they are receiving messages from outer space) and hallucinations (for example, that there are voices in their head). Furthermore, schizophrenia appears to be largely a genetically based disorder, running strongly in families.

Schizophrenia generally begins very gradually and not suddenly (such as during a panic attack). Additionally, because it runs in families, only a certain proportion of people can become schizophrenic. In other people, no amount of stress will cause the disorder. A third important point is that people who become schizophrenic will usually show some mild symptoms for most of their lives (unusual thoughts, flowery speech, etc.). Thus, if this has not been noticed in you yet, then the chances are you will not become schizophrenic. This is especially true if you are over 25, since schizophrenia generally first appears in the late teens to early twenties. Finally, if you have been through interviews with a psychologist or psychiatrist, then you can be fairly certain that they would have known if you were likely to become schizophrenic.

Losing Control

Some people during a panic attack believe they are going to lose control. Presumably, they mean that either they will become totally paralyzed and not be able to move, or they will not know what they are doing and will run around wildly killing people or yelling out obscenities and embarrassing themselves. Alternatively, they may not know what to expect but may just experience an overwhelming feeling of impending doom.

From our earlier discussion, we now know where this feeling comes from. During anxiety the entire body is prepared for action, and there is an overwhelming desire to escape. However, the fight/flight response is not aimed at hurting other people (who are not a threat) and it will not produce paralysis. Rather, the entire response is simply aimed at getting the organism away. In addition, there has never been a recorded case of someone "going wild" during a panic attack. Even though the fight/flight response makes you feel somewhat confused, unreal, and distracted, you are still able to think and function normally. Simply think of how seldom other people even notice that you are having a panic attack.

Nervous Collapse

Many people are frightened about what might happen to them as a result of their symptoms, perhaps because of some belief that their nerves may become exhausted and they may collapse. As discussed earlier, the fight/flight response is produced chiefly through activity in the sympathetic nervous system, which is counteracted by the parasympathetic nervous system. The parasympathetic nervous system is, in a sense, a safeguard to protect against the possibility that the sympathetic nervous system may become "worn out." Nerves are not like electrical wires, and anxiety cannot wear out, damage, or use up nerves. The absolute worst that could happen during a panic attack is that an individual could pass out, at which point the sympathetic nervous system would stop its activity and the person would regain consciousness within a few seconds. However, actually passing out as a result of the fight/flight response is extremely rare, and if it does occur, it is adaptive, since it is a way of stopping the sympathetic nervous system from going "out of control."

Heart Attacks

Many people misinterpret the symptoms of the fight/flight response and believe they must be dying of a heart attack. This is probably because many people do not have enough knowledge about heart attacks. Let us look at the facts and see how heart disease differs from panic attacks.

The major symptoms of heart disease are breathlessness and chest pain as well as occasional palpitations and fainting. These symptoms are generally directly related to effort, that is, the harder you exercise, the worse the symptoms, and the less you exercise, the better. The symptoms will usually go away fairly quickly with rest. The symptoms associated with panic attacks, on the other hand, often occur at rest and seem to have a mind of their own. Certainly, panic symptoms can occur during exercise or can be made worse during exercise, but they differ from the symptoms of a heart attack, since they can occur equally often at rest. Of most importance, heart disease will almost always produce major electrical changes in the heart, which are picked up very obviously by the EKG. In panic attacks the only change that shows up on the EKG is a slight increase in heart rate. Thus, if you have had an EKG and the doctor has given you the all-clear, you can safely assume you do not have heart disease. Also, if your symptoms occur in various situations and not only upon exertion, this is additional evidence against your having a heart attack.

CHAPTER FIFTEEN

Medication

———»○«———

As noted in the introductory chapter, psychopharmacology and the biochemical understanding of anxiety disorders have become crucial aspects of treatment. Major innovations and improvements in pharmacotherapy are continuing in an explosion of new research.

This chapter has been revised from the first edition to provide an up-to-date, practical orientation to the medications currently in use, with special emphasis on medication for obsessive-compulsive disorder.

———»○«———

Medication

ERIC HOLLANDER
BONNIE R. ARONOWITZ
DONALD F. KLEIN

INTRODUCTION

Pharmacological treatment of the anxiety disorders can be a gratifying experience for the informed psychiatrist. Rarely does a group
of disorders have such a clear response to medication or show such
dramatic relief in patients' subjective distress.

This chapter will summarize current approaches to the pharmacological treatment of panic disorder, generalized anxiety disorder, social phobia, and obsessive-compulsive disorder. Rather than
providing an exhaustive review of controlled studies, it describes
practical approaches and common pitfalls.

GENERAL PRINCIPLES

Treatment approaches differ for different types of anxiety disorders.
This makes precise differential diagnosis crucial prior to treatment.
Treatments highly effective for one type of anxiety may be ineffec-

tive for another. In addition, it is imperative to rule out underlying medical conditions that might masquerade as anxiety disorders. These include, but are not limited to, thyroid and parathyroid disease, pheochromocytoma, cardiac abnormalities and arrhythmias, temporal-lobe epilepsy, alcohol and substance abuse and withdrawal (cocaine in particular), and caffeinism.

Since anxiety patients are often extremely sensitive to medication and may actually experience a paradoxical exacerbation of symptoms early in treatment, especially if initial doses are too high, one must begin with very low doses, and the patient should be warned about this possibility. Another treatment problem frequently encountered is the use of inadequate doses of medication or duration of treatment. Patients should receive an adequate trial of a given medication prior to the decision to change medication. Thus the maxim "start low, go high, and persist" is appropriate.

MEDICATION TREATMENT
OF PANIC DISORDERS

Pharmacological treatment of panic disorder is based on the three-stage model of panic developed by Klein (1981). The core or primary symptom is recurrent, spontaneous panic attacks. Repeated experience of unexpected panic attacks leads to anticipatory anxiety or dread about when or where the next attack will occur. Many patients then begin to avoid situations in which help might be unavailable or escape difficult if a panic attack occurs. This is the agoraphobic complication of panic disorder.

The initial goal of treatment is to block the spontaneous panic attacks with medication. Achieving this usually takes several weeks. Patients are then encouraged to re-enter phobic situations. This will confirm that the patient no longer panics in the feared situation, and this assurance will help extinguish the avoidance behavior. Persistent absence of panic in spite of return to normal activity extinguishes the anticipatory anxiety as well.

The patient must learn to distinguish between panic and anticipatory anxiety, since many medications block panic but not anticipatory anxiety. In measuring effects of drug treatment, it is necessary to specifically inquire about spontaneous panic attacks, anticipatory anxiety, and phobic avoidance. The patient needs to keep a daily diary of anxiety symptoms and episodes during the course of treatment. Often patients will state that they are unimproved because of persisting anticipatory anxiety, but a diary review shows sharp improvement in the panic attacks themselves.

A central feature of panic is fear of loss of control. It is helpful to provide reassurance that medication specifically tailored to panic attacks will not affect patients' ability to control themselves or the environment. It is also important to discuss possible early side effects of the medication, so that patients do not interpret somatic sensations as signs of imminent panic.

Before initiation of treatment, an individualized medical evaluation is necessary to rule out other illnesses masquerading as panic or anxiety, as discussed above, and to determine the presence of preexisting medical illnesses that might be exacerbated by treatment (i.e., tricyclic antidepressants) such as cardiac conduction defects and narrow-angle glaucoma. Other illnesses may preclude specific treatments, such as asthma precluding MAO inhibitors.

Antidepressants

Tricyclics

The central feature in the treatment of panic disorder is the pharmacologic blockade of the spontaneous panic attacks. Several classes of medication are effective in accomplishing this. The most widely studied are the tricyclic antidepressants, especially imipramine, desipramine, and clomipramine. Other tricyclics, including nortriptyline and amitriptyline, have not been systematically studied. Monoamine oxidase inhibitors (MAOIs) are effective anti-panic drugs but are usually reserved for patients who do not respond to tricyclic antidepressants. The presence of depressed mood is not a requirement for any of these drugs to be effective in blocking panic attacks.

Imipramine has been the most extensively studied tricyclic. Klein (Klein and Fink 1962, Klein 1964) first noted the anti-panic effects of imipramine in studies of hospitalized phobic anxiety patients. Imipramine blocked panic but had little effect on anticipatory anxiety or phobic avoidance. Subsequent double-blind studies confirmed the superiority of imipramine compared to placebo (Sheehan et al. 1980, Zitrin et al. 1978). Patients with panic attacks but without agoraphobia respond equally as well as agoraphobics with panic (Garakani et al. 1984). The anti-panic effect of imipramine has been demonstrated to be independent of the presence of depression (Mavissakalian and Michelson 1986, Zitrin et al. 1983). There is some evidence that higher doses yield better outcomes (Mavissakalian and Perel 1985, Zitrin et al. 1983).

When initiating a drug regimen, it is crucial for the patient to understand that the drug will block the panic attacks but not necessarily decrease the amount of intervening anticipatory anxiety. Therefore, patients may also require a benzodiazepine for a short time to reduce the level of anticipatory anxiety.

Some patients with panic disorder display an initial hypersensitivity to tricyclic antidepressants and monoamine oxidase inhibitors in which they complain of jitteriness, agitation, a "speedy" feeling, and insomnia. This is transient, but it is recommended that patients with panic disorder be started on lower doses of tricyclics or monoamine oxidase inhibitors than would be given to depressed patients.

One regimen is to start the patient at a dosage of 10 mg daily, at night, of imipramine and increase the dose by 10 mg every other night until 50 mg is reached. The dosage may be administered all at once. Since imipramine tends to be sedating, bedtime dosing is helpful for insomnia and for reducing daytime drowsiness. The occasional patient who is overstimulated can take the medication in the morning. If 50 mg is inadequate for full panic blockade, the dosage is raised by 25 mg increments every 3 days or by 50 mg weekly to as high as 300 mg. Most patients require a minimum of 150 mg daily of tricyclics. Unfortunately, underdosage commonly occurs. In some cases a dosage of imipramine over 300 mg is necessary. This requires monitoring of the electrocardiogram. Panic patients not responding to 300 mg/day of imipramine should have blood tricyclic levels measured. Often, blood levels will be disproportionately low for the dose, suggesting rapid metabolism, excretion, malabsorption, or noncompliance.

Patients who experience excessive anticholinergic side effects to imipramine may instead be administered desipramine. Desipramine treatment is often accompanied by less dry mouth, blurred vision, and constipation. In addition, there is less sedation, so that daytime drug administration is possible.

Once full remission of panic attacks has been accomplished, it is recommended that the patient be maintained on medication for 6 months to a full year to prevent early relapse. After this, it is reasonable to taper the patient from medication. Although, for many, panic disorder tends to be a recurrent condition, several studies suggest that up to two-thirds of patients will not relapse immediately after cessation of medication (Cohen et al. 1984, Zitrin et al. 1983). Further studies in this area are needed.

Preliminary studies have indicated that tricyclic antidepressants may also be effective in treating chronically anxious patients who have neither depression nor panic.

MAO INHIBITORS

Since monoamine oxidase inhibitors (MAOIs) have the additional rare side effect of hypertensive crises, they are regarded as a second-line treatment for panic disorder. To prevent the possibility of hypertensive crisis, it is important to review a list of foods and medications that must be avoided. Foods that contain tyramine are avoided, since with the blockade of intestinal monoamine oxidase, the enzyme that normally degrades tyramine, the blood pressure may rise to dangerous levels. These foods include, but are not limited to, aged cheeses, smoked or processed meats or fish, and red wine. Tyramine is a product of protein fermentation. Other medications that are sympathomimetic should also be avoided. These include epinephrine, often used in dental procedures, or phenylpropanolamine, an over-the-counter stimulant. Illicit drugs such as cocaine and the marketed analgesic medication Demerol also must be avoided.

However, MAO inhibitors are quite effective and should be considered for those patients who do not respond to tricyclics, cannot tolerate them, or have coexistent atypical depression or social phobia, for which MAOIs may be the treatment of choice. Available MAOIs include phenelzine (Nardil), isocarboxazid (Marplan), and tranylcypromine (Parnate). In our experience the antihypertensive pargyline (Eutonyl) is also effective.

In a double-blind placebo-controlled comparison of imipramine and phenelzine in agoraphobic patients, phenelzine was slightly better than imipramine and had fewer side effects (Sheehan et al. 1980).

Phenelzine is often the MAOI used first. However, if sedation and weight gain are of great concern, tranylcypromine, which is less sedating and sometimes decreases appetite, can be administered. Phenelzine may be initiated at 15 mg daily, in a morning dose. The dose may be raised by 15 mg every 4 to 7 days, as tolerated, to a maximum dose of 90 mg. Tranylcypromine (Parnate) is begun at 10 mg in the morning. The dose may be raised by 10 mg every 3 to 4 days, as needed, to a maximum of 80 mg per day.

After informing the patient about the common side effects, as well as the rare but potentially life-threatening side effect of hypertensive crises, treatment with monoamine oxidase inhibitors may begin. Common side effects include daytime sedation, nighttime insomnia, and orthostatic hypotension. These side effects, if they arise, may be managed by reduction of the dosage. Daytime sedation may be effectively treated with the addition of caffeine in moderation or methylphenidate. Nighttime insomnia can be managed by adding 25 to 50 mg of trazodone at bedtime. Orthostatic hypotension is treated by adding salt to food, using salt tablets, or adding the mineralocorticoid florinef, 0.1 mg, 1 to 3 times per day. Other possible side effects include dry mouth, constipation, blurred vision, sweating, tremor, palpitations, urinary hesitancy, sexual side effects, anorgasmia, and liver toxicity. Pyridoxine (vitamin B6) deficiency has also been reported, presenting with numbness and tingling, and may be treated by adding B6, 100 to 300 mg per day.

The hypertensive reaction may present with a severe throbbing headache, nausea, vomiting, pounding chest and high blood pressure. While the incidence of paroxysmal headaches is about 2 percent, progression to intracranial bleeding or myocardial infarction is very rare, with the fatality rate less than one in 1,000,000 (Klein et al. 1980). Patients who experience the symptoms described should proceed to an emergency room to have their blood pressure monitored. If blood pressure is elevated, intravenous phentolamine, an alpha antagonist, is the treatment of choice. Patients may also be advised to carry a 20 mg capsule of the antianginal medication nifedipine (Procardia). At the first sign of a hypertensive reaction they chew the capsule, which rapidly lowers blood pressure. It is important to note that the risk of hypertensive crises continues for 2 weeks after discontinuation of an MAOI, so the diet must be continued during this time. Also, concomitant use of different MAOIs are incompatible, so in switching from one to the other, a 2-week washout is required. The serotonin reuptake blocker fluoxetine (Prozac) is also contraindicated for 2 weeks following discontinuation of a MAOI. In addition, one must wait 6 weeks after the discontinuation of fluoxetine, prior to beginning a MAOI.

Reversible MAOIs are new medications that hold the promise of a significant decrease of side effects over old MAOIs. An example of a reversible MAOI is moclobemide (Aurorix). Since these reversible MAOIs do not permanently inhibit the MAO enzyme, there is substantially less risk of a hypertensive reaction at therapeutic doses and therefore no dietary restrictions are required at these doses. The usual initial dose of moclobemide is 150 mg, which may be raised by 150 mg every 4 to 7 days as tolerated, to a maximum dose of 600 mg. Use of serotonin reuptake blockers, however, is contraindicated during moclobemide treatment due to the possibility of the development of a serotonin syndrome.

BENZODIAZEPINE DERIVATIVES

Panic Disorder. The high potency benzodiazepine alprazolam (Xanax) is an effective anti-panic drug and has been extensively studied. There is less data about the efficacy of the other high potency benzodiazepines, clonazepam (Klonopin) and lorazepam (Ativan), but what exists is promising. These medications have fewer initial side effects than tricyclic antidepressants and monoamine oxidase inhibitors, have a more rapid onset of action, and effectively treat the anticipatory anxiety and phobic avoidance components in addition to the acute panic attacks themselves. However, they require longer periods for withdrawal (.25 mg every 7 days is usually a safe regimen) and there is the potential for dependency and withdrawal symptoms. Doses ranging from 1 mg to 10 mg daily in divided doses are generally sufficient. Alprazolam may occasionally cause mania and clonazepam depression (Herman et al. 1987).

The major drawback of these medications is the substantial risk of withdrawal symptoms during taper (Fyer et al. 1987). In severe cases, delirium and seizures have been reported with abrupt withdrawal. Alprazolam's short duration of action may necessitate every-4-hour dosing. Because of this short half-life, the phenomenon of "clock-watching" has been reported. The patient may notice an increased level of anxiety prior to his next dose. This is less of a problem with clonazepam, which has a longer half-life. Another early side effect of these agents is sedation, which may decrease with time.

Generalized Anxiety Disorder. Generalized anxiety disorder (GAD) is characterized by persistent anxiety and worrisomeness lasting at least 6 months. Symptoms include motor tension, autonomic hyperactivity (sweating, heart pounding, and frequent urination), apprehensive expectation, and vigilance and scanning (insomnia, difficulty concentrating). The pharmacologic treatment of GAD is somewhat less well established than that of panic disorder. Traditionally, chronically anxious patients have been placed on benzodiazepines. However, it is unclear whether benzodiazepines are more effective than other drugs or treatment methods in patients specifically diagnosed with GAD. One study suggests that benzodiazepines such as chlordiazepoxide may peak in effectiveness after 4 weeks of treatment, and that tricyclics such as imipramine may be more effective for patients with generalized anxiety over the longer term (Kahn et al. 1986). However, the study may have included panic patients and thus requires replication.

Although generally safe, with side effects limited mainly to sedation, there is growing concern that some patients may become tolerant or even physiologically dependent on benzodiazepines. Available data indicate that most patients are able to stop taking them without serious sequelae and that the problem of frank addiction is substantially overestimated. It is probably limited to an addiction-prone population (e.g., past history of alcoholism) or to patients with panic disorder who often escalate standard benzodiazepine usage in unsuccessful attempts at self-medication. Withdrawal symptoms of insomnia, agitation, irritability, and sensory disturbances can occur and are considerably lessened by gradual tapering of the medication. The distinction between actual withdrawal and a simple recrudescence of the original anxiety symptoms when the benzodiazepine is discontinued is sometimes difficult to determine. However, the onset of insomnia is a useful clue for withdrawal. A few preliminary studies have shown continued efficacy of these drugs at the same dose level up to 6 months after beginning treatment.

Buspirone, a nonbenzodiazepine serotonin (5 HT) 1a agonist, is an antianxiety agent with fewer sedative properties and less potential for abuse than the benzodiazepines. It has been shown clinically efficacious in GAD but not in panic disorder. The problem is a slow onset of action and lack of subjective feeling of relaxation. 30 to 60 mg per day of buspirone in divided doses is often required for a full antianxiety effect.

SELECTIVE SEROTONIN REUPTAKE INHIBITORS

There has been a great deal of interest lately in the use of selective serotonin reuptake inhibitors for the treatment of panic disorder. Studies with a specific serotonin receptor agonist, m-CPP, have shown that panic patients have greater anxiety reactions than controls in response to this challenge (Kahn et al. 1988), suggesting some level of serotonergic hypersensitivity. Early studies with fluoxetine (Prozac) reported that many panic patients could not tolerate the 20 mg initial dose (Gorman et al. 1987). However, those who tolerated this initial dose often showed improvement. Recent studies report that the serotonin reuptake blockers fluvoxamine

(Luvox) and clomipramine (Anafranil) are equally effective in panic disorder treatment, but that clomipramine had a better antidepressant effect (Den Boer 1988). A controlled comparison of selective serotonergic (Fluvoxamine) and noradrenergic (maprotiline) antidepressants in panic disorder reported superiority for the serotonergic agent fluvoxamine (Luvox) (Den Boer 1988). In a double-blind placebo-controlled study of fluvoxamine and ritanserin (a specific 5HT-2 receptor antagonist) in panic disorder, fluvoxamine resulted in a profound reduction in the number of panic attacks, followed by a subsequent decrease in agoraphobic avoidance behavior. Treatment with ritanserin appeared ineffective (Den Boer 1988) In our clinical experience, panic disorder patients show a good response to fluoxetine (Prozac) if treatment is initiated at a low dose of 2.5 to 5 mg. The 20 mg capsule may be dissolved in water to attain this dose, or a liquid form is available. In addition to fluoxetine (Prozac) and fluvoxamine (Luvox), other serotonin reuptake inhibitors are currently on the market. These include paroxetine (Paxil) and sertraline (Zoloft), which may also have good anti-panic effects. As with fluoxetine, it is recommended to initiate treatment of the selective serotonin reuptake inhibitors at a very low dose and to gradually increase to a moderate dose, as tolerated. However, given that some panic disorder patients are particularly sensitive to the stimulating side effect of serotonin reuptake inhibitors, a new medication, nefazadone (Serzone) may be an advance. The serotonin (5 HT) 2 antagonist properties of this medication may aid in blocking the jittery side effects of serotonin reuptake inhibitors in panic patients, but requires further investigation.

OTHER MEDICATIONS

Beta-adrenergic blocking drugs, such as propranolol, are said by some to be useful in a variety of anxiety disorders but there is no proof that they are specifically effective in blocking spontaneous panic attacks. Our impression is that they are only occasionally active and work less well than tricyclic antidepressants, monoamine oxidase inhibitors, or alprazolam. They are not to be used as primary, first-choice drugs.

Clonidine, which quiets locus ceruleous discharge, would seem for theoretical reasons to be a good anti-panic drug. Although in a small series, two-thirds of patients responded (Liebowitz et al. 1981), for several the therapeutic effect was lost in a matter of weeks despite dose continuation. This, plus a number of bothersome side effects, makes clonidine a poor initial choice for panic disorder. One controlled 2-week crossover study found clonidine to be efficacious for both panic disorder and GAD (Hoehn-Saric 1981). However, Hoehn-Saric agrees that the effects are lost with time.

MEDICATION TREATMENT OF PHOBIC DISORDERS

Agoraphobia

The clinical picture in agoraphobia consists of fears and avoidance behaviors that center around three main themes: (1) fear of leaving home, (2) fear of being alone, and (3) fear of being in a situation where escape is difficult or help is unavailable. There is some disagreement as to the best method for treatment of agoraphobia with panic attacks. One widely employed strategy is the use of medication to block panic attacks followed by a psychoeducational intervention that encourages the patient to re-enter phobic situations. (For a discussion of the pharmacotherapy of panic attacks, see the panic disorder section of this chapter.) A second strategy uses behavioral psychotherapy alone in the treatment of these patients. Lately there has been a shift from exposure to phobic situations to exposure to panic-like sensations, in an attempt to prevent catastrophizing. Comparative controlled trials are under way.

The treatment for agoraphobia without panic attacks is behavioral psychotherapy including the encouragement of exposure to phobic situations. Limited symptom attacks, however, should be treated like panic attacks, and in our experience are most uniformly present in so-called agoraphobia without panic.

Social Phobia

In social phobia, the central fear is of humiliation or embarrassment in front of others. This may be generalized (occurring in most social situation) or discrete (occurring only in performance situations, such as public speaking). Medication studies in social phobia are few. Analogue (nonclinical samples with performance or social anxiety) studies suggest beta-blocker efficacy, particularly when used acutely prior to a performance (Liden and Gottfries 1974). Many performing artists or public speakers find that oral propranolol 10 to 20 mg one hour before stage time reduces palpitations, tremor, and "the butterfly feeling." Fluoxetine (Prozac) has been demonstrated as effective in the treatment of social phobia (Schneier et al. 1992) as has buspirone (Schneier et al. 1993).

The MAO inhibitor phenelzine was initially found effective in mixed agoraphobic–social phobic samples (Tyrer et al. 1973) and in an open trial of social phobics (Mountjoy et al. 1977). In this trial a number of patients with generalized social phobia (also meeting criteria for avoidant personality) became much more socially comfortable and outgoing within 6 weeks on phenelzine 45 to 90 mg per day. Cessation within 6 months was followed by relapse, and more chronic treatment requires study. Liebowitz and colleagues (1992) conducted a double-blind, placebo-controlled comparison of phenelzine and the beta blocker atenolol in a large sample of carefully diagnosed social phobics. Phenelzine was superior in the vast majority of patients with generalized social phobia. Atenolol was helpful for some subjects with discrete social phobia, such as public speaking. Further studies are required to compare the efficacy and possible synergism of medications and behavioral treatments of social phobia.

Simple Phobia

Simple phobias are circumscribed fears of specific objects, situations, or activities. The fears are usually not of the objects themselves but of some dire outcome that may result from contact with the objects. Examples are fear of snakes, heights, driving, and enclosed spaces. In the limited number of studies to date tricyclics, benzodiazepines, and beta blockers generally do not appear useful for simple phobics. Exposure therapy is often effective.

MEDICATION TREATMENT OF OBSESSIVE-COMPULSIVE DISORDER

Recent advances in the pharmacotherapy of obsessive-compulsive disorder (OCD) have generated a great deal of excitement in the study of this disorder, and have led to a re-evaluation of the etiology of OCD.

The first promising development in OCD was with the tricyclic antidepressant clomipramine (Anafranil) (CMI) which was available in Canada and Europe for many years, but was not easily available in the United States. Since the 1970s, a number of uncontrolled studies from these countries have documented improvement in primary OCD patients with clomipramine.

More recently a series of well-controlled double-blind studies have documented that clomipramine is more effective than placebo in reducing OCD symptoms (Clomipramine Collaborative Study Group 1991). Clomipramine is equally effective for OCD patients with pure obsessions and those with rituals, in contrast to behavioral treatments, which are less useful for patients with obsessions not accompanied by rituals.

In a review of seven CMI studies with a total of 106 patients, two-thirds were found to be significantly improved on blind ratings (Insel and Zohar 1987). Some patients show an almost complete remission, others little or no improvement. Overall, there appears to be an average reduction of OCD symptoms of more than 40 percent. There is a relatively slow improvement with CMI, with a maximum improvement occurring after 6 to 12 weeks of treatment. While one study found a greater effect of CMI compared to placebo only in the most depressed subgroup (Marks et al. 1980), the majority of studies find specific antiobsessional effects irrespective of depressive symptoms. Controlled studies also suggest CMI is more effective than other antidepressants. Clomipramine was also more effective than alprazolam in the treatment of OCD (Stein et al. 1992).

Studies with selective serotonin reuptake inhibitors such as fluvoxamine (Goodman et al. 1990, Rasmussen et al. 1993) and fluoxetine (Liebowitz et al. 1989) have also demonstrated specific antiobsessional effects in uncontrolled and controlled trials.

The most extensively studied selective serotonin reuptake inhibitor is fluvoxamine (Luvox). In a 10-week multicenter controlled trial, fluvoxamine was found significantly better than placebo in the treatment of 160 OCD patients (Rasmussen et al. 1993). Fluvoxamine was also found to be significantly better than the norepinephrine reuptake inhibitor desipramine in OCD (Goodman et al. 1990).

Currently, the serotonin reuptake inhibitors are considered the treatment of choice for OCD. However, because of the chronic refractory nature of OCD, a wide variety of other medications had been used in its treatment. Thus, prior case reports documented a response to lithium, trazadone, alprazolam, phenelzine, tranylcypromine, imipramine, amphetamine, and tryptophan in individual OCD patients, without the use of controls.

Pharmacologic factors in treatment-resistant OCD include insufficient dosage (less than 250 mg clomipramine equivalent), slow response onset (12 weeks are often required), inadequate treat-

ment duration (an initial treatment of 12 months is often necessary), and symptom relapse following medication discontinuation.

Treatment-resistant OCD may be due to inadequate treatment
of coexisting personality disorder, social phobia, tics, or neurological
disorders. Obsessions of delusional severity may also contribute to
treatment resistance. Uncontrolled series have demonstrated improvement with MAO inhibitors in those patients with coexistent panic
attacks (Jenike et al. 1983) or social phobia (Carrasco et al. 1992).
Neuroleptics may be a useful augmentation strategy in partially responsive patients with comorbid tics, schizotypal personality disorder, or delusions (Hollander and Cohen 1993). There are also reports
of improvement in OCD symptoms following oral (Knesevich 1982)
and intravenous (Hollander et al. 1988) clonidine, although this effect
appears to be transient. Intravenous clomipramine has met with success in some patients refractory to oral clomipramine (Warnecke
1985, Fallon et al. 1992).

Other strategies for treating partially refractory OCD patients
include addition of a variety of agents to selective serotonin reuptake
inhibitors (SSRIs) or combining clomipramine with another SSRI.
Carbamazepine (Tegretol; 400–1200 mg/day) or lithium for bipolar or depressed OCD patients (Rasmussen 1984), and clonazepam (Klonopin; 2–8 mg/day) (Hewlett et al. 1990) or buspirone
(Buspar; 30–60 mg/day), (Jenike et al. 1991) for anxious OCD
patients, may be helpful augmentation strategies. The noradrenergic antidepressant desipramine (Norpramine; 10–30 mg/day) (Hollander et al. 1991), and the appetite suppressant fenfluramine (Pon-
dimin; 20–60 mg/day) (Hollander and Liebowitz 1988) have been
useful augmentation strategies for depressed OCD patients. Partially
selective serotonin reuptake inhibitors such as clomipramine or the
new venlafaxine (Effexor; 225 mg/day) may also be used. With
motor symptoms (such as tics or Tourette's syndrome), delusional
symptoms, or schizotypal personality disorder, a low-dose high-
potency neuroleptic such as haloperidol (Haldol) (McDougle et al.

1990) or pimozide (Orap) (Stein & Hollander, 1992) may be added (see Table 15–1 for augmentation strategies for the treatment of OCD). All of the above have been reported as helpful augmentation strategies in some refractory OCD patients.

When adding a second SSRI such as fluoxetine, fluvoxamine, sertraline, or paroxetine to clomipramine, it is important to follow the combined clomipramine and desmethylclomipramine blood levels. These should not exceed a combined level of 1000 ng/mL to avoid increased risk of seizures. Since intensive behavior therapy is also effective in OCD treatment, this may be considered the first augmentation strategy for refractory OCD (Foa et al. 1984).

Finally, alternative treatment for refractory OCD include MAOIs, intravenous clomipramine (Fallon et al. 1992, Warneke 1985) antiandrogens, and neurosurgery (including capsulotomy or cingulotomy (Jenike et al. 1991).

It is of great interest that oral m-CPP (m-chlorophenyl piperazine), a selective 5HT antagonist, has been found to increase obsessions in a subgroup of OCD patients when given acutely (Hol-

Table 15–1. Augmentation Strategies for Treatment
of Obsessive-Compulsive Disorder

Strategy	Dose Range (mg)
Add to clomipramine or SSRI	
Buspirone	30–60
Fenfluramine	20–60
Desipramine	10–30
Clonazepam	2–4
Carbamazepine	400–1200
Intensive behavior therapy	
Combined clomipramine	50–100
and SSRI	20

Notes: SSRI = selective serotonin reuptake inhibitor. Combined clomipramine + desmethylclomipramine blood levels < 1000 ng/mL.

342 Specific Treatment Techniques

lander 1992). This behavioral exacerbation has been shown to
decrease after chronic treatment with clomipramine (Zohar et al.
1988) or fluoxetine (Hollander et al. 1991), suggesting that chronic
treatment may correct the serotonin dysregulation via adaptive
downregulation of 5HT receptors. Treatment with serotonin reuptake inhibitors also seems to be effective in OCD related disorders
(Hollander 1993) such as trichotillomania (Stein & Hollander
1992), sexual obsessions, sexual addictions, and paraphilias (Stein
et al. 1992), and pathological gambling (Hollander et al. 1992).

Case Management Approach

Patient cooperation is an invaluable aid to treatment with psychotropic agents. A common cause of treatment failure is noncompliance—not taking the medication. One reason for resistance is that
accepting medication forces the patient to admit that he is sick.
Some patients also fear loss of control to the medication.

Building of rapport between doctor and patient is of great
importance. Empathy, reassurance, and clarification from the physician will enable most patients to take medication regularly and
without undue anxiety. However, severe cases may require added
interventions. Arranging for the patient to talk with another anxiety disorder patient who has previously taken the medication is
helpful. Participation in a short-term educational support group with
other patients who are currently starting medication is also helpful.

A psychoeducational approach involves describing to the
patient the entire course of treatment as envisioned. This includes
the period of time before clinical improvement is expected, the frequency in changes of drug dosage, the eventual dose that probably
will be attained, and the expected length of drug treatment. Possible and expected side effects should be described to help prevent
catastrophizing as a result of new somatic sensations and to build
confidence in the treatment.

The patient should be instructed to notify his doctor immediately of any unusual side effects. The physician should be very available for telephone coverage during the initial phases of treatment. This is an extremely reassuring experience, and most patients do not abuse this practice.

Sometimes problems arise if the psychotherapist is covertly competitive with the effectiveness of drug treatment. This may lead to low dose and premature termination of medication. Therefore, there most be good rapport between psychotherapist and psychopharmacologist.

For most patients, the combination of medication, education about the illness, and supportive encouragement are sufficient. For others, adjunctive treatment (behavioral or cognitive exercises) may be required. Treatment failures are most commonly due to inadequate dose, insufficient medication trial, or misdiagnosis of concomitant psychiatric disorder, rather than the refractory nature of the illness. Fortunately, most anxiety disorder patients can be effectively treated with specific medication which targets their core anxiety symptoms. This makes accurate diagnosis, appropriate treatment and good communication between psychopharmacologist and psychotherapist essential.

REFERENCES

Carrasco, J., Hollander, E., Schneier, F., and Liebowitz, M. R. (1992). Treatment outcome of obsessive-compulsive disorder with comorbid social phobia. *Journal of Clinical Psychiatry* 53:387–391.

Clomipramine Collaborative Study Group. (1991). Clomipramine in the treatment of patients with obsessive-compulsive disorder. *Archives of General Psychiatry* 48:730–738.

Cohen, S. D , Moneiro, W., and Marks, I. M. (1984). Two-year follow-up of agoraphobics after exposure and imipramine. *British Journal of Psychiatry* 144:276–281.

Den Boer, J. A. (1988). Serotonergic mechanisms in anxiety disorders: an inquiry into serotonin function in panic disorder. *Cip-Gegevens Koninklijke Bibliotheek, Den Haag.*

Fallon, B. A., Campeas, R., Schneier, F R., et al. (1992). Open trial of intravenous clomipramine in five treatment-refractory patients with obsessive-compulsive disorder. *Journal of Neuropsychiatry and Clinical Neurosciences* 4:70–75.

Foa, E. B., Steketee, G., Grayson, J. B., et al. (1984). Deliberate exposure and blocking of obsessive-compulsive rituals: immediate and long-term effects. *Behavior Therapy* 15:450–472.

Fyer, A. J., Liebowitz, M. R., Gorman, J. M., et al. (1987). Discontinuation of alprazolam treatment in panic patients. *American Journal of Psychiatry* 144:303–308.

Garakani, H., Zitrin, C. M., and Klein, D. F. (1984). Treatment of panic disorder with imipramine alone. *American Journal of Psychiatry* 141: 446–448.

Goodman, W. K., Price, L. H., Delgado, P. L., et al. (1990). Specificity of serotonin reuptake inhibitors in the treatment of obsessive-compulsive disorder: comparison of fluvoxamine and desipramine. *Archives of General Psychiatry* 47:577–585.

Gorman, J. M., Liebowitz, M. R., Fyer, A. J., et al. (1987). An open trial of fluoxetine in the treatment of panic attacks. *Journal of Clinical Psychopharmacology* 7:329–332.

Herman, J. B., Rosenbaum, J. F., and Brotman, A. W. (1987). The alprazolam to clonazepam switch for the treatment of panic disorder. *Journal of Clinical Psychopharmacology* 7:175–178.

Hewlett, W. A., Vinogradov, S., and Agras, W. S. (1990). Clonazepam treatment of obsessions and compulsions. *Journal of Clinical Psychiatry* 51:158–161.

Hoehn-Saric, R., Merchant, A. F., Keyser, M. L., et al. (1981). Effects of clonidine on anxiety disorders. *Archives of General Psychiatry* 38: 1278–1282.

Hollander, E. (1993). *Obsessive-Compulsive Related Disorders.* Washington, DC: American Psychiatric Press.

Hollander, E., and Cohen, L. J. (1994). The assessment and treatment of refractory anxiety. *Journal of Clinical Psychiatry* 55(2 suppl):27–31.

Hollander, E., DeCaria, C., Gulley, R., et al. (1992). Serotonergic function in obsessive compulsive disorder: behavioral and neuroendocrine responses to oral m-CPP and fenfluramine in patients and healthy volunteers. *Archives of General Psychiatry* 49:21–28.

Hollander, E., DeCaria, C. M., Schneier, F. R., et al. (1990). Fenfluramine augmentation of serotonin reuptake blockade antiobsessional treatment. *Journal of Clinical Psychiatry* 51:119–123.

Hollander, E., Fay, M., Cohen, B., et al. (1988). Serotonergic and noradrenergic sensitivity in obsessive-compulsive disorder: behavioral findings. *American Journal of Psychiatry* 145:1015–1017.

Hollander, E., Fay, M., and Liebowitz, J. R. (1988). Clonidine and clomipramine in obsessive-compulsive disorder. *American Journal of Psychiatry* 145:388–389.

Hollander, E., Frenkel, M., DeCaria, C. M., et al. (1992). Treatment of pathological gambling with clomipramine. *American Journal of Psychiatry* 149:710–711.

Hollander, E., and Liebowitz, M. R. (1988). Augmentation of antiobsessional treatment with fenfluramine. *American Journal of Psychiatry* 145:1314–1315.

Hollander, E., Mullen, L., Skodol, A., et al. (1991). Obsessive-compulsive disorder, depression, and fluoxetine. *Journal of Clinical Psychiatry* 52: 418–422.

Insel, T. R., and Zohar, J. (1987). Psychopharmacological approaches to obsessive compulsive disorder. In *Psychopharmacology*, vol. I, *A Generation of Progress*, ed. H. Meltzer. American College of Neuropsychopharmacology. New York: Raven.

Jenike, M. A., Baer, L., Ballantine, H. T., et al. (1991). Cingulotomy for refractory obsessive-compulsive disorder: a long-term follow-up of 33 patients. *Archives of General Psychiatry* 48:548–555.

Jenike, M. A., Baer, L., and Buttolph, L. (1991). Buspirone augmentation of fluoxetine in patients with obsessive compulsive disorder. *Journal of Clinical Psychiatry* 52:3–14.

Jenike, M. A., Surman, O. S., Cassem, N. H., et al. (1983) Monoamine oxidase inhibitors in obsessive-compulsive disorders. *Archives of General Psychiatry* 43:79–85.

Kahn, R. J., McNair, D. M., Lipman, R. S., et al. (1986). Imipramine and chlordiazepoxide in depression and anxiety disorders. *Archives of General Psychiatry* 46:79–85.

Kahn, R. J., Wetzler, S., Van Praag, H. et al. (1988). Behavioral indication of serotonergic supersensitivity in panic disorder. *Psychiatry Research* 25:101–104.

Klein, D. F. (1964). Delineation of two drug-responsive anxiety syndromes. *Psychopharmacologia* 5:397–408.

——— (1981). Anxiety reconceptualized. In *Anxiety: New Research and Changing Concepts*, ed. D. F. Klein and J. G. Rabkin. New York: Raven.

Klein, D. F., and Fink, M. (1962). Psychiatric reaction patterns to imipramine. *American Journal of Psychiatry* 119:432–438.

Klein, D. F., Gittleman, R., Quitkin, F., et al. (1980). *Diagnosis and Drug Treatment of Psychiatric Disorder: Adults and Children*, 2nd ed. Baltimore: Williams & Wilkins.

Knesevich, J. W. (1982). Successful treatment of obsessive-compulsive disorder with clonidine hydrochloride. *American Journal of Psychiatry* 139:364–365.

Liden, S., and Gottfries, C. G. (1974). Beta-blocking agents in the treatment of catecholamine-induced symptoms in musicians. *Lancet* 2:529.

Liebowitz, M. R., Fyer, A. J., McGrath, P., and Klein, D. F. (1981). Clonidine treatment of panic disorder. *Psychopharmacology Bulletin* 17:122–123.

Liebowitz, M. R., Gorman, J. M., Fyer, A. J., et al. (1988). Pharmacotherapy of social phobia: an interim report of a placebo controlled comparison of phenelzine and atenolol. *Journal of Clinical Psychiatry* 49:252–257.

Liebowitz, M. R., Hollander, E., Schneier, F., et al. (1989). Fluoxetine treatment of obsessive compulsive disorder: an open clinical trial. *Journal of Clinical Psychopharmacology* 9:423–427.

Liebowitz, M. R., Quitkin, F., Stewart, J. W., et al. (1984). Phenelzine versus imipramine in atypical depression: a preliminary report. *Archives of General Psychiatry* 120:669–677.

Liebowitz, M. R., Schneier, F. R., Campeas, R., et al. (1992). Phenelzine vs. atenolol in social phobia: a placebo controlled comparison. *Archives of General Psychiatry* 49:290–300.

Marks, I. M., Stern, R., Mawson, D., et al. (1980). Clomipramine and exposure for obsessive compulsive rituals. *British Journal of Psychiatry* 136:1–25.

Mavissakalian, M., and Michelson, L. (1986) Two year follow-up of exposure and imipramine treatment of agoraphobia. *American Journal of Psychiatry* 143:1106–1112.

Mavissakalian, M., and Perel, J. (1985). Imipramine in the treatment of agoraphobia: dose-response relationships. *American Journal of Psychiatry* 142:1032–1036.

McDougle, C. J., Goodman, W. K., Price, L. H., et al. (1990). Neuroleptic addition in fluvoxamine-refractory obsessive-compulsive disorder. *American Journal of Psychiatry* 147:652–654.

Mountjoy, C. Q., Roth, M., Garside, R. F., and Leitch, I. M. (1977). A clinical trial of phenelzine in anxiety depressive and phobic neuroses. *British Journal of Psychiatry* 131:486–492.

Rasmussen, S. A. (1984). Lithium and tryptophan augmentation in clomipramine-resistant obsessive-compulsive disorder. *American Journal of Psychiatry* 141:1283–1285.

Rasmussen, S. A , Eisen, J. L., and Pato, M. T. (1993). Current issues in the pharmacologic management of obsessive compulsive disorder. *Journal of Clinical Psychiatry* 54(suppl):4–9.

Schneier, F. R., Chin, S., Hollander, E., and Liebowitz, M. R. (1992). Fluoxetine and social phobia. *Journal of Clinical Psychopharmacology* 12:62–64.

Schneier, F. R., Saoud, J. B., Campeas, R., et al. (1993). Buspirone in social phobia. *Journal of Clinical Psychopharmacology* 13:251–256.

Sheehan, C. V., Ballenger, J., and Jacobsen, G. (1980). Treatment of endogenous anxiety with phobic, hysterical, and hypochondriacal symptoms. *Archives of General Psychiatry* 37:51–59.

Stein, D. J., and Hollander, E. (1992). Low-dose pimozide augmentation of serotonin reuptake blockers in the treatment of trichotillomania. *Journal of Clinical Psychiatry* 53:123–126.

Stein, D. J., Hollander, E., Anthony, D., et al. (1992). Serotonergic medications for sexual obsessions, sexual addictions and paraphilias. *Journal of Clinical Psychiatry* 53:267–271.

Stein, D. J., Hollander, E., Mullen, L., et al. (1992). Comparison of clomipramine, alprazolam and placebo in the treatment of obsessive-compulsive disorder. *Human Psychopharmacology* 7:389–395.

Thoren, P., Asberg, M., Bertilsson, L., et al. (1980). Clomipramine treatment of obsessive-compulsive disorder. II. Biochemical aspects. *Archives of General Psychiatry* 37:1289–1294.

Tyrer, P., Candy, J., and Kelly, D. (1973). A study of the clinical effects of phenelzine and placebo in the treatment of phobic anxiety. *Psychopharmacology* 32:237–254.

Warneke, L. B. (1985). Intravenous clomipramine in the treatment of obsessional disorder in adolescence: case report. *Journal of Clinical Psychiatry* 46:100–103.

Zitrin, C. M., Klein, D. F., Woerner, M. G., and Ross, D. C. (1983). Treatment of phobias. I. Comparison of imipramine and placebo. *Archives of General Psychiatry* 40:125–138.

Zitrin, C. M., Klein, D. F., Woerner, M. G., et al. (1978). Behavior therapy, supportive psychotherapy, imipramine, and phobias. *Archives of General Psychiatry* 35:307–316.

Zohar, J., Insel, T. R., Zohar-Kadouch, R. C., et al. (1988). Serotonergic responsivity in obsessive-compulsive disorder: effects of chronic clomipramine treatment. *Archives of General Psychiatry* 45:167–172.

CHAPTER SIXTEEN

Medication Discontinuation in Panic Disorder

In the 1970s and 1980s a controversy raged as to whether psycho-pharmacology or talking therapy was the better treatment. At this point, most experts accept that both are effective, and combined treatment can be the most effective in many cases. However, one of the main disadvantages of medication remains the potential for relapse once the medication is withdrawn. Drs. Ballenger, Pecknold, Rickels, and Sellers's consensus paper addresses this issue with particular regard to benzodiazepine discontinuation.

Medication Discontinuation in Panic Disorder

JAMES C. BALLENGER
JOHN PECKNOLD
KARL RICKELS
EDWARD M. SELLERS

This chapter addresses current issues associated with medication discontinuation in panic disorder, with specific focus on one of the most frequently used medication classes for this indication, the benzodiazepines. Identification of the principal issues associated with the discontinuation phase of benzodiazepine treatment of panic disorder is the primary focus of this chapter, but it also addresses common misperceptions, how they developed, and the risk issues involved.

The following areas were identified as potentially controversial:

1. Confusion related to the terminology used when describing discontinuation symptoms

2. Negative misperceptions, shared by a broad group of people, including health professionals, patients, lay public, and the media, regarding the syndrome associated with benzodiazepine discontinuation

3. Actual efficacy of the medication, duration of efficacy, and mechanism of action

4. Nature of the illness and its psychopathology

5. Determination of the optimal time for discontinuing medication, appropriate reasons for doing so. how discontinuation should be approached. and expected outcomes

After review of the literature and discussion focused on these issues, the authors concluded that the majority of patients, when slowly tapered, are able to discontinue the benzodiazepines without a great deal of trouble, particularly after short-term therapy. Patients treated with long-term therapy at high therapeutic doses may experience greater difficulty with discontinuation. If patients are appropriately and adequately prepared and if discontinuation efforts employ a slow, gradual taper schedule, discontinuation symptoms, if they occur, are transient, mild to moderate in severity, and generally tolerable by the average patient.

This chapter discusses these conclusions and issues associated with discontinuation, beginning with reasons for discontinuation, how to conduct discontinuation, discontinuation outcomes, management of discontinuation symptoms, and conclusions that can be drawn from the data presented. In addition, it provides information on the relatively small subset of patients who have significant problems with medication discontinuation and discusses possible reasons for this occurrence.

TREATMENT OPTIONS
FOR THE PANIC DISORDER PATIENT

After conducting an in-depth history and arriving at a diagnosis of panic disorder, the physician must determine with the patient which of the available treatments (generally medication, behavioral or cognitive therapy, or a combination) seems most appropriate and offers the best chance for recovery. There are few data available on those patient characteristics that may predict better response to a particular treatment. Therefore, if medications are to be utilized, the physician generally weighs the pros and cons of each of the classes of medicines that are known to be effective and makes the most appropriate choice for treatment. This should be done flexibly, allowing for modifications in treatment or changes in the medication if treatment efficacy is not achieved in a reasonable time.

There are three classes of medicines that have been demonstrated in controlled trials to be effective in the treatment of panic disorder: the monoamine oxidase inhibitor (MAOI) antidepressants, the tricyclic antidepressants (TCAs), and the benzodiazepines. The selective serotonin reuptake inhibitors (SSRIs) appear to be effective, but conclusive evidence remains limited. Each of these groups of medicines has definite advantages and disadvantages, which are briefly reviewed (Ballenger 1986, 1991b, 1992, Schatzberg and Ballenger 1991).

The MAOIs, TCAs, and SSRIs share the disadvantage of delayed onset of action (4 to 12 weeks), so for the patient in acute crisis needing rapid relief they would probably not be the drugs of choice. In addition, the currently available MAOIs require strict dietary restrictions and have a number of other side effects which include: risk of developing hypertensive, hyperpyrexic reactions; insomnia; orthostatic hypotension; weight gain; interference with sexual function; and, in some patients, mania. On the other hand, for those patients who suffer from recurrent depression as well as panic disorder, the MAOIs, TCAs, and, probably, the SSRIs offer antidepressant effects, and some studies show that they may offer better antiphobic relief (Sheehan et al. 1980).

The TCAs afford the patient a number of advantages, including once-daily dosing and antidepressant effects, and in some cases are available in generic form at reduced cost to the patient. In addition, the TCAs are the best studied of the medications effective in panic disorder. Disadvantages include many of those seen with the MAOIs, such as orthostatic hypotension, sexual dysfunction, anticholinergic side effects, and mania in bipolar patients. Further, when medication treatment is first initiated, some patients experience stimulant-like symptoms, which can be severe enough to lead to discontinuation if not dealt with properly.

The benzodiazepines have fewer side effects than the MAOIs and TCAs, and therefore are generally better tolerated (Cross National Collaborative Panic Study 1992, Rickels et al. 1993, Schwerzer et al. 1993), and also provide relief rapidly, with improvement usually beginning within the first week of treatment. In addition, they reduce anticipatory anxiety, and some are available in generic form. Their disadvantages include multiple daily dosing, risk of sedation and cognitive and psychomotor impairment during acute treatment, sexual side effects, and risk of withdrawal symptoms upon discontinuation.

The SSRIs generally have fewer side effects than the TCAs or MAOIs (e.g., less weight gain, postural hypotension, anticholinergic effects), but like these agents can also be administered once daily and should have comparable antidepressant efficacy. Their principal disadvantages include relatively slow onset of action, initial stimulatory type side effects, and expense.

Many clinicians and patients choose treatment with the benzodiazepines (Rickels et al. 1993, Schweizer et al. 1993), and the remainder of this paper deals with issues relevant to these agents. Despite the obvious advantages of benzodiazepines, their use is viewed as controversial by many. We will first discuss the basics of treatment with the benzodiazepines, as well as the issues to be addressed in order to discontinue them with minimal difficulty. The controversy surrounding their use will be addressed within these sections as appropriate and in more depth following the description of the treatment/discontinuation process.

Treatment with Benzodiazepines

As with the other pharmacotogic agents used for the treatment of panic disorder, the benzodiazepines must be administered at doses high enough for an adequate period of time to achieve clinically important improvement. The benzodiazepine used most frequently and studied most extensively for this indication is alprazolam, which is also the only medication currently approved by the Food and Drug Administration for a panic indication. Both the Phase I and II Cross National Trials provided definitive proof of the efficacy of alprazolam, its rapid onset of action, and minimal side effects (Ballenger et al. 1988, Cross National Collaborative Panic Study 1992, Rosenberg et al. 1991).

The Phase I data showed that at an average dose of 5.4 mg/day at Week 4 and 5.7 mg/day at Week 8, significant clinical efficacy was achieved, with reduction in symptomatology seen in the first week of treatment and maintained throughout the 8-week trial. At the end of the study, 92 percent of the patients treated with alprazolam for the full 8 weeks were moderately improved or better. This dosage range and efficacy level are consistent with those found in other tnals (Cross National Collaborative Panic Study 1992, Rickels et al. 1993, Schweizer et al. 1993).

A subsequent dose-comparison study of 6 mg of alprazolam versus 2 mg of alprazolam and placebo again demonstrated greater improvement for the two drug groups. There were few clinically significant differences in the two dosage groups, therefore suggesting that there are many patients who are responsive to lower doses of alprazolam (Lydiard et al. 1992).

The Phase I results were essentially replicated in the Phase II study which compared placebo and imipramine with alprazolam (Cross National Collaborative Panic Study 1992, Rosenberg et al. 1991). Utilizing the largest patient sample to date (1,168 in 12 centers), the Phase II study showed alprazolam to be more effective than placebo, with efficacy in the first week, which was again sustained throughout the 8-week trial. Significant clinical improvement did not occur with imipramine until Week 4, but by the end of the study efficacy was roughly comparable for both drugs. The principal differences between the two drugs were that alprazolam was better tolerated than imipramine and onset of efficacy was seen significantly earlier in treatment. Similar findings were recently reported (Schweizer et al. 1993).

PATIENT DIFFICULTIES WITH MEDICATION TREATMENT

The clinician should be alert to the fact that many panic disorder patients have an exaggerated concern regarding the use of medications. Education, physician availability, and continued reassurance are often necessary to reduce these concerns What may seem like exaggerated measures are often necessary to deal with this over-concern and are perhaps best illustrated by the physician who actually administers the first dose of medicine in his office, staying with and reassuring the patient that the medicine is safe and will not harm him or her.

The Dependence Controversy

Concern over benzodiazepine use is often greater with long-term pharmacotherapy. However, clinical evidence indicates that panic disorder is not a short-term condition, and long-term treatment is recognized as appropriate in many cases (Ballenger 1991a, Curtis et al. 1993, Gorman and Papp 1990, Pollack 1990, Mavissakalion and Perel 1992a,b, Salzman 1990). Despite the lack of evidence of negative physical effects associated with long-term medication treatment, the patient may not be completely reassured. The fear of the medicine itself may shift to concern, often shared by the patient, family, and even physician, that the patient may become "dependent" on the medicine, which in this context is often erroneously equated with "addiction" and drug abuse (Shader and Greenblatt 1993). These issues are also discussed in Sellers and colleagues (1993).

Unfortunately, attitudes similar to those described in patients and family members are also shared by many members of the health care professions and are apparent in the use of misleading terminology, like "getting hooked," when referring to medically appropriate long-term treatment with benzodiazepines. Other groups have contributed to these exaggerated ideas as well. For instance, Peter Tyrer in his guest editorial for *Stress Medicine* refers to statements made by the lay press such as, "It is more difficult to stop tranquilizers than to come off heroin" (Tyrer 1991). These concerns about drug abuse remain prevalent despite evidence to the contrary from multiple studies, including several large studies that found no evidence of benzodiazepine abuse or addictive behavior in panic disorder patients treated long-term with these agents (Cross National Callaborative Panic Study 1992, Katschnig et al. 1991, Nagy et al. 1989, Noyes et al. 1988, Sellers et al. 1993, Shader and Greenblatt 1993).

Scientific data document that the main issue contributing to this controversy is that a significant number of patients after long-term use of benzodiazepines will experience withdrawal symptoms (and/or relapse) upon discontinuation. This is incorrectly viewed as evidence of benzodiazepine abuse or addiction (Sellers et al. 1993). Although the neuroadaptation that occurs with benzodiazepines and that may result in withdrawal symptoms on discontinuation is correctly termed *physical dependence*, this phrase is also widely misunderstood and incorrectly thought to represent drug dependence/addiction or abuse.

Benzodiazepine Use/Abuse in Clinical Samples

Benzodiazepine abuse is actually very rare in clinically treated samples. Romach and colleagues (1992) studied long-term alprazolam users in the community. Community surveys were conducted at three separate time points (1988, 1989, and 1990). For the purpose of this study, long-term was defined as use for at least 3 months.

They found: (1) Despite long-term use, there was no escalation in dosage to suggest abuse or development of tolerance. These findings were confirmed in the large Phase I and II Cross National Trials with alprazolam where there was no evidence of abuse or escalation in dosage (Ballenger et al. 1988, Cross National Collaborative Panic Study 1992, Rosenberg et al. 1991). (2) The majority of respondents (61 percent) took alprazolam as prescribed, but many patients actually took less than prescribed by switching to an "as needed" schedule for symptom control. (3) Over two thirds of these patients (71 percent) had tried to discontinue alprazolam at least one time, and symptoms were reported by 85 percent of the respondents when decreasing or discontinuing alprazolam. It is impossible to know from this study whether these were withdrawal symptoms, relapse, or a combination of the two. (4) Only 16 percent of the physicians discussed duration of drug use: 32 percent, decreasing dosage, and 31 percent, discontinuation; and 49 percent provided no information on how to discontinue. (5) An additional question was added to the 1990 survey which showed that 79 percent of these patients were receiving alprazolam from their family practitioner, 34 percent from their psychiatrist, and some from both. (6) Finally, this group of patients had significant history of previous psychoactive medication use indicative of previous and persisting psychopathology. In summary, the results of this study, consistent with evidence for other benzodiazepines, show that long-term alprazolam use is not associated with drug dependence/addiction or abuse.

Investigators in a prescription-event monitoring study conducted in Britain collected and analyzed data on 10,895 patients who had been prescribed alprazolam (Edwards et al. 1991). This study reported no serious side effects or adverse events. Drowsiness and depression were reported infrequently, although it was their assessment that depression was due to the primary condition being treated and was not a side effect of the drug (Edwards et al. 1991).

Terminology

It is important to clarify the very real differences between drug abuse, dependence/addiction, and appropriate long-term use of benzodiazepines when a patient is treated for an illness that requires and responds to pharmacologic intervention (Sellers et al. 1993). Education in this area is therefore critical and should be focused toward the health care professional, particularly nonpsychiatric clinicians. Erroneous labeling of *dependence* as a synonym for benzodiazepine *abuse* or *addiction* has negatively heightened public awareness and has contributed to sensationalistic media coverage. This terminology developed in work with drug addicts abusing opiates and is generally not applicable in this context in which a therapeutic benefit is derived, i.e., prescription use (Sellers et al. 1993).

In the field, the following terms and definitions have reached general acceptance:

1. *Physical dependence* refers to the neuroadaptive processes that occur when certain drugs are repeatedly administered and which lead to the characteristic syndrome of withdrawal symptoms when the drug is discontinued or significantly reduced.

2. *Drug dependence* is the syndrome of compulsive, harmful drug use, attempts to stop, frequent relapse, and an extremely high priority for drug use. *Addiction* is the term referring to the

extreme end of drug dependence, usually characterized by overwhelming involvement in obtaining and using the illegal drug,
escalation of dose, and high relapse.

3. *Drug abuse* (or harmful use) is defined as repeated drug use
despite harmful medical, legal and/or social consequences, but
use which falls short of compulsive use.

An important distinction must be made between drug abuse
and addiction and the benign need for a medication which may
produce physical dependence and therefore withdrawal symptoms
on discontinuation. This latter state is a type of nonpharmacologic,
psychological dependence or clinical requirement for the medication. As briefly reviewed above, abuse of benzodiazepines is very
rare and occurs almost exclusively in alcoholics or drug addicts who
also abuse illegal drugs like cocaine or heroin. The term *abuse* should
be reserved for drug use to "get high," use stimulated by craving
for the drug, and use that has harmful medical effects and social
consequences. The word *addiction* should be reserved for the overwhelming preoccupation with obtaining and using the drug of abuse.
Physical dependence is the accurate term, although widely misapplied,
to describe the process of neuroadaptation to a drug that then leads
to a withdrawal state consisting of characteristic signs or symptoms
when the medication is discontinued abruptly or too rapidly. It is
important to remember that this adaptive process and withdrawal
syndrome occur with many classes of medications including
antiepileptics and cardiovascular medications, not just the benzodiazepines. The occurrence of such a state (physical dependence/
withdrawal symptoms) has no known relationship to drug abuse in
benzodiazepine-treated patients. Unfortunately many lay and even
professional people confuse these terms and issues and believe that
benzodiazepines have strongly "addictive" properties and that the
process by which patients become physically dependent on (adapted
to) these medications represents "drug abuse" rather than the

expected adaptation to the medication akin to the body "getting used to" any medication.

Misunderstanding also is widespread about return of the original condition (relapse) after medication is discontinued or reduced. After discontinuation, relapse may occur, and through no moral or characterological weakness, the panic disorder patient may need to resume medication treatment in order to enjoy a relatively symptom-free life. Rather than providing confirmation of a "drug addiction or habit," this underscores the chronic and relapsing nature of this disorder and the beneficial effects of the drug. Follow-up studies conducted over 5 years after treatment found that only a minority (15 to 30 percent) of patients were without symptoms (Coryell et al. 1983, Katschnig et al. 1991, Rickels et al. 1993). However, to confirm that symptoms that have occurred after benzodiazepine treatment of panic disorder are symptoms of relapse and not transient withdrawal symptoms that are often indistinguishable from panic disorder symptoms, patients need to be entirely off benzodiazepine treatment long enough for withdrawal symptoms to clear. This can take 2 to 3 weeks or occasionally longer.

REASONS FOR DISCONTINUATION

Definitive evidence is not yet available regarding the optimal length of treatment, although one recent study documented that 8 months of treatment led to greater improvement than 2 months (Curtis et al. 1993), and this certainly is in keeping with the experience of most clinicians. Another recent study compared short-term versus extended maintenance treatment in panic disorder patients treated with imipramine and demonstrated that the group who received 12 months of maintenance treatment following 6 months of acute treatment had significantly less relapse at follow-up than did the group who received only 6 months of acute treatment (Mavissakalian and Perel 1992a,b).

After 6 to 18 months of effective pharmacotherapy of panic disorder, most clinicians attempt to taper and discontinue medications (Ballenger 1991, Gorman and Papp 1990, Mavissakalian and Perel 1992a,b, Pollock 1990). One might question the utility of discontinuing treatment that has proved effective and that has allowed the patient to return to near normal levels of functioning. However, once the patient has maintained maximal improvement for at least 6 months and has re-established his or her previous state of functioning and confidence, there are several appropriate reasons for reassessing continuing need for treatment, which can only be accomplished by discontinuing the medication.

The best reason is that treatment may no longer be necessary. Also, problematic side effects, the wish to conceive or unexpected pregnancy, or emergence of alcohol or drug abuse are all valid reasons for attempting to discontinue effective treatment. Other less important but real reasons include the expense and inconvenience involved in taking the benzodiazepines multiple times a day and issues of self-esteem. Finally, the least appropriate reasons to consider discontinuation include: concern over physical effects caused by the medicine; unfounded concerns that may be shared by the patient, his or her physician, and family members regarding "drug addiction/abuse"; the erroneous belief that panic disorder is a short-term condition; and an issue frequently seen in panic disorder patients, i.e., their wish not to be "dependent on medications." In this group's opinion, concern over serious adverse physical effects or a fear of developing problematic dependence or drug abuse/addiction with long-term benzodiazepine therapy is not justified by the data.

Discontinuation Process

The decision to discontinue medicines should be a mutual one between patient and doctor, and patients should be reassured that for most, discontinuation is actually not difficult nor problematic.

The issue of eventual discontinuation should be addressed early in treatment, and the patient should be educated about what to expect during this process.

It is critical that the medication be tapered slowly and gradually; this minimizes the severity of any withdrawal symptoms that may occur with discontinuation. The patient should be reassured that he or she may reexperience some anxiety symptoms, but that for most, these will resolve within 1 to 3 weeks (Pecknold et al. 1988). The patient should also be reassured that if after an adequate period of time during which treatment need is reassessed, it is determined that the patient continues to require pharmacologic treatment, medication can be reinstated.

Timing is also critical when attempting discontinuation. This should be attempted at a relatively unstressful time in the patient's life. For example, one should not consider discontinuation in a patient who is a student when exams are scheduled. Similarly, it would be inappropriate to begin taper for the businessman when he has an important presentation pending or a critical business trip to make.

Discontinuation Outcomes

Several related and sometimes confusing outcomes may occur when benzodiazepines are discontinued. The first and obviously most desirable is that the patient remains asymptomatic. However, many patients can expect to experience transient withdrawal symptoms or rebound panic, both of which generally resolve within 1 to 3 weeks after complete discontinuation of the benzodiazepine. Finally, the patient may fully or partially relapse, with return to original symptomatology that does not resolve, and that may require treatment, either with the original medicine, another agent, or nonpharmacologic treatment.

Data on the prevalence of these outcomes are widely divergent, indicating that anywhere from 20 percent to 80 percent of patients remain well, and the extent of relapse also varies widely from patient to patient (Rickels et al. 1993, Sheehan 1986, Versiani et al. 1987, Zitrin et al. 1983). However, recent evidence suggests that 30 percent to 45 percent of panic disorder patients remain well (Ballenger 1991, Rickels et al. 1993).

As mentioned earlier, education is critical to successful discontinuation. If patients are prepared for the possibilities that withdrawal symptoms and panic rebound may occur during discontinuation, they are usually able to tolerate the symptoms. Data show that at least some withdrawal symptoms can be seen in as many as 35 percent to 90 percent of patients discontinued from benzodiazepines. (Noyes et al. 1991, Pecknold et al. 1988, Rickels et al. 1993). Given this anticipated outcome, the patient should be reassured that if symptoms occur, they are not life-threatening, are generally mild to moderate, and should resolve within a few days or weeks. Again, the patient should understand and agree that taper will be accomplished slowly, with gradual decreases in dosage to minimize any return of symptoms.

The time frame within which discontinuation is completed is probably the most important factor in the success of this process. When patients from the Phase I Cross National Trial were discontinued rapidly (less than a month) from alprazolam after 8 weeks of treatment, 35 percent experienced transient rebound panic and withdrawal symptoms (Pecknold et al. 1988). This was recently replicated by Rickels and colleagues (1993) with an even more rapid taper. Rebound panic can be especially frightening to the patient. since it often occurs with more intensity than the original panic.

Much of the clinical data available on discontinuation, unfortunately, reflects the outcome following relatively rapid discontinuation of drug. However, there have been some studies that compare rapid versus gradual discontinuation. Generally patients discontinued abruptly experienced more symptomatology than those discontinued gradually (Laughren et al. 1982, Rickels et al. 1990, Schweizer et al. 1990). In one study, 44 percent of the abruptly discontinued patients suffered rebound anxiety compared to none of the gradually tapered group (Fontaine et al. 1984).

More recently, Pecknold and colleagues (1993) compared three methods of alprazolam discontinuation at three sites. Patients were treated for 6 weeks and then were tapered at different rates at each of the three sites. In this study, the 39 percent of the patients who were rapidly withdrawn from medication experienced rebound panic and 11 percent to 14 percent rebound symptoms of anxiety. This is comparable to the earlier findings of Pecknold and colleagues (1988), where 27 percent of the patients reported panic rebound and 13 percent reported anxiety rebound. In the current study. (Pecknold et al. 1993), however, the incidence of withdrawal, even in the rapidly tapered group (17 percent and 22 percent) was lower than that demonstrated in the Cross National Trial (35 percent) (Pecknold et al. 1988). If the same indicator symptoms from the Cross National Trial are utilized, the incidence was only 13 percent and 7.7 percent, suggesting that the incidence and severity of withdrawal symptoms can be greatly reduced by slower, more flexible taper schedules.

Recently, Tyrer (1991) described a late and persisting "benzodiazepine post-withdrawal syndrome," separate from the typical syndrome that occurs during or immediately after benzodiazepine discontinuation and resolves over a 1 to 2 week period. He described a clinical picture in which patients experienced symptoms that generally began 1 to 3 months following withdrawal and were very similar to the original illness state and did not remit as do the initial transient withdrawal symptoms. It would seem more likely and it is the consensus of the authors that given the chronic and relapsing nature of panic disorder, what Dr. Tyrer is actually describing is relapse, or a return to the original illness state.

Severe Withdrawal Symptoms

There have been limited published reports of severe reactions such as seizures and deliria when benzodiazepines are discontinued, which are summarized in the recent American Psychiatric Association Task Force Report (Salzman 1990). In a case report conducted by Noyes and colleagues (1986), a patient developed seizures within 24 hours following discontinuation of alprazolam. It should be noted that development of seizures occurred during a very rapid taper, with reduction of 1 mg every 3 days. A case report was recently published describing the development of seizures in a patient following abrupt discontinuation of alprazolam, which ultimately may have contributed to the patient's death (Haque et al. 1990). However, the patient in the report had been tapered successfully to a daily dose of 1 mg/day when seizures developed. Confounding the potential implications of this report was the postmortem finding of severe cardiac disease and the sudden discontinuation of metoprolol, a β-blocker. Another report of seizures following abrupt discontinuation of diazepam was made by Tyrer and colleagues (1983).

In postmarketing surveillance efforts by Upjohn, spontaneous reports of seizures have been received from around the world. These reports are uncontrolled, often impossible to fully evaluate, and provide no estimate of the incidence nor the causality of the event; however, they do provide some valuable suggestions. Of the 274 reported seizures, the overwhelming majority (234) occurred during withdrawal (data on file, The Upjohn Co.). Fully 47.9 percent occurred after abrupt alprazolam discontinuation and 9.4 percent with taper schedules out of insert guidelines. In another 32.1 percent, the withdrawal method or regimen was unknown. However, 3.8 percent occurred when withdrawal tapers were within insert guidelines and 2.6 percent when the patient "missed" a dose during continued therapy. These last two categories represent real risk and require further close study, although their incidence is presumably quite low. However, the bulk of these data again underscore the importance of a slow, gradual, and flexible taper.

SUMMARY

The following conclusions can be drawn from the available literature on benzodiazepine use.

1. Benzodiazepines are used frequently and worldwide, with approximately I in 10 North Americans having used a benzodiazepine in the last year (Balter et al. 1984).

2. Despite their frequent use, there is little to no evidence that benzodiazepines are overprescribed or abused in routine medical practice (Rickels 1981, Uhlenhuth et al. 1988).

3. Much of the controversy attributed to benzodiazepine use is the result of (a) confusion in terminology and (b) misunderstanding and mishandling of withdrawal. Drug *dependence/ addiction* and *abuse* and *physical dependence* are often used interchangeably, albeit incorrectly. The terms *drug dependence, addiction,* and *abuse* should only be used to describe *DSM-III-R* criteria which typically include dose escalation, harmful consequences, and drug-seeking behavior in an inappropriate, damaging, and dangerous way. On the other hand, physical dependence can and does develop in a therapeutic setting, is appropriate and expected, and is not indicative of addiction or abuse. The real issue, the risk of withdrawal symptoms on discontinuation (i.e., physical dependence), should be discussed with the patient at the outset of benzodiazepine therapy for both clinical and medico-legal reasons. Although not indicative of abuse, benzodiazepine physical dependence can and does lead to mild to moderately severe withdrawal symptoms that can complicate or make difficult the discontinuation of benzodiazepines.

4. Benzodiazepines are effective antianxiety agents, with a more favorable side effect profile than the TCAs or MAOIs generally used in the treatment of panic disorder. In addition, they have a more rapid onset of action, with improvement generally beginning within the first week of treatment.

5. Benzodiazepine treatment should be reassessed periodically, to determine if the medication is still necessary. The major purpose of a trial of discontinuation is to determine if continued pharmacotherapy is needed.

6. Most patients can discontinue benzodiazepines with little to no problem, if the medication is tapered slowly, gradually, and flexibly, usually over a 2- to 4-month period.

7. Discontinuation is an important risk issue in benzodiazepine treatment, and should be discussed in detail at the beginning of treatment.

8. If patients are educated about the potential outcomes associated with discontinuation and have adequate support available from their clinician, they are generally able to tolerate this process with little problem.

9. There is a subset of patients who have significant problems with discontinuation. Those who have difficulty include patients with a previous history of psychopathology, relapse back into the original condition, passive-dependent-neurotic personality makeup, or comorbid substance abuse problems.

Finally, the benzodiazepines occupy an important and appropriate place in the treatment of the anxiety disorders. They have proven efficacy and work quickly, and many of the problems associated with discontinuation can be eliminated or reduced if this process is managed correctly.

REFERENCES

Ballenger, J. C. (1986). Pharmacotherapy of the panic disorders. *Journal of Clinical Psychiatry* 47(6, suppl):27–32.

—— (1991a). Long-term pharmacologic treatment of panic disorder. *Journal of Clinical Psychiatry* 52(2, suppl):18–23.

—— (1991b). Treatment of panic disorder and agoraphobia. In *The Clinical Management of Anxiety Disorders*, ed. W. Coryell and W. Winokur, pp. 41–62. New York: Oxford University Press.

—— (1992). Medication discontinuation in panic disorder. *Journal of Clinical Psychiatry* 53(3, suppl):26–31.

Ballenger, J. C., Burrows, G. D., DuPont, R. L., et al. (1988). Alprazolam in panic disorder and agoraphobia: results from a multicenter trial, I: efficacy in short-term treatment. *Archives of General Psychiatry* 45: 413–422.

Balter, M. B., Manheimer, D. I., Mellinger, G. D., et al. (1984). A cross-national comparison of anti-anxiety/sedative drug use. *Current Medical Research Opinion* 4:5–18.

Coryell, W., Noyes, R., and Clancy, J. (1983). Panic disorder and primary unipolar depression: a comparison of background and outcome. *Journal of Affective Disorders* 5:311–317.

Cross National Collaborative Panic Study, Second Phase Investigators. (1992). Drug treatment of panic disorder: comparative efficacy of alprazolam, imipramine, and placebo. *British Journal of Psychiatry* 160: 191–202.

Curtis, G. C., Massana, J., Udina, C., et al. (1993). Maintenance drug therapy of panic disorder. *Journal of Psychiatric Research* 27(suppl): 127–142.

Edwards, J. G., Inman, W. H. W., Pearce, G. L., et al. (1991). Prescription-event monitoring of 10,895 patients treated with alprazolam. *British Journal of Psychiatry* 158:387–392.

Fontaine, R., Chouinard, G., and Annable, L. (1984). Rebound anxiety in anxious patients after withdrawal of benzodiazepine treatment. *American Journal of Psychiatry* 141:848–852.

Gorman, J. M., and Papp, L. A. (1990). Chronic anxiety: deciding the, length of treatment. *Journal of Clinical Psychiatry* 51(1, suppl):11–15.

Haque, W., Watson, D. J., and Bryant, S. G. (1990). Death following suspected alprazolam withdrawal seizures: a case report. *Texas Medicine* 86:44–47.

Katschnig, H., Stolk, J., and Klerman, G. L. (1991). Discontinuation experiences and long-term treatment follow-up of participants in a clinical drug trial for panic disorder. In *Biological Psychiatry International Congress, Series 968*, vol. 1, ed. G. Rascagni, N. Brunello, and T. Fakuda, pp. 657–660. New York: Elsevier.

Laughren, T. P., Battey, Y., Greenblatt, D. J., et al. (1982). A controlled trial of diazepam withdrawal in chronically anxious outpatients. *Acta Psychiatrica Scandinavica* 65:171–179.

Lydiard, R. B., Lesser, J. M., Ballenger, J. C., et al. (1992). A fixed-dose study of aprazolam 2 mg, alprazolam 6 mg, and placebo in panic disorder. *Journal of Clinical Psychopharmacology* 12:96–103.

Mavissakalian, M., and Perel, J. M. (1992a). Clinical experiments in maintenance and discontinuation of imipramine therapy in panic disorder with agoraphobia. *Archives of General Psychiatry* 49:318–323.

—— (1992b). Protective effects of imipramine maintenance treatment in panic disorder with agoraphobia. *American Journal of Psychiatry* 149:1053–1057.

Nagy, L. M., Krystal, J. H., Woods, S. W., et al. (1989). Clinical and medication outcome after short-term alprazolam and behavioral group treatment of panic disorder: 2.5-year naturalistic follow-up study. *Archives of General Psychiatry* 46:993–999.

Noyes, R., Jr., DuPont, R. L., Jr., Pecknold, J. C., et al. (1988). Alprazolam in panic disorder and agoraphobia: results from a multicenter trial, II: patient acceptance, side effects, and safety. *Archives of General Psychiatry* 45:423–428.

Noyes, R., Jr., Garvey, M. J., Cook, B., et al. (1991). Controlled discontinuation of benzodiazepine treatment for patients with panic disorder. *American Journal of Psychiatry* 148:517–523.

Noyes, R., Perry, P. J., Crowe, R. R., et al. (1986). Single case study: seizures following the withdrawal of alprazolam. *Journal of Nervous and Mental Disease* 174:50–52.

Pecknold, J. C., Alexander, P. and Munjack, D. (1993). Alprazolam XR in the management of anxiety: discontinuation. *Psychiatric Annals* 23(10, suppl):38–44.

Pecknold, J. C., Swinson, R. P., Kirch, K., et al. (1988). Alprazolam in panic disorder and agoraphobia: results from a multicenter trial, III: discontinuation effects. *Archives of General Psychiatry* 45:429–436.

Pollack, M. H. (1990). Long-term management of panic disorder. *Journal of Clinical Psychiatry* 51(5, suppl):11–13.

Rickels, K. (1981). Are benzodiazepines overused and abused? *British Journal of Clinical Psychopharmacology* 11:71S-83S.

Rickels, K., Schweizer, E., Case, W. G., et al. (1990). Long-term therapeutic use of benzodiazepines, I: effects of abrupt discontinuation. *Archives of General Psychiatry* 47:899–907.

Rickels, K., Schweizer, E., Weiss, S., et al. (1993). Maintenance drug treatment of panic disorder, II: short- and long-term outcome after drug taper. *Archives of General Psychiatry* 50:61–68.

Romach, M. K., Somer, G. R., Sobell, L. C., et al. (1992). Characteristics of long-term alprazolam users in the community. *Journal of Clinical Psychopharmacology* 12:316–321.

Rosenberg, R., Ottosson, J. O., Bech, P., et al., eds. (1991). Alprazolam, imipramine and placebo treatment of panic disorder in Scandinavia. *Acta Psychiatrica Scandinavica* (suppl) 364(83).

Salzman, C. S. (1990). *Benzodiazepine Dependence, Toxicity, and Abuse: A Task Force Report of the American Psychiatric Association.* Washington, DC: American Psychiatric Press.

Schatzberg, A. F., and Ballenger, J. C. (1991). Decisions for the clinician in the treatment of panic disorder: when to treat, which treatment to use, and how long to treat. *Journal of Clinical Psychiatry* 52(2, suppl):26–31.

Schweizer, E., Rickels, K., Case, W. G., et al. (1990). Long-term therapeutic use of benzodiazepines, II: effects of gradual taper. *Archives of General Psychiatry* 47:908–915.

Schweizer, E., Rickels, K., Weiss, S., et al. (1993). Maintenance drug treatment of panic disorder, I: results of a prospective, placebo-controlled comparison of alprazolam and imipramine. *British Journal of Psychiatry* 50:51–60.

Sellers, E. M., Ciraulo, D. A., DuPont, R. L., et al. (1993). Alprazolam and benzodiazepine dependence. *Journal of Clinical Psychiatry* 54(10, suppl):64–75.

Shader, R. I., and Greenblatt, D. J. (1993). Use of benzodiazepines in anxiety disorders. *New England Journal of Medicine* 328:1398–1405.

Sheehan, D. V. (1986). Tricyclic antidepressants in the treatment of panic and anxiety disorders. *Psychosomatics* 27(suppl):10–16.

Sheehan, D. V., Ballenger, J. C., and Jacobsen, G. (1980). Treatment of endogenous anxiety with phobic, hysterical and hypochondriacal symptoms. *Archives of General Psychiatry* 37:51–59.

Tyrer, P. (1991). The benzodiazepine post-withdrawal syndrome [editorial]. *Stress Medicine* 7:1–2.

Tyrer, P., Owen, R., and Dawling, S. (1983). Gradual withdrawal from diazepam after long-term therapy. *Lancet* 1:1402–1406.

Uhlenhuth, E. H., DeWit, H., Balter, M. B., et al. (1988). Risks and benefits of long-term benzodiazepine use. *Journal of Clinical Psychopharmacology* 8:161–167.

Versiani, M., Costa e Silva, J. A., and Klerman, G. A. (1987). *Treatment of panic disorder with alprazolam, clomipramine, imipramine, tranylcypromine, or placebo.* Paper presented at the 26th Annual Meeting of the American College of Neuropsychopharmacology, San Juan, PR, December.

Zitrin, C. M., Klein, D. F., Woermer, M. G., et al. (1983). Treatment of phobias, I: comparison of imipramine hydrochloride and placebo. *Archives of General Psychiatry* 40:125–138.

CHAPTER SEVENTEEN

Bibliotherapy

—————————

Dr. Weekes, an Australian psychiatrist, was the first to write self-help books on phobias. Despite her geographical and historical isolation, her books, with quaint titles such as *Peace from Nervous Suffering* and *Hope and Help for your Nerves*, were widely read, and seemed to be universally regarded as among the most comforting, supportive, and useful of self-help books. The books are now unfortunately out of print.

A brief paper is reprinted here to give a sense of the tone she strikes that achieves such wide patient acceptance. Her key concepts are "first and second fear" and "floating through." She advocates facing the anxiety, experiencing it, and accepting it. She says that it is only by this means, without distractions, that the patient learns the dimensions of the panic and is able to tolerate it without fears of disintegration.

—————————

Bibliotherapy

CLAIRE WEEKES

Nothing in life is to be feared. It is only to be understood.

—Marie Curie

Agoraphobia—the condition in which a patient suffers incapacitating anxiety in public places or anywhere outside his own home—is a common syndrome affecting thousands of people in Britain. Optimism in treating it is contrary to much current opinion. However, after many years of practice with a special interest in the anxiety state of which agoraphobia has often been a major symptom, and especially after the results of my last 10 years' experience concerned almost exclusively with treating agoraphobic people, an optimistic approach is in my opinion justified.

A brief outline is offered here of my method of treating agoraphobia. The special difficulty of treating the disorder is that inability to travel to the doctor's office is often so much part of the agoraphobic's illness that he may rarely, perhaps never, succeed in making the journey. In these circumstances, offering a satisfactory program of treatment and in addition giving the frequent encouragement and reassurance the agoraphobic patient needs present special difficulties, while to treat a patient adequately at home is surely asking too much from a busy practitioner.

The treatment described here overcomes these difficulties. It does not require the personal presence of the doctor. It is available when needed (which may be many times during one day) either at home, or away from home when the patient's agoraphobic fears are at their worst. In addition, the cost is negligible.

Treatment is in the form of two books (Weekes 1962, 1972), two long-playing records (Weekes 1967), quarterly magazines sent to 1,800 agoraphobic men and women in Great Britain and Ireland during the four years 1969–1972, and a cassette (Weekes n.d.) for a small portable tape player. This remote "control" (perhaps "direction" would be a more accurate word) has made it possible to treat people living not only in distant parts of Great Brirain but also in other countries.

The books are available in most libraries, the recordings and cassette are available from Charlotte Radeau, Living Growth Foundation, 6800 14th Avenue North, St. Petersburg, FL. 33710, and the quarterly magazines (1969–1972) have been published in book form (Weekes 1972).* In psychiatric clinics in Great Britain where the recordings are used, patients are encouraged to bring their tape recorders and make copies, and no objections are raised. The condition is explained to the patients in the following way.

EXPLANATION TO PATIENTS

Understanding by the patient of the cause of agoraphobia is essential for successful treatment, and the key lies in understanding the state in which the nervous reaction to stress is unusually intense and

---

Editor's note: At the time of this printing, Dr. Weekes's books and recordings are no longer available.

swift. This I term *sensitization*, and I explain that when mildly sensitized, nerves feel on edge and little things upset too much, too easily. Severe sensitization can be more disturbing, even alarming. An ordinary spasm of fear may be felt as an "electrifying" flash of panic, which may come in response to no more than the shock of a slamming door, or, more bewildering still, for no apparent reason other than thinking of it. A slightly quickly beating heart may feel like an acute attack of palpitations, irregular beats like a sudden descent in a lift, a mild attack of faintness like impending death, and so on. Such intense responses so impress the sufferer he thinks they must be unique to him. He rarely recognizes them as part of the usual pattern of stress exaggerated.

Sudden severe sensitization can follow the shock of physical stress, such as a severe hemorrhage, a difficult confinement, or a surgical operation. Gradual sensitization may accompany continuous domestic stress or debilitating illness—anything that puts a patient under stress for a long time.

I also explain to patients that where a special problem has started the illness and helps to keep a person sensitized, understanding sensitization and knowing how to cope with it is itself a step toward recovery, because the sufferer may become as much concerned with the state he is in as with the original problem. Sensitization resolves naturally if not kept alive by bewilderment and fear. Bewilderment acts by placing a sensitized person constantly under the strain of asking himself why he is like this, why he cannot be his old self, and what could happen next. The more he struggles to be the person he was, the more exasperation and tension he adds and so the more stress. While in his bewilderment he feels he cannot adequately direct his thoughts and feelings, he stands vulnerable to fear, which seems to overwhelm him before he has time to reason with it.

Sensitization, bewilderment, and fear are three reactions leading to an anxiety state of which agoraphobia, when present, is the most crippling symptom. Often the first attack of the disorder in a

man or woman takes the form of panic or palpitations or severe
giddiness or a feeling of weakness or collapse while out of doors.
Such an attack probably follows any of a variety of stresses. If a
woman (almost 90 percent of agoraphobic patients arc women) has
had a frightening attack of palpitations or a weak "turn" or panic
while away from home and yet one day manages, in spite of this,
to walk as far as the supermarket, how natural when immobilized
in a long line at the checkout to be suddenly smitten with the fear
of having one of her spells. The panic and mounting tension that
follow may so stiffen her muscles that she may feel unable to move
and may cling desperately to the nearest support.

After a few such attacks, she either avoids supermarkets—or
any place where she feels restricted by a crowd—tries to take someone to shop with her, or becomes finally housebound when she dis-
covers that "paralysis" may strike anywhere away from the house.
When patients understand severe sensitization, what may have
seemed incredible behavior becomes a more understandable human
reaction.

PRACTICAL APPROACH

Some therapists search for a deep-seated cause for agoraphobia,
believing that unless this is found and treated, the illness cannot be
cured. In my experience, while finding an original cause for sensitization has been intellectually interesting, it has rarely been essential for cure. Agoraphobia persists because the habit of fear—and,
because of this, sensitization—remains. This must be cured. The
sensitized person has become afraid of so much. He sits near the
door in a restaurant, at the back of the hall at a meeting, always leaving a way open for quick escape should, as he thinks may occur, his
fear grow beyond him.

After relieving a patient's bewilderment by adequate explanation of his illness, I follow with a program of treatment based on

the four principles of facing, accepting, "floating," and letting time pass. Many people sink deeper into their illness by doing the opposite. The nervously ill person notices each symptom with alarm and withdraws from it, afraid to examine it too closely for fear of making it worse He may agitatedly seek occupation to try to force forgetfulness. This is running away, not facing. He may try to cope by teasing himself against unwelcome sensations, trying to "get the better of them." This is fighting, not accepting. "Floating" implies going along with the feelings without resistance, as if floating on the sea, submitting to the undulation of the waves. The thought of floating lessens tension that may inhibit action. Letting time pass is an important concept, since so many patients worry because much time has passed and they are still ill. They are impatient with time, and this impatience increases tension and anxiety.

COPING WITH PANIC

To help the patient cope with panic I explain that when he panics he feels not one fear, as he supposes, but two separate fears—a first and second fear. First-fear comes to any of us in response to danger. It is normal in intensity and passes with the danger. However, the "electric" flash of first-fear that the sensitized person feels is so out of proportion to the danger causing it that he recoils and as he does so he adds a second flash—fear of the first fear. He may be more concerned with the feeling of panic than with the original danger. And because sensitization prolongs the first flash, the second flash may join in and the two fears seem as one. Though he may have no control over the first fear, and this is often true, with practice he can learn how to control the second fear—and it is the second fear that is helping to keep the first fear alive and keeping him sensitized and ill.

The agoraphobic person hemmed in at the school meeting has only to feel trapped to experience first-fear and then to immediately follow with second-fear and an urge to escape from the building. As the panic grows, he feels his mind goes numb and is sure something terrible will happen. He does not understand that it is the second-fear he adds himself that may finally drive him to seek refuge outside.

To cope while inside the hall he should practice seeing panic through with as much acceptance as he can muster (usually aided by sedation in the early stages of treatment). It is important for him to appreciate that his body has a limited capacity to produce panic, so that panic always comes in a wave, which will pass if he waits. If he remains seated and tries to relax to the best of his ability, even lets his body slump in the seat and is prepared to let panic do its very worst, it will not mount. His sensitized body may continue to have flashes of panic from time to time, but these will be bearable and he will be able to see the function through. The realization that they have been bluffed by physical feeling has been enough to cure some people.

The patient should be taught the difference between true acceptance and just "putting up with." "Putting up with" means bearing panic with clenched teeth, hoping that it will get it over quickly and not come again. True acceptance means recognizing second-fear (which can be prefixed by "Oh, my goodness" and "What if?"), and adding as little as possible. It also means learning to regard panicking as yet another opportunity to practice coping with it until it no longer matters. This can be done. I have watched many agoraphobics come through panics to lasting cure in this way, even those who thought courage was not their strong point.

However, before a patient should be expected to face and accept his nervous symptoms (not only panic), they should be fully explained to him. While I hesitate to make the following elementary suggestions, I am reminded of the many anxious patients who have complained that they had never previously been given such explanations and who began to recover afterward.

SPECIFIC SYMPTOMS

For example, I keep crackers in my surgery for the nervous person with difficulty in swallowing solid foods and hence with a habit of avoiding eating in public places. At the sight of a dry cracker he usually recoils; I then suggest that he chew, not swallow. As soon as the softened, moistened cracker reaches the back of his tongue, his swallowing reflexes take over and some of the cracker is automatically on its way down. When the patient understands that he needs only to chew and that swallowing will look after itself, some of the fear and tension goes and swallowing becomes easier.

Again I hesitate to discuss such a common symptom as hyperventilation. However, I am reminded of a young girl sent to me by her general practitioner because she had been breathing shallowly almost constantly for a year. She entered my office in distress. I explained the respiratory center's automatic control of breathing, how it worked during sleep and unconsciousness. To illustrate its action I asked her to hold her breath as long as she could. When she found that she was soon forced to take a deep breath almost against her will, she appreciated the control beyond her control and saw the folly of her struggle. Some months later her doctor reported that she was cured. He had thought of every treatment except simple explanation. Every nervous symptom has explanation. It is not enough to say it is "only nerves."

RESPONSE TO TREATMENT

In my opinion, dependence on constant medication to tranquilize nervous symptoms or on learning how to avoid having them—for example, avoiding waiting in a queue—carries the danger of leaving the patient vulnerable to the return of symptoms at any time, in any place. Dr. Isaac Marks has stressed the disadvantages of the unexpected return of panic after weeks of present-day treatment of agoraphobia by medical desensitization (Marks 1969). A patient must be taught to cope with his symptoms. If a technique needs a name, perhaps mine could be called *coping through understanding.*

There are many ways to help understanding beside those already mentioned—for example, stressing the difference between testing and practicing. The thought of testing brings tension, whereas the thought of practicing holds no urgent demand. Also, testing followed by failure brings an acute sense of defeat, whereas failure while practicing means merely the necessity to practice again.

Again, it helps the sufferer to understand that the symptoms of stress are part of life and that the illness is their exaggeration in his sensitized body, not simply their occurrence; that therefore cure lies not in their complete elimination, as he probably believes and hopes, but in their reduction to normal intensity.

RELAPSE

Even months after a patient is desensitized and thinks he is cured, the sudden return of his symptoms in an exaggerated way in response to stress can so shock the sufferer he may think he has "slipped right back." He should be taught to understand the traps memory can set and try to accept the setbacks it may bring, until he knows the way out of setbacks so well that he no longer fears the way in. Indeed, the definition of recovery should include having setbacks and knowing how to cope with them, so that neither doctor nor patient becomes too discouraged by them.

In this short chapter I have not mentioned the complications sometimes associated with agoraphobia: indecision, suggestibility, loss of confidence, feeling of unreality, feeling of disintegration, obsession, and depression. These too may develop following a set, logical pattern, and this pattern, with treatment, is discussed in my books and recordings.

Finally, I stress that repetition of advice is the crux of treatment of the agoraphobic. He finds achievement difficult because he remembers past failures and how he felt then, so that when he thinks of facing similar experiences, his reactions are automatically those of withdrawal, fear, and despair. With enough repetition of the right advice new association paths are established, which ultimately replace the old automatic flashback reactions of panic and withdrawal when the patient is stressed. I call this *right reaction-readiness* and know of no better way of establishing it than by using records and tape cassettes, which can not only be played immediately before the patient sets out to practice but also (with cassettes) while he is out.

RESULTS

In 1970–1971, questionnaires were filled in by 528 agoraphobic people in Great Britain and Ireland whom I had treated for periods varying from a few months to 6 years using the method outlined above, without any personal contact. Of these, 60% had been agoraphobic for 10 years or more and 27% for 20 years or more, so that most could be classed as chronic agoraphobics. For their present illness 65% had had treatment from one or more psychiatrists and 30% from their general practitioner alone. Previous treatment had included almost every known orthodox method. This group offered a challenge to treatment without the personal supervision of a doctor.

Of the patients aged 14–29, the results were satisfactory or good in 73%; of those aged 30–39 similar good results were found in 67%, and in those aged 40–49 in 55%. Of the older and therefore more difficult group aged 50–74, good progress was made by 49%. As so many of these people were chronically ill (only 27 had been ill for less than 3 years), the chances of spontaneous recovery irrespective of treatment were negligible.

REFERENCES

Marks I. M. (1969). *Fears and Phobias*. London: Heinemann.

Weekes, C. (n.d.). *Moving Towards Freedom and Going on Holiday* (cassette). St. Petersburg, FL: Living Growth Foundation.

—— (1962). *Self Help for Your Nerves*. London: Angus and Robertson.

—— (1967). *Hope and Help for Your Nerves* (record album). St. Petersburg, FL: Living Growth Foundation.

—— (1972). *Peace from Nervous Suffering*. London: Angus and Robertson.

CHAPTER EIGHTEEN

Identifying and Treating Phobias Following a Trauma

⸺⟫●⟪⸺

This contribution by Sally Winston expands upon treatment for post-traumatic stress disorders, which had been omitted from the first edition. It presents the clinical observation that phobias originating from post-traumatic stress are different from phobic disorders in certain fundamental ways and require different assessment and treatment techniques.

⸺⟫●⟪⸺

Identifying and Treating Phobias Following a Trauma

SALLY WINSTON

Most people who treat anxiety disorders are quite familiar with effective psychopharmacological and cognitive-behavioral treatment for panic and phobic disorders but tend to be less familiar with both theory and treatment of the traumatic stress disorders. Nevertheless, since hyperarousal, panic attacks, and phobias are often sequelae of trauma, and trauma is ubiquitous in our society, phobia therapists often encounter these phenomena. This paper will advance the thesis that phobic reactions which arise from traumatic origins may present differently and may require different or additional treatments. Because post-traumatic stress disorder (PTSD) tends to be a chronic disorder, many patients whose anxiety problems are trauma-related do not make any conscious connection between their current struggles with panic and avoidance behaviors and the original traumatic events, which may have occurred years before. In addition, many people who have survived trauma earlier in their lives are left with residual symptoms of hyperarousal and phobia, which then acquire a life of their own. This chapter will introduce the reader to such patients, help to raise awareness regarding trauma-based symptoms, and provide some direction for handling phobias which arise in this context. A full discussion of PTSD, an entire field of inquiry in and of itself, is not intended here. The reader is encouraged to pursue more comprehensive works listed at the end of the chapter and Chapter 8 in this volume.

The following cases illustrate a number of phenomena which characterize trauma-based panic attacks and phobic behaviors. These may not be as responsive to standard behavioral therapies and cognitive interventions for panic disorder, social phobia, or specific phobias of non-traumatic origin.

PANIC ATTACKS WHICH DO NOT HABITUATE MAY BE FLASHBACKS.

> Case 1: A 51-year-old Vietnam veteran has been hospitalized for major depression. Early in his stay, he "creates a ruckus" in the cafeteria. He tries returning there repeatedly but panics and is inconsolable each time. He acknowledges to nursing staff that "sometimes he gets phobias like this." In interview, he denies being afraid of the sensations of the panic attack, shows little concern about social embarrassment, and expresses anger about not being allowed to just eat his meals alone in his room. Eventually, after several meetings, he asks if you realize "that a fork going into a baked potato feels just like a bayonet going into a human body."

This patient may not be suffering from a misattribution of danger to sensations of arousal, as is common in phobias secondary to panic disorder, but from a *re-experiencing* of extreme terror or helplessness which was at the time a *totally appropriate response to real danger*. At the time they are panicking, PTSD patients may not seem to be fully with you while you talk with them—they are back in time to some degree and may seem dissociated. They may speak in a "little voice" like a child, or seem unresponsive to logical conversation. Reassurance that symptoms are not dangerous, and help with breathing and non-catastrophic thinking, so helpful with panic attacks, are not really useful. Techniques which focus on grounding, returning to the present time and place, or decreasing the affective impact of the flashback experiences will be more helpful.

To help orient a patient in present time, such techniques as carrying a transitional object (perhaps something small from your office, or something that is a powerful reminder of the patient's present life) may be useful. Continuous simple verbal reminders of the actual date, time, and place may be needed. With prior permission of the patient, physical touch may keep some patients grounded during flashbacks.

Since flashbacks may occur in any sensory modality (visual, olfactory, auditory, kinesthetic), techniques which diminish their impact are those which decrease their intensity. One might teach the patient to "place" a vivid disturbing image on an imaginal small black-and-white television screen. One might help the patient to "de-focus" attention that is riveted on a horrible image by widening the peripheral vision and looking at what else is in the scene being re-experienced. One might have the patient practice standing apart from particular sensations and observing and reporting them. Sometimes auditory flashbacks are less distressing if they can be shifted in terms of the apparent direction of their source. Sometimes patients can learn to "turn down the volume" by imagining that the sounds are coming from a radio whose dial they control.

Sometimes it is possible to "bypass" the impact of a flashback with an illogical or abrupt transition that calls upon intact functional aspects of the patient. An example of this might be to suddenly begin talking about something in the patient's present life that has nothing to do with traumatic material, or asking the patient for advice about something related to his or her work. What works for one patient may not work for another. How to handle flashbacks must be collaboratively and empirically developed with the patient, often in retrospective analysis of what was helpful and what was not at critical moments.

Patients who are experiencing flashbacks ask for help in preventing their occurrence and in stopping them once they start. At this point, there are really no known ways of stopping intrusive re-experiencing as a sequela to trauma. The most that can be done is to minimize the known triggers whenever possible, decrease the impact when they occur, reduce the degree of distress they engender, and learn to interpret their meaning in a non-judgmental fashion. It is sometimes helpful to talk about flashbacks as the mind's attempt to grasp and process something too difficult to assimilate all at once. Flashbacks are vivid remembering, often accompanied by the "freezing" response or overwhelming terror and helplessness that occurred at the time of the trauma.[1] Intentional suppression of flashbacks works paradoxically to increase their frequency. It is often helpful for the patient to know that flashbacks occur thousands of times a day at first, gradually become less frequent, and eventually only occur when specifically triggered by a reminder, either something experienced in the present or a bodily state of arousal similar to the state the body was in during the original emer-

---

1. Because of the tendency to freeze and dissociate during vivid re-experiencing, there are safety issues which are not typical of panic disorder or other phobic patients. Patients can in fact drive dangerously, come to a stop in the middle of the road, walk into dangerous environments, act impulsively, and even enact elaborate sequences of behavior such as finding a gun and shooting a family member. Because trauma may produce a tendency towards rigidified and hypervigilant response to threat, patients may overreact to mild cues of rejection and behave abusively, or automatically submit to the demands or expectations of authority figures or current abusers. Some may be revictimized partly because of an impaired ability to judge danger.

gency. This is why triggers can be as dissimilar as too much caffeine, a man who has the same hairstyle as the rapist, a car of the same make or color as the one that caused the accident, or a news report about a tornado or a murder. Panic attacks can and often do occur both as a reaction to and in anticipation of flashbacks.

Phobic Avoidance Which Seems Based on Shame, Guilt, or Revulsion rather than on Fear May Be Trauma-Related.

> Case 2: A woman who is almost housebound with agoraphobia will only come to see you after hours, when there will be no other patients who might see her. She arrives in dark glasses that she keeps on throughout the interview. She tells you that she is afraid to leave her house since she was raped four years ago by a friend of a friend. She denies being afraid that she will be attacked again. She does have panic attacks if she watches the eleven o'clock news, but she denies being afraid of panic outside her house. She says that she does not want to see anyone who might know her, because they might ask her how she's been or why she quit her job. She has never told anyone about the rape, except her doctor.

Avoidance behavior may be an attempt to avoid not fear but other strong feelings which are relevant to the trauma and its meaning to the patient. Again, interventions which are focused on reduction of fearful attributions and decreased physiological arousal may not be helpful. Dealing with the meaning the patient has developed of what occurred is essential in the recovery process. Survivors of trauma deal with guilt associated with their own self-preservation behavior or thoughts or affects at the time of the emergency. They may suffer from the aftereffects of physical or psychological defilement. They may describe feeling like "damaged goods." They may be struggling with levels of anger or rage they never thought possible. They may be experiencing a spiritual crisis or loss of faith. Patients may feel that their "core" has collapsed and they are helpless, without purpose, or "banned" from regular human connections. They often feel that they can no longer relate to "innocents," or people who have not been through similar events, particularly if the trauma was a deliberate act of a human perpetrator.

IDIOSYNCRATIC TRIGGERS MAY INDICATE A CONDITIONED RESPONSE ACQUIRED AT THE TIME OF THE TRAUMA AND GENERALIZED ALONG PHYSICAL, TEMPORAL, OR SYMBOLIC DIMENSIONS.

> Case 3: A man who was forcibly raped years ago has a phobia of people in uniform, and experiences severe anxiety in their presence. He is able to relate this to an episode with a homophobic, abusive police detective who detained him at the police station for hours of provocative questioning the night the rape occurred.

The patient will often feel less "crazy," and panic will seem less random, if the connection to the original trauma can be made. This can decrease the patient's negative self-judgment for having overreacted or having become irrational when triggered. Identifying triggers in the environment such as news reports, anniversaries of particular events, and stimuli that are relevant because of their similarity to or association with the trauma is often helpful. Unlike in exposure therapies, patients may be encouraged to avoid such stimuli where possible, particularly when they are flooded or overwhelmed by them. On the other hand, triggers cannot be fully avoided because they will frequently be part of unavoidable or unpredictable circumstances. It supports self-esteem and decreases bewilderment to identify triggers, even after the fact.

When a patient develops agoraphobia secondary to panic disorder, there is an inherent logic to the avoidances—basically any place or situation in which the patient feels trapped, or believes that a panic attack would be particularly dangerous or the escape to a safe place or person would be difficult. Thus, for example, avoiding bridges, tunnels and highways with no shoulders makes sense. Similarly, a person may not want to be solely responsible for children, or may avoid the dentist's chair because a panic attack not well handled might create problems. On the other hand, if a person in addition has a problem with women in blue dresses or red smeary stains or crying babies, one might wonder about one-trial traumatic conditioning.[2] Panic attacks can also be produced simply by having the body be in a similar state to the way it felt at the time of the original stressor, so that fatigue, hunger, sleep deprivation, or just physical arousal due to excitement can trigger panic or even flashbacks.

THE PRESENCE OF SEVERAL COMORBID DIAGNOSES, ESPECIALLY SUBSTANCE ABUSE, EATING DISORDERS, AND PERSONALITY DISORDERS, AS WELL AS A HISTORY OF SELF-MUTILATION, PARASUICIDAL BEHAVIOR, CHRONIC DYSPHORIA OR ANGER, MULTIPLE LIFETIME VICTIMIZATIONS, AND EXTREME NARCISSISTIC VULNERABILITY MAY REQUIRE A DIFFERENT TREATMENT APPROACH.

> Case 4: A woman who has been referred for treatment of her debilitating panic attacks has not been able to follow through on any homework assignments and seems to have one crisis after another in her relationships that must be addressed. She is often despairing and wonders if it is worth it to be in treat-

---

2. It is interesting, by the way, to consider the first out-of-the-blue panic attack in subsequently phobic patients as meeting the technical criteria for a traumatic stressor: it is a sudden event in which the person believes he may die and experiences intense fear and helplessness. In most PTSD, the initial reaction is to fear it may happen again, and the intense anticipatory anxiety of panic disorder patients certainly follows this pattern.

ment at all. She reveals that there is one form of anxiety relief that she has no intention of giving up: she lifts her long sleeves to reveal hundreds of delicate self-cuts in various stages of healing.

A number of elements in a history or presentation may be cues that the patient could be dealing with prolonged or repetitive traumatic experiences in childhood, and is suffering from the chronic aftereffects described by Herman as "complex PTSD" (1992) or by van der Kolk as "disorders of extreme stress (DES)" (1993), including: problems with affect regulation, self-destructiveness and impulsivity; alterations in consciousness; self-perception as damaged, helpless, or special; problems with trust, intimacy, and revictimization; and somatization. If such cues exist but conscious memories of trauma are not present, it does not imply that treatment should then embark upon a memory retrieval course (one fraught with extreme potential hazards). However, such cues in a panic or phobic patient do imply that a more cautious treatment approach may be required, particularly regarding deliberate arousal of anxiety, direct exposure work, and managing the therapeutic relationship itself.

NOTHING CAN BE ACCOMPLISHED UNTIL THE PATIENT FEELS SAFE.

For patients suffering from the aftereffects of trauma, this means not only safe at home, but safe with the therapist and safe with the affects and impulses which may arise during treatment. Patients who respond to increased levels of arousal produced by exposure to trauma-related stimuli need to be taught methods of self-soothing, containment, and grounding or they may become overwhelmed, impulsive, or dysfunctional. This may mean delaying exposure work until some skills have been learned, or until the therapeutic alliance is more solidly established. Note, by the way, that self-soothing techniques may in some cases *not* include relaxation, since trauma patients often feel safer when feeling empowered, strong, or connected to others, rather than at ease, unguarded, and relaxed. Also, because of the sometimes exquisite levels of sensitization and arousal in these patients, treatment may need to proceed at a slower pace. Sessions may need to be longer in order to accommodate a sufficient "cool-down," with debriefing and a self-care homework discussion, particularly after doing any sort of exposure or memory processing work.

MANY PATIENTS MUST DEAL WITH SECONDARY WOUNDING ISSUES BEFORE THEY CAN CONFRONT THEIR FEARS.

> Case 5: A man entered treatment for insomnia and general irritability. He had been waking up with nightmares ever since he witnessed the traumatic death of his girlfriend in a freak accident 3 years ago. He developed a phobia of sleeping, and can only fall asleep on the couch with the TV on. He misses his girlfriend and has been unable to date or care about anyone or anything. Recently he has had a strange urge to revisit the scene of the accident, but family members are telling him that he is torturing himself and needs to put it behind him. He continues to obsess about how unsupportive they have been, and can talk about little else when he comes to talk to you. He is particularly upset with their statements that it was God's will.

What the police, family members, press, friends, clergy, or courts do may be even more preoccupying and painful than the original trauma, and may in and of themselves provoke anxiety, rage, or despair. Needing to talk about feeling betrayed, abandoned, or hurt in the sequelae of the trauma is not simply avoidance of confronting the phobic stimuli.

EXPOSURE TECHNIQUES CAN BE USED IN A VARIETY OF WAYS WITH TRAUMA SURVIVORS.

With patients who have established required safety criteria, exposure techniques, whether imaginal or in vivo, can be used to process and habituate to traumatic stimuli, eventually leading to reduced intrusive re-experiencing and to less phobic avoidance. Standard desensitization techniques can certainly be utilized for phobic phenomena that are now functionally autonomous. Sometimes revisiting the scene of the traumatic event, or writing about it, or doing historical research into the details (police records, press reports, diaries) will assist the patient to remember and work through unfinished business, re-own dissociated affects, or take back a previously split off part of their lives.

MANY PATIENTS WHO ARE SUFFERING WITH INTRUSIVE RECOLLECTION, PANIC, AND PHOBIA ARE ALSO INTERMITTENTLY OR CONCURRENTLY STRUGGLING WITH THE NUMBING PHENOMENA THAT ARE PART OF THE BIPHASIC NATURE OF PTSD.

Patients may seem unmotivated because they are feeling dead inside, have a restricted range of affect (particularly for soft or loving feelings), or may be amnesic for part or all of the traumatic experience. They may also be suffering from a concurrent depressive disorder that is masked by the more attention-provoking symptoms of hyperarousal, panic, and irritability. A loss of meaning may lead to a "why bother" attitude towards treatment.

ONCE TRAUMA-BASED PANIC OR PHOBIC PHENOMENA ARE DISCOVERED, WHAT SHOULD THE NEXT STEPS BE?

Case 6: A woman in treatment for classic panic disorder with agoraphobia has been doing well. She understands the biological predisposition she probably inherited from her agoraphobic mother. She feels confident about handling anticipatory anxiety and has only very rare panic attacks. One day her husband calls you for emergency help with some sort of setback or "mega-panic attack" that she is having. She went into a fast-food restaurant and suddenly became terrified. She was not able to articulate what happened and had not calmed down at all when they left the restaurant. He couldn't seem to reach her; she was hyperventilating and weeping like a child, and kept saying she was going to throw up. Later that day she tells you about memories that suddenly came rushing forward of abuse by a teacher in a preschool, when she was forced to eat greasy food, vomited, and had to wear her soiled clothes all day. That night, she sleeps well for the first time in years.

It is possible, of course, for trauma-based and non-trauma-based symptoms to co-exist in the same individual. Careful assessment will be needed to understand the differences. It needs to be determined to what extent the current anxiety disorder symptoms are related to or are functionally autonomous from the original trauma. Is it possible to proceed successfully with cognitive-behavioral therapies surrounding current symptomatology without disturbing or unearthing past memories or issues? What is the simplest and most effective way of meeting the patient's request for help? How well has the patient worked out his or her own recovery and re-integration from the trauma, except for residual symptoms of hyperarousal? These questions should be shared openly and explicitly with the patient, including frank discussions of the potential pain and disruption that can be created while working through and assimilating traumatic memories. A careful assessment needs to be made of the patient's present capacity for tolerating negative affects without becoming behaviorally dysfunctional or risking real present-life adjustment. And, of course, no form of therapy should ever be used with a trauma survivor without his or her explicit informed permission. It may be possible to proceed with phobia therapy as one might with any patient, with the additional element of good psychoeducational information regarding the typical aftereffects of trauma.

REFERENCES

Herman, J. (1992). *Trauma and Recovery: The Aftermath of Violence—From Domestic Abuse to Political Terror.* New York: Basic Books.

van der Kolk, B. (1987). *Psychological Trauma.* Washington, DC: American Psychiatric Press.

SUGGESTED READING

Matsakis, A. (1994). *Post-Traumatic Stress Disorder: A Complete Treatment Guide.* Oakland, CA: New Harbinger Publications.

Meichenbaum, D. (1994). *A Clinical Handbook/Practical Therapist Manual for Assessing and Treating Adults with Post-Traumatic Stress Disorder (PTSD).* Waterloo, Ontario: Institute Press.

Ochberg, F., ed. (1988). *Post-Traumatic Therapy and Victims of Violence.* New York: Brunner/Mazel.

CHAPTER NINETEEN

Psychoanalytic Psychotherapy

———⟶⟩●⟨———

Dr. Abend presents in this chapter a brief outline of the fundamental assumptions of psychoanalytic psychotherapy concerning the dynamic structure of a phobia. He then presents an illustrative case report in which the interpretive sequence enables the patient to overcome her phobia.

The relationship between psychoanalysis and phobia therapy is remote, because the fundamental assumptions underlying the two schools are contradictory. The phobia therapists point to the research showing their techniques are more efficient and expedient. The psychoanalysts consider that they are treating the person as a whole, rather than allowing the symptom to define the person. Further, the psychoanalyst has a basic mistrust of behaviorism as simplistic and violating the principle of "neutrality." The phobia therapist believes that when a patient comes to him seeking symptom relief, the patient has made the decision to change that behavior and the therapist should use all his skill to effect that change. The psychoanalyst would reply that the patient's desire to change is often complicated by unconscious factors, which might prove to be quite contradictory to his or her announced intention.

As so often occurs in developing sciences, there has been a gradual shift of both positions toward the center. Psychoanalysts are more frequently making referrals for symptom relief, either concurrent with, or preceding, more intensive therapy. Phobia specialists are finding that a psychodynamic understanding may inform all phases of treatment, and such psychotherapy techniques may be important in managing other aspects of the therapist's interaction with the phobic patient, even when symptom-focused techniques are being employed.

Psychoanalytic Psychotherapy

SANDER M. ABEND

The treatment of phobias by psychoanalysis, or by psychodynamic psychotherapies derived from psychoanalysis, rests on the assumption that all phobias are defensively altered representations of underlying unconscious conflicts. The essence of the treatment consists in the uncovering and working through of these unconscious determinants; if successfully accomplished, this can alleviate their surface manifestations, the phobic symptoms themselves.

Thus, just as the analytic therapies regard the contents of dreams reported in a session as a perfect point of departure for analytic investigation, the surface texts of phobic concerns are similarly understood as the starting points for exploration of unconscious concerns and the fantasies that express them. Often, to begin with at least, the suffering patient may have no awareness of the existence of these underlying conflicts, much less of their relationship to the phobic symptoms to which they have given rise. The resolution of these unconscious stresses will often result in the disappearance of the phobia to which they are related.

Perhaps the best-known case of phobia ever reported in the psychoanalytic literature was that of Little Hans, a 5-year-old boy who developed a paralyzing fear of horses. The monograph in which the unraveling of his phobias is described, entitled *Analysis of a Phobia in a Five-Year-Old Boy* (1909), is one of five famous lengthy clinical reports published by Sigmund Freud. Psychoanalytic theory and practice have evolved since the case of Little Hans first appeared in print, hence some of Freud's observations and explanations have been superseded by later findings and modifications. For our present purposes, two points are worthy of note:

1. Freud classified phobias as closely related to what he called at the time *anxiety hysteria*, noting that the little boy's phobia only began some time after a more generalized anxiety state had made its appearance.

2. The "phobia" was not a single consistent fear of horses, but instead turned out to be a set of different, rather specific ideas, all involving horses, that frightened the little boy. These included (a) that a horse would bite him, (b) that only a big white horse was likely to bite him, (c) that a horse would fall down dead in the street, (d) that a horse would enter his room at night, and (e) that horses were to be feared only if they were pulling heavily laden carts or wagons. These individual variations, or refinements, of the patient's fears gradually came to light as the treatment progressed.

Freud did not conduct Little Hans's treatment himself. The boy was "analyzed," after a fashion, by his own father, with some help from Freud, at a time when no organized technique for psychoanalysis or psychotherapy of children had yet been developed, and when even the treatment of adults by psychoanalysis was at a very early stage of development. Even so, the material of the case led Freud to state with some confidence that many layers of unconscious meaning were all *condensed*, thus contributing in conjunction to the form of the phobic symptoms, and that in phobias the fearful situation was *projected* outside the individual's mind and onto an aspect of the environment that could then be avoided, thus enabling the patient to substitute a degree of constriction of life for what might otherwise be an intolerable and unavoidable subjective state of psychic discomfort. Although he did not use the precise term *displacement* at that time to explain the formation of the phobic symptoms, it is clear from his clinical descriptions that the horses, wagons, and so forth all stood for other persons or objects associated with them only by unconscious connections.

Freud's explanatory formulations in the Little Hans case stressed childhood sexual wishes and the conflicts stemming from them. His main purpose in writing up and publishing the case, however, was to lend support to his thesis about the potential pathogenic significance of infantile sexual concerns and theories. One can find, in the detailed clinical descriptions, hints of what analytic theory would only much later incorporate more explicitly: the role played by aggressive wishes and conflicts in phobia formation. One may also detect, in the explication of the case material, evidence of the contribution of preoedipal constellations and issues, of unconscious need for punishment, and of the secondary gains obtainable by manipulation of persons in the patient's environment.

It is also important to keep in mind that Freud's first theory of anxiety held sway when this report was written. At that time, anxiety was believed to be the end product of some quasi-biological alteration in the libido, conceived of rather concretely as if it were a physical substance. The transformation of libido into anxiety was somehow caused by the repression of the forbidden sexual wishes that were thought to be energized by this mysterious libido. Since anxiety was thought to be produced by repression, treatment was aimed at restoring health through the lifting of the repressions, which was gradually to be achieved by the psychoanalytic work.

Although theories and schools of psychoanalytic thought have multiplied since Freud's day, any statement of the current psychoanalytic understanding of the treatment of phobias would certainly include the principle that the symptom itself is overdetermined— a number of levels of meaning are likely to be found in the course of its successful unraveling. Accordingly, no matter what general description of a phobia is obtained at the outset of treatment from a patient, analytic therapists expect that it will be revised in the course of treatment into several, perhaps even many, more specific subtexts, each of which will be related to some aspect or aspects of the unconscious significance of the symptom.

The assumption that phobic symptoms all have unconscious underpinnings still characterizes the psychoanalytic theory of phobias. In pursuit of the sources of specific phobias, analytic therapists are likely to seek associative evidence indicating the nature of their linkage to the unconscious wishes, fears, and fantasies they have come to represent, rather than to pursue a cognitive elaboration of the reality situation that obtained when the symptoms first appeared. It would be anticipated, as a matter of course, that sexual and aggressive wishes and their associated conflicts, stemming from all developmental levels, invariably including certain manifestations of guilt such as restitution or punishment, will combine together to contribute to the establishment and maintenance of any phobia.

It is often stated that separation anxiety is likely to play an important role in phobia. It should be realized that *separation anxiety* does nor refer merely to the real or imagined loss of an attachment. It is instead a kind of shorthand term for anxiety associated with a whole variety of real or fantasied losses. The complexity of unconscious mental activity is such that any perceived or dreaded loss may represent symbolically any or all the varieties of childhood danger situations and is not to be understood invariably to refer to loss of the mother or other primary caretaker.

As is well known, the therapeutic emphasis on discovering the unconscious meanings behind the surface phobic symptoms leads to a specific technical posture on the part of the analytic therapist. Efforts are directed toward uncovering the unconscious conflicts that give rise to the phobic concerns, rather than focusing primarily on the manifest descriptions and consequences of the phobias themselves or on efforts at reassuring, educating, or otherwise encouraging patients to combat or overcome their problems. It is no longer even considered appropriate analytic technique to urge patients to enter the avoided phobic situations, although that was at one time accepted practice, even among psychoanalysts of the most traditional stripe. The change in technique reflects strongly the accumulated and more accurate understanding arrived at in the recent period of psychoanalytic theory, which holds that the patients' defenses, manifested in treatment as resistance to progress, cannot merely be swept aside or overpowered. Resistance, too, like the forbidden wishes for sexual or aggressive gratification, and like the multiple influences of the patient's internalized moral system, must all receive equal and careful attention from the therapist in order to determine their respective roles in the symptoms and other aspects of the patient's psychological functioning.

In summary then, psychoanalytic therapists regard symptoms as providing a variety of manifest texts that one must attempt to understand and interpret. Treatment consists of as thorough an uncovering of their unconscious significance as is possible to achieve. The hidden significance will in all cases turn out to be complex; many levels of conflict, elaborated into unconscious fantasies, are likely to be incorporated into the formulation of phobic symptoms.

Perhaps the clearest and most comprehensive way to understand matters is to think of the phobias as compromise formations. This means the symptoms are the psychological resultant of the interplay between (1) certain sexual and aggressive wishes of childhood mental life, (2) the anxiety to which these give rise, (3) various expressions of superego reaction to these forbidden wishes, in the forms of punishment, undoing, restitution, and placation of the internalized moral authority, and (4) a panoply of defenses that may be mobilized against either the forbidden wishes, the anxiety, the superego influences, or some combination of all these forces.

Among the ego mechanisms that are used defensively, those most commonly associated with the formation of phobic symptoms are condensation, displacement, and projection, but many other aspects of psychological functioning can also serve defensive ends.

The tracing out of these unconscious elements and their interrelationships is likely to take many months, even years, and if the effort is successful, the potential benefits of the treatment usually go far beyond the relief of the specific phobia or other symptoms. Patients today generally recognize both the longer time frame and the broader goals of psychoanalysis and psychoanalytic psychotherapy, so it would be unusual for a patient to seek such treatment or accept a recommendation for it solely for the relief of even the most troublesome phobia. These days, the analytic understanding of phobic symptoms most often comes about during the course of a treatment that was initially undertaken for other reasons, or at least for reasons in addition to the phobic complaints themselves. Conversely, patients who are solely interested in the relief of a specific phobia, and who have no apparent awareness of other coexistent problems, as a rule do not seek psychoanalytically oriented treatment.

Only therapists with a thorough grounding in psychoanalytic conceptualization and techniques are likely to utilize this therapeutic approach to the treatment of patients' phobias. Such therapists and their patients will be prepared for the possibility that, even in successful therapies, improvement may come very slowly and gradually. This is not invariable, however, and in some cases improvement may be quite rapid. It is impossible to predict the rate and degree of change in a given symptom at the outset of analytic treatment, especially since the unconscious determinants of the problems often cannot be guessed at, nor can the patient's genuine motivation for change be accurately assayed from what he or she says to the therapist at the beginning of therapy.

The following brief clinical vignette will serve to illustrate some of the points mentioned.

A divorced woman in her early thirties, a successful junior executive in a multinational corporate enterprise, sought treatment because a flying phobia threatened to limit her career advancement. She revealed to the consultant who evaluated her that she had also had a bout of severe anxiety associated with flying some years earlier, this had subsided in the course of a limited psychotherapy that was a mixture of support and exploration. The symptoms had returned about a year ago, but this time a brief course of treatment similar to her earlier, successful, limited-goal therapy did not bring relief. If anything, the anxiety associated with flying seemed to be worsening. The patient added that she had an ongoing relationship with a man she valued highly; she wanted some help to try to assure that problems of hers that she thought had contributed to her previous marital failure did not spoil her present prospects for happiness. Both the patient and the consultant thought that a more intensive psychoanalytically oriented therapy was indicated at this time.

Despite many difficulties in immersing herself freely in the treatment, the patient's persistent and conscientious work gradually permitted a progressive unfolding of the many levels of meaning of her phobia about flying, accompanied by relief to the point of full recovery. (Certain other dimensions of her treatment were also successful but will not be described in the context of this illustration.)

The first level of understanding to emerge was that the patient used her anxiety before and during flights as a way of tormenting and punishing herself unmercifully. This punishment came to be seen as related to her career ambitions, which she imagined would necessarily involve intense and deadly competition, especially with men. As this configuration became clearer, the patient became able to report a more precise description of her anxiety about flying. She was terrified that in the course of a flight her discomfort would grow so intense that she would lose control of herself and become hysterical. Such an outburst would be intensely humiliating to her, especially if it were to occur in the company of a male co-worker. Eventually she was able to elaborate her view that such a hysterical loss of control as she imagined, and dreaded, would characterize her as a weak, contemptible female, destroying the image of the competent, firm, rational, and composed person (qualities she attributed to men) that she wished to present to the world. This disgrace would be a fit punishment for her ruthlessly defeating the males she competed with, which she imagined humiliated them terribly. In time it also became clear how these conflicts resonated with issues in her childhood relationship to her father, a successful businessman.

After this was worked out, she was able to recall that the current outbreak of flying phobia had commenced after a particular flight during which a male co-worker accompanying her party had regaled them with war stories, consisting of harrowing tales of his heroism while in military service as a flyer. She had responded to his boasting with a mixture of inner fury, envy, and the conviction that she would not have been able to stand such experiences.

By this time in the therapy she was able to fly without experiencing much, if any, anxiety, but she still had considerable anticipatory dread. She noted that the dread was much worse before flights home than it was when going elsewhere on business or vacation. This observation ushered in an elaboration of a new level of meaning of her phobic anxiety. She now had thoughts of panic and loss of control as a consequence of being confined within the plane with no way to get out, even if she became upset. Claustrophobic feelings led to a fuller exploration of her ambivalent relationship with her mother and to rivalrous feelings toward siblings of both sexes. In one session she described a fantasy that the airplane she was in might break apart, spilling her to her death. This led to associations about pregnancy, delivery, and abortion.

These subjects were also on her mind as she was considering alternatives to her business career, since she and her boyfriend were contemplating marriage. In the course of exploring these issues she revealed she had long held a conviction that her mother had come to wish she had aborted the patient, who had been a troublesome and difficult child. This idea about her mother, which was never confirmed, was expressed symbolically in the patient's fear that the plane would open up, dropping her to her death. With this reconstruction, the flying phobia improved still more.

One last level remained to be clarified. It came up in the course of the patient's description of her preflight ritual. Whenever she noted stirrings of anxiety, she thought of the therapist and usually experienced immediate relief. When she was asked why she thought she needed to evoke his image, since she had obviously done much of the work of overcoming her problem herself, she became flustered and angry. She revealed that she believed she would always need treatment, and she berated her therapist for seeming to take away her comfort and undermining her peace of mind. It took some further time to clarify that she liked the idea of not being alone, especially when she felt possible danger to be present. This meant to her that the therapist had assumed the role of the wished-for benevolent and protective mother, in place of her real mother, with whom she had so unsatisfactory a relationship. When the therapist questioned her need for this fantasy relationship, the patient experienced this questioning as tantamount to rejecting her. The thought of ever ending treatment also carried that connotation. After a mild and brief regression, however, her phobic symptoms again disappeared as work toward termination proceeded.

The foregoing case demonstrates a number of features described in the introductory material. Several different specific versions of fear were incorporated in this woman's flying phobia. Various conflicts contributed to it, and these could only gradually be teased out of the material as treatment progressed. The transference dimension of her phobic structure came to light at the last, but it was clearly essential to be included in the treatment, or else the potential for another serious relapse in the future, after termination, would obviously have been much greater.

It should be added that this patient at all times considered her phobia to be irrational, and she clearly remembered her earlier success in overcoming it. Only in retrospect could she see that her lack of confidence in being able to maintain mastery over her symptoms on her own was itself a symptom, having a specific unconscious meaning, and one that had to be worked through in its turn. Only then could she begin to see the future more optimistically, with some sense that she now possessed the capability for mastering her phobia herself.

CREDITS

5

Credits

"Cognitive Therapy for Evaluation Anxieties," from *Anxiety Disorders and Phobias: A Cognitive Perspective*, by Aaron T. Beck and Gary Emery with Ruth L. Greenberg. Copyright © 1985 by Aaron T. Beck, M.D., and Gary Emery, Ph.D. Reprinted by permission of BasicBooks, a division of HarperCollins Publishers. Inc.

"Medication Discontinuation in Panic Disorder," by James C. Ballenger, John Pecknold, Karl Rickels, and Edward M. Sellers, in *Journal of Clinical Psychiatry* 54(10): supplement, 15–21. Copyright © 1993 *Journal of Clinical Psychiatry*.

"Bibliotherapy," by Claire Weekes, formerly titled "A Practical Treatment of Agoraphobia," in *British Medical Journal* 2:469–471. Copyright © 1973 *British Medical Journal*.

INDEX